GR72L66Y91

EPIC SINGERS AND ORAL

LORD ALBERT B

DATE DUE

Brodart Co.   Cat. # 55 137 001   Printed in USA

MYTH AND POETICS

A series edited by
GREGORY NAGY

Epic Singers and Oral Tradition
by ALBERT BATES LORD

Also in the series

Poetry and Prophecy: The Beginnings of a Literary Tradition
edited by James Kugel

The Language of Heroes: Speech and Performance in the Iliad
by Richard P. Martin

Greek Mythology and Poetics
by Gregory Nagy

Homer and the Sacred City
by Stephen Scully

EPIC SINGERS AND ORAL TRADITION

ALBERT BATES LORD

CORNELL UNIVERSITY PRESS

ITHACA AND LONDON

First published 1991 by Cornell University Press.

International Standard Book Number 0-8014-2472-0 (cloth)
International Standard Book Number 0-8014-9717-5 (paper)
Library of Congress Catalog Card Number 90-55888
Printed in the United States of America
Librarians: Library of Congress cataloging information
appears on the last page of the book.

Excerpt from "The Waste Land" in *Collected Poems 1909–1962* by T. S. Eliot, copyright 1936 by Harcourt Brace Jovanovich, Inc., copyright © 1964, 1963 by T. S. Eliot, is reprinted by permission of the publisher.

Excerpt from "The Wanderings of Oisin" is reproduced from W. B. Yeats, *The Poems: A New Edition*, edited by Richard J. Finneran (New York: Macmillan, 1983).

Excerpt from *There Was a King in Ireland* by Myles Dillon, published 1971 by University of Texas Press, is reprinted by permission of the publisher.

⊛The paper in this book meets the minimum requirements
of the American National Standard for Information Sciences—
Permanence of Paper for Printed Library Materials, ANSI Z39.48–1984.

For Mary Louise

Contents

Foreword

Gregory Nagy

Epic Singers and Oral Tradition, by Albert B. Lord, is a particularly distinguished entry in the Myth and Poetics series. My goal, as series editor, has been to encourage work that helps to integrate literary criticism with the approaches of anthropology and pays special attention to problems concerning the nexus of ritual and myth. A model of such integration and emphasis is Lord's 1960 classic study of the mechanics and aesthetics of oral-traditional poetry, *The Singer of Tales*. With the appearance, some thirty years later, of *Epic Singers and Oral Tradition* in the present series, we now have a new model. Representing as it does the wide chronological span of Albert Lord's scholarly activity and an even wider geographical span of his diverse cultural interests, this book constitutes a definitive introduction to the man and his work.

"Although much talked about in negative criticism," Lord writes in his introduction, "living oral-traditional literature is still not very well known, and I try over and over again in the course of this book to acquaint the reader with some of the best of what I have had the privilege to experience and to demonstrate the details of its excellence." Lord speaks from experience, the experience of fieldwork in living oral traditions, and this background confers on him a profound authority, despite his modesty about his work. *Epic Singers and Oral Tradition* makes plain, once and for all, the legitimacy and importance of exploring the oral-traditional heritage of Western literature.

Acknowledgments

I thank the good friends and colleagues who urged me to publish a selection of my papers, especially most recently James Hankins, Richard Janko, and Jan Ziolkowski. I am also grateful to Gregory Nagy for encouragement and for accepting the volume into the series Myth and Poetics of which he is editor. I deeply appreciate his gracious foreword, and thank him for many other kindnesses over the years.

In preparing the published articles for reprinting, I found Kenneth Morrell's skill and generosity with the scanner indispensable for the speedy accomplishment of a task that would otherwise have taken many days and weeks; for all this I thank him.

The Cornell University Press and particularly Bernhard Kendler have been courteous and understanding hosts. Carol Betsch and Adrienne Mayor guided me with dexterity and patience through the intricate process of putting a not too easy manuscript into proper shape for printing.

I am grateful to Matthew W. Kay and Russell Edward Martin of the Graduate School of Arts and Sciences for helping in preparation of the manuscript and for their expertise with computers. Matthew also assisted in framing correspondence and obtaining permissions to reprint previously published articles. I am indebted also to the original publishers for allowing those papers to appear again and have acknowledged their courtesy in the individual chapters.

Mary Louise Lord came to my aid at every stage of the undertaking, from the choice of selections to editing and reediting. Her scholarly acumen and her experience with medieval Latin manuscripts were invaluable in dealing with this manuscript also. Her love and devotion have kept the whole enterprise alive.

ALBERT BATES LORD

Cambridge, Massachusetts

EPIC SINGERS AND
ORAL TRADITION

Introduction

It is of the nature of things that Homer and his poems should play some role, directly or indirectly, in all the articles in this volume. It is not surprising, either, that South Slavic oral-traditional epic should loom large in them as well. Since my graduate work was also seriously concerned with medieval English and Germanic epic, some of the writings included here represent that field. Because the methodology that I inherited from my teacher Milman Parry is, I believe, applicable to many other narrative poetries, references to them are not infrequent. Finally, in pursuit of the sources and history of epic poetry in the Balkans from Homer's times to the present, I have turned my attention to Byzantium and to the Near and Middle East, whence have come, together with the migrations of people over a long period of time, styles and stories that we observe in the Balkan peninsula today.

Another subject that appears several times in the course of the volume is the high quality of some of the oral-traditional literature of the world. That literature and its representatives from the Slavic Balkans have, I feel, been misjudged for various reasons, one result of which being that they have not been studied and analyzed as they should be. To the class-conscious they belong to the lower classes, that is, to the illiterate and uneducated, and they have, therefore, been thought beneath the notice of serious scholars of literature.

Along these lines, D. H. Green, paraphrasing Eric Havelock, has complained that the "oral theory" "lumps together two different poetic situations, one where the oral technique of a Balkan peasantry was no

I

longer central to the culture in which they lived and one where the
poetry of a Homeric governing class represented the main vehicle of
significant communication in its society."[1]

One might point out that in the case of the Moslem poetry in
Yugoslavia at least some of the singers for some five hundred years, up
to the end of World War I, belonged to the governing class, and the
Moslem epic of the Sandjak of Novi Pazar (South Serbia), Bosnia, and
Hercegovina, was the poetry of that class. Avdo Međedović's *The Wedding of Smailagić Meho* is a strong affirmation of the moral values and
aspirations of the community. It performed the very function that
Havelock assigned to the Homeric poems: "Literate societies [conserve
their mores] by documentation; pre-literate ones achieve the same result
by the composition of poetic narratives which serve also as encyclope-
dias of conduct."[2]

The Christian poetry, too, represented the ideals of the governing
class in the Middle Ages—I am thinking, for example, of the times of
the emperor Dušan in the fourteenth century—and of the rebellious
leaders of the eighteenth and nineteenth, as parts of Serbia began to be
liberated from the Ottoman empire by the emerging kings and princes
who were not ousted until World War II. Both the Moslem and the
Christian poetry expressed the ideals of the governing class even when it
was out of power.

Although much talked about in negative criticism, living oral-
traditional literature is still not very well known, and I try over and over
again in the course of this book to acquaint the reader with some of the
best of what I have had the privilege of experiencing and to demonstrate
the details of its excellence.

The first article in this volume was the keynote address at a conference
in 1985 at the University of Natal in Durban, South Africa, "Oral
Tradition and Literacy: Changing Visions of the World," and while
focusing on Homer and South Slavic, it deals with some general questions that plague those of us who work with oral-traditional literature.
In it, for example, I stoutly defend the legitimacy of the term "oral
literature," and I also emphasize that the method of composition of oral-
traditional narrative poetry is not "improvisation" but a special form of
"composition in performance" that uses units called "formulas" and
"themes," to which I have more recently added the highly important

[1] Green, 1990, 270. Havelock, 1963, 93–94.
[2] Havelock, 1978, 4.

concept of "blocks of lines." In one guise or another, this topic runs through all the papers.

This is not the place to go into the details of the controversy over the term "oral poetry." I should like to note here, however, that one must distinguish between the literal and the specialized use of the word "oral" in this connection. Some scholars have been deceived by Ruth Finnegan's confusing assertions that there are oral poetries that are not composed in performance.[3] This is true, but those poetries generally consist of short nonnarrative songs and not of long epics. It is the mode of composition that is crucial, not the mode of performance. If one forgets that, one arrives at the absurd conclusion that Virgil's *Aeneid* becomes an oral poem when someone reads it aloud or memorizes parts of it, or the whole, if that were feasible, and the reader or memorizer becomes an oral poet! This is patently ridiculous. The distinctive style of which Parry wrote came into being because of the necessities of composition in performance of long narrative poems. The necessity of composing rapidly called forth a special kind of style, which Parry called a "necessary style."

The second article is the fifth and last of a group of papers read at the annual meetings of the American Philological Association. The first three followed a plan and titles that Parry had already sketched before his death in December 1935 as a series of "Homer and Huso" articles.[4] The first, in 1936, was "Homer and Huso I: The Singer's Rests in Homer and Southslavic Heroic Song." In Parry's notes dictated in the winter and spring of 1935, under "Date of writing, January 20, 1935," he wrote several paragraphs under the heading "The Falsity of the Notion of the Chants of the Homeric Poems."[5] Following Parry's scheme, I kept the "Homer and Huso" titles for two more papers in *Transactions of the American Philological Association (TAPA)*, one in 1938, with the subtitle "II: Narrative Inconsistencies in Homer and Oral Poetry," and

[3] Finnegan, 1977, 18–22 and 1988, 86–109. See also Green, 1990, 270–272.

[4] Ćor Huso was a blind singer (*ćor* is Turkish and means "blind in one eye") from whom a number of Parry's singers from Novi Pazar and Bijelo Polje had learned some of their songs. To Parry he was a kind of legendary singer perhaps kin to Homer. For the three articles see Lord, A., 1936, 1938, and 1948.

[5] Parry bound the typed form of these notes under the title "Ćor Huso, A Study of Southslavic Song." Sitting at the table in the window of the Parry dining room in Dubrovnik, I typed those notes from the wax cylinders on which they were recorded. They have not yet been published in full, but some excerpts appeared in Parry, A., 1971, 437–478. For the subject of Homeric chants and singer's rests see Parry, A., 1971, 454–455.

the other, after World War II, in 1948, "III: Enjambement in Greek and Southslavic Heroic Song." This, too, Parry had written of in his Ćor Huso notes.[6] Although the next paper, presented at the meetings three years later, in 1951, dropped "Homer and Huso" from the title "Composition by Theme in Homer and Southslavic Epos," it continued the comparison of techniques of composition and their effect in the two traditions.

In 1953, "Homer's Originality: Oral Dictated Texts" rounded off the series; it was the second to be presented without the "Homer and Huso" rubric but the first to draw on the experience of field collecting. Here too, however, Parry had written in his notes dictated in 1935 about the effect of the process of dictating on the epic singer who was asked to do so for the collector.[7] The paper aroused some totally unexpected, and to me still not quite explicable, controversy. Although the case in the paper is somewhat overstated, I continue to believe firmly in its basic tenets. Assuming that Homer was an oral poet, I could see no other way for his poems to be written than that he dictate them to someone to write down, even as I had witnessed the process in Yugoslavia. One might put the pen in Homer's hand, but he would find it awkward and the whole process would entail knowledge and purposes on his part that would be anachronistic. It should not be thought that the dictating process suddenly turns the singer from an oral-traditional poet to a T. S. Eliot. That is the height of naiveté! I deal with this problem in "Homer as an Oral-Traditional Poet," the fifth paper in this book.

The third paper, "Homeric Echoes in Bihać," dates from about the same time as "Homer's Originality: Oral Dictated Texts." It is an early example of my interest in mythic patterns and their persistence in time and across language barriers in contiguous traditions. It appeared two years after *The Singer of Tales* and was one of my first attempts to study mythic patterning. The conclusion that elements in the patterns involved had survived, without the intervention of the poems of Homer themselves, since Homeric times and earlier was almost irresistible.

Chapter four speaks for itself and needs no special explanations other than to stress the significance of Avdo Međedović in Parry's experience. Unfortunately, Milman Parry did not live to give his own account of Avdo.

[6]Parry, A., 1971, 462–464.
[7]Ibid., 450–451.

With the fifth article, "Homer as an Oral-Traditional Poet," read at a classics symposium at the University of Pennsylvania that, unofficially, I seem to remember, had the idea of evaluating Homeric scholarship "after the oral theory," I attempt to correct some of the misunderstandings of Parry's "oral theory." The paper has not been published before. In it the subjects I spoke of earlier, such as improvisation and the quality of South Slavic oral-traditional poetry, come to the fore. It was a memorable symposium, with papers by, among others, Jasper Griffin, Richard Janko, Joseph Russo, and Laura Slatkin. In my contribution I took Albin Lesky gently to task for judging "The Wedding of Smailagić Meho" on the basis of a summary of the poem that I had given to C. M. Bowra, without Lesky's ever reading the poem himself. I also have taken issue with George Goold over his interpretation of the passages in the Homeric poems which are repeated verbatim, or almost so. He has claimed that such nearly exact repetitions are characteristic of written style and are thus proof that Homer wrote his poems. Since it is not unusual to find such passages in pure oral-traditional songs, and since editors, and even collectors, tend to "standardize" repeated passages, I do not find that his arguments agree with the facts.

"The Kalevala, the South Slavic Epics, and Homer" was read at an exciting International Folk Epic Conference held at University College, Dublin, in September 1985 to celebrate the hundred and fiftieth anniversary of the publication of the Kalevala (1835) and the fiftieth of the establishment of the Irish Folklore Commission (1935), which was to become the Department of Irish Folklore, the organizer of the conference. The Homeric poems and the Liedertheorie of K. Lachmann played a part in Lönnrot's conception of the Kalevala, a concatenation of shorter poems of various kinds to form a long epic.

When I returned with Milman Parry from Yugoslavia in September 1935, it was decided that I should work for a doctorate in comparative literature, with a major in English and minors in ancient Greek and Serbo-Croatian. My graduate adviser during my first year was George Lyman Kittredge, whose place was taken after his retirement by Fernand Baldensperger. Sitting with me on the steps of Warren House, Kittredge assigned me to take Anglo-Saxon and Middle English. The following year I was to add Old Norse with F. Stanton Cawley, and eventually Middle High German with Taylor Starck. The first semester in Anglo-Saxon was taught by Francis Peabody Magoun, Jr., and the second, devoted entirely to *Beowulf*, by Kittredge himself; this was his last class before retiring. For Middle English, including Chaucer, my teachers that year were first John Livingston Lowes and second Fred Norris Robinson. Magoun was one of the readers of my doctoral dissertation, "The Singer of Tales"; the others were Roman Jakobson for Slavic and John H. Finley, Jr., and C. M. Bowra, who was then visiting professor at Harvard, for Greek. I cite all this to explain how someone who was essentially a classicist found himself studying Germanic, particularly medieval English, epic poetry and Old Norse sagas in addition to South Slavic.

The seventh, eighth, and ninth chapters in this book are concerned with *Beowulf* and other Anglo-Saxon poems and continue an interest in them that first saw publication in the section on *Beowulf* in the chapter titled "Some Notes on Medieval Epic" in *The Singer of Tales* in 1960. Students in my seminar on medieval epic very often analyzed formulas and themes in Anglo-Saxon and Middle English poetry, and I regularly lectured on *Beowulf* and *Maldon* in my courses in comparative literature, and even included in later years the *Alliterative Morte Arthure*. Both the seminar and the course on the comparative study of oral-traditional epics dated from the early 1950s. In 1965 I was asked to contribute an article to a festschrift for Francis Peabody Magoun, Jr., and "Beowulf and Odysseus" was written for that volume. "Interlocking Mythic Patterns in *Beowulf*" was read at the Old English Colloquium at Berkeley in the late 1970s and published in 1980.

When I was revising my dissertation (1949) for publication as *The Singer of Tales*, I began gradually to feel that although analysis of formulas and even themes was interesting and valuable, I was not learning more about the deeper meaning of the poetry. Influenced by Gertrude Levy's book *The Sword from the Rock*, among others, I came to believe that much of oral-traditional poetry was of mythic origin.[8] I touched on this briefly in *The Singer of Tales*. It was under that spell that both "Beowulf and Odysseus" and "Interlocking Mythic Patterns in *Beowulf*" were conceived. They were part of my ongoing endeavor to answer the question of what such poems as *Beowulf* are about, or, to put the question as Milman Parry did, how they should be understood if they are oral-traditional poems. In my teaching of comparative epic I

[8]Levy, 1953.

had the good fortune to include *Gilgamesh* and *Enuma Elish* as well as the *Iliad* and the *Odyssey*, and I thought that I could see patterning of incidents in some medieval poems that was similar to that in the ancient poetries. It was not a matter of direct influence, of course, but of the persistence, in traditions of peoples contiguous to one another, of meaningful elements and sequences of elements over long periods of time, persistence of significant items even through change because they were meaningful and deemed essential to the societies that fostered them. These two papers on *Beowulf* belong to that endeavor.

The ninth paper, "The Formulaic Structure of Introductions to Direct Discourse in *Beowulf* and *Elene*," has a different history, although it too goes back to my dissertation and to *The Singer of Tales*. I was invited to give a paper at the annual International Congress on Medieval Studies at Kalamazoo, Michigan, in 1982. At the time of the Old English Colloquium at Berkeley, I was also asked to give a public lecture in which, for the first time, I attempted to answer the criticisms that Larry Benson made in an article in *Publications of the Modern Language Association* in 1966. In 1981 the tape of my lecture was transcribed. Even though I was not satisfied with my comments, I decided that at Kalamazoo I would return to formula studies of *Beowulf*. I had checked Benson's statistics and could not fault them. On the other hand, I was thoroughly convinced that the formulaic style originated in the "oral period"—Benson had not questioned that—and was characteristic of oral-traditional narrative song. I set out then to see if I could differentiate between the formulaic style of *Beowulf* and that of other Anglo-Saxon poems.

As I indicate in Chapter 9, a certain amount of published research had continued to concern itself with the study of the formulaic style. In my own thinking, I had been expanding the boundaries of the formula so that they included phrases of more than one hemistich or of more than one line. I also became interested in larger syntactic units, even whole sentences, as the units of composition. In the Kalamazoo paper I began to apply those concepts to the structure of introductions to speech in *Beowulf* and *Elene*. I had also accumulated information about *Andreas, Christ, Phoenix*, and other poems as well. I have continued to deepen and widen my investigations of introductions to speech and of sentences beginning in the b) verse. Those studies will be reported on at a later date. The paper in the present volume, therefore, represents only the beginning of an ongoing research project that began in 1982.

The Milman Parry Collection was made for purposes of experimentation with the intent to learn how a living oral tradition operated. Chapter 10, written for a volume of papers to honor Roman Jakobson, was the result of research, using materials in the Parry Collection, into the effect of a fixed text on the compositional technique of oral-traditional singers of epic narrative. What happened when a published, fixed text came into the possession of traditional singers? When they began to memorize that text, what were the results? In the collection we had songs that had been gathered and published in the nineteenth century and had become known in fixed texts to traditional singers in the 1930s. One summer I experimented with comparing the texts that Parry had collected with those written down in the early 1800s by Vuk Stefanović Karadžić from one of his best singers, Tešan Podrugović of Gacko. This paper, "The Influence of a Fixed Text," is an example of one of the kinds of experimentation that the Parry Collection was intended to make possible.

The final three papers in this volume are concerned with the relationship between the South Slavic oral-traditional epics and other modern traditions, Greek and Asiatic. The first of the three dates from the early 1950s, when I was deeply involved in the Slavic department while Michael Karpovich was its chairman and Roman Jakobson and Dmitri Čiževsky were very active. Volume 2 of the *Harvard Slavic Studies* (1954) dealt partly with Byzantine-Slavic relations, since it honored Father Francis Dvornik, historian and professor at Dumbarton Oaks. This paper differs somewhat from the other comparative papers because it focuses attention not on mythic patterns—it was written before that time in the development of my ideas—but on a motif. Moreover, it makes use of written authors, such as Vergil and Lucretius, as well as traditional poems such as the Homeric and Serbo-Croatian epics and the Byzantine epic of *Digenis Akritas*. I have revised the paper to some extent (this is true of most of the papers in this volume), but I have not changed its general thrust.

In contrast to "Notes on *Digenis Akritas* and Serbo-Croatian Epic," the last two papers in the volume stem from the 1980s and treat of relations with Central Asiatic epic traditions. The first of these is a kind of "archaeology" aimed at digging out long-forgotten and far-distant meanings from Bulgarian songs of this century. It started with my curiosity about an anomaly, as was the case with several other papers. In *Beowulf* it was the anomaly of a guest who was gratuitously insulted, as was Beowulf in the court of Hrothgar, an episode that called to mind the scene in Phaeacia in the *Odyssey* in which Odysseus was insulted by one of Alcinous's sons. There is another instance of anomaly in the *Odyssey*, when Odysseus's young companion, Elpenor, fell from the roof and broke his neck. This death seemed to make little sense unless one fitted it into a mythic pattern in which a companion's death led to the hero's journeying to the land of the dead seeking answers to questions of mortality. This occurs in the case of the Bulgarian song in which an eagle brings the wounded hero water in its beak in return for the hero's once having saved the eagle's children from death. What is that all about? I chanced upon an incident in the Turkic epic of Er Töshtük which I believe suggests a plausible answer and in turn sheds light on one of the sources of the Balkan epic tradition.

The final paper also looks to Central Asia and, among other things, focuses on horses and types of stories. The latter is, of course, related to my concern with sequences of incidents in narrative and mythic patterning. The former arises from my long-time interest in the importance of horses in epic poetry in the Balkans, where horses are not especially native, and in Central Asia, where they are at home on the steppes. Coupled with this anomaly is the fact that a great many words for horses of many kinds are of Turkic or Persian or Arabic origin, and our journey to Central Asia via Anatolia and points in between is not only a natural one but also inevitable.

Of the papers that I finally decided not to reprint, I was sorry to omit the two or three that I had published in the field of biblical studies. The Bible was a part of my upbringing, and I was overjoyed at the great opportunity given me by William O. Walker, Jr., at Trinity University in San Antonio, Texas, to participate in May 1977 in an extraordinary "Colloquy on the Relationships among the Gospels." This invitation led me to study the synoptic gospels from the point of view of oral-traditional literature.[9]

---

[9]Lord, A., 1978b, 33–91. I learned much at the Texas conference and cherish the friendships made there. The paper that I wrote for it is too long to be included in this volume. I also contributed an article to *Semeia* (Lord, A., 1976a) on the question of whether the parallelisms in the Old Testament were in some way related to the concept of formulas in oral-traditional literature. As part of a group of articles on several aspects of the same subject, the paper did not seem to make the best of sense when taken from its context and so was not included here. At the invitation of Susan Niditch I participated in a conference, "The Hebrew Bible and Folklore," at Amherst College in April 1988, with a paper titled "Patterns of Lives of the Patriarchs from Abraham to Samson and Samuel." See Niditch, 1990.

Also omitted with regrets is any representative of my articles on the composer Béla Bartók, who transcribed the music of many of the recordings in the Milman Parry Collection, a selection of which he published in *Serbo-Croatian Folk Songs*, for which I provided texts and translations.[10]

In December 1986, an international conference, "Texts, Tones, and Tunes," was sponsored by the Committee on Ethnomusicology of the American Institute of Indian Studies (of which Daniel M. Neumann of the University of Washington, Seattle, is chairman). The conference took place in New Delhi, and I was asked to give the opening address, which I titled "Text, Tone, Tune, Rhythm, and Performance in South Slavic Sung Narrative." This paper was a challenge for a nonspecialist in musicology, but I was aided by the fact that the members of the conference represented several different fields and geographical areas, including Russian opera and Chinese songs (discussed by my Harvard colleague, Rulan Pian); Anthony Seeger, an expert on South American music, and musicologist Bruno Nettl of Indiana University also presented papers. Needless to say, for many of us the most important papers were those by our Indian hosts, who opened up for us new aspects of thought and music. The kind invitation of Komal Kothari to his Folklore Institute at Burunda broadened my perspectives still further. There I heard many musicians, both at the institute and at Dr. Kothari's home in Jodhpur; most notable for me was the singing of Pabuji and Bagrawat epics in front of the *par*, the cloth on which are painted episodes in the narratives.[11]

It has been a strange experience to review my past writings, some of them going back more than fifty years. The earliest papers in this vol-

[10] Bartók and Lord, 1951. My paper "Béla Bartók as a Collector of Folk Songs," which was read at a conference on Bartók at the University of Washington in Seattle, was published in *Cross Currents* in 1982, and my article "Béla Bartók and Text Stanzas in Yugoslav Folk Music" appeared in a festschrift for Professor John Milton Ward of the music department at Harvard in 1985. See Lord, A., 1982, 295–304; Lord, A., 1985a, 385–403. A paper on the Latvian *dainas* as oral-traditional literature was read at a conference at the University of Montreal in October 1985, organized by Vaira Vīķis-Freibergs in honor of Krišjānis Barons, the collector of the *dainas* in the nineteenth century. See Lord, A., 1989; *Latvian Folk Songs*, 1989, 35–48.

[11] The paper read at the New Delhi Conference is forthcoming in a volume edited by Bonnie Wade of the University of California at Berkeley. Many years ago I wrote a long paper on the catalogues in the epic songs of Avdo Međedović. It was intended to provide comparative material for the study of the famous catalogue of ships in the *Iliad* and also of catalogues in other epic poems, especially the *chansons de geste*. I hope to publish it later, after expanding and revising it.

ume were published more than thirty-five years ago; others represent research in progress. They were addressed to a variety of audiences in places as distant from one another as Berkeley, California; Philadelphia; Dublin; and Durban, South Africa. Sometimes, needless to say, they reflect controversies pertinent to the times and places where they were delivered. Much has been written on most of the subjects treated, and I have tried to learn from what I have read of both positive and negative criticism of Parry's ideas as well as of my own attempts to follow them. I feel it necessary to move further, in directions that the epic singers and their songs indicate, toward an understanding of the meaning of oral-traditional epic poetry. Naturally enough, I have found it necessary to edit and to revise the papers, at times considerably, because I did not want to say anything with which I no longer agreed. For the most part, however, the revision has been stylistic or concerned with a shift of emphasis; I have made very little substantive change.

As I point out in the notes, my paper from 1953, "Homer's Originality: Oral Dictated Texts," is reprinted nearly exactly. It has been included in several anthologies of articles on Homer, notably those by Geoffrey S. Kirk in England (1964) and Joachim Latazc in Germany (1979). I include it here in spite of the fact that I have some fear, not entirely unjustified, that it may continue to give rise to misunderstandings of what the specific advantages may be that can accrue to the dictating singer. Under the circumstances of a "dictating performance" the singer can expand his song, as I have demonstrated. He also, it appears, can enter into a different rhythm of composition from that of his singing performance. This facet of dictating, strangely enough, has not been thoroughly investigated, possibly because collectors at the present time do not write down songs from dictations but record them on tapes, including videotapes or cassettes. The rhythm of dictation may induce, or enhance, structures that are endemic to traditional poetics, such as parallelisms and other paratactic arrangements of ideas and words. Just as the singing brings with it sequences of rhythmic and melodic patterns, so the dictating may have its own distinct structures.

As I reconsidered very recently the stylization of a passage from Salih Ugljanin's "Song of Bagdad" which was found in a dictated version but not in two sung texts, I was suddenly aware of the experience of listening to Salih dictate. In my memory I could envisage a room in Novi Pazar on a series of rainy days, and I could see him sitting at the table at which Nikola Vujnović was writing and hear him speak the lines rapidly but with a deliberate tempo; a line, a pause, then another line, as he watched Nikola set it down on the paper. But the pauses did not interrupt either his thought or his syntax. The measured delivery made the parallelisms in the following lines of the passage I just referred to almost inevitable:

>Kad tatarin pod Kajniđu dođe,
>Pa eto ga uz čaršiju prođe,
>
>When the messenger came to Kajniđa,
>Then he passed along through the market place.
>When . . . to Kajniđa he came,
>Then . . . along the market place he passed.

This kind of construction may emerge more clearly in the mannered dictating than in the necessary flexibility of composition in the hurly-burly of the live singing performance.

One might think that dictating gave the singer the leisure to plan the words and their placing in the line, that the parallelism was due to a careful thinking-out of the structure. First of all, however, dictating is not a leisurely process; neither the singer nor the scribe has patience for long pauses for deliberation. The hours pass and the lines accumulate as the song is set down. But more especially, a mood and a tempo, as I have suggested, are established which produce the balanced utterances of the poet. Not conscious planning but the rhythm of that particular process of composition calls forth the structures. I might add that not all singers can dictate successfully. As I have said elsewhere, some singers can never be happy without the *gusle* (a one-stringed bowed instrument) accompaniment to set the rhythm of the singing performance.

One of the most striking and valuable features of the Milman Parry Collection is that it brings to the fore the singer and performance. The collection must be approached with the realization that each text in it represents a performance, whether sung, recited, or dictated; and every performance is unique and has its singer. When studied in that way, it can teach us much about the life of the South Slavic oral epic tradition and, if we are willing, by extension, it may suggest much about other traditions as well. That it has done so is clear from the variety of cultures, ancient, medieval, and modern represented in this volume. It is even more dramatically demonstrated by the annotated bibliography *Oral Formulaic Theory and Research* assembled by John Miles Foley and published in 1985.[12]

Scope alone, however impressive, and performance alone, however spectacular it may be, constitute but the outward trappings of the study of oral-traditional epic song. It is the singer and what is sung that count. They are strongly affected by the traditional setting of performance and by the traditional audience, but those alone do not create the singer, or the words, or what they relate. It is the mind of the composing traditional singer that we must seek to comprehend both at the moment of performance and even when it is seemingly at rest. The epic tradition lies in the myths and tales stored in the minds of all the singers past and present, the least as well as the greatest. It is this that one learns "in the field," that is, in listening to and talking with singers. I had the great privilege of apprenticeship, short as it was, with Milman Parry; it was from him I absorbed a feeling for the epic songs of the Slavic Balkans, and it was with him that I came to know and to listen to many singers telling urgent stories of olden times.

On another level I learned from Parry the necessity of careful field recording so that the texts thus obtained would reflect accurately the words of the singer rather than those put there by the collector. To reach valid conclusions about the process of composition of oral-traditional narrative song, conclusions that could be used for comparative research, one had to have reliable texts. I hope that I acquired from Parry some degree of fastidiousness in that regard.

Parry came to know many varieties of singers, skillful and otherwise, and at least one of genius. I think that perhaps he found two Homers in those years. One, whom he has remembered in the title of his field writings, namely, Ćor Huso Husein of Kolašin, an almost legendary figure from the past who had died before Parry's collecting years, but of whom Parry heard from those who had listened to his singing and had learned songs from him. Had Parry had time, he would have written more about Ćor Huso. The other great singer was Avdo Međedović, whose name reverberates everywhere in this volume; for him Parry lingered in Bijelo Polje during the summer of 1935. It is fitting that the

---

[12]Foley, 1985. See also the journal *Oral Tradition*, founded by John Miles Foley in 1986.

two generations should have been represented so well among the South Slavic peoples in the 1930s, because any tradition's chances of immortality rest upon the desire of the younger singers to continue to tell the myths and histories of their elders, and upon the ability of the older generation to inspire that yearning for knowledge.

Before I close, I should like to pay tribute to Gregory Nagy's volume in this present series, *Greek Mythology and Poetics*. In emphasizing the significance of myth as a source of the Homeric epic, he points directly to what, I believe, gives the *Iliad* and the *Odyssey* both deep structure and deep meaning. Reading them as traditional poems expressive of sacred realities, we can appreciate their religious—in the broadest sense—dimension, extending back to their origins.

In another book, appearing at the same time, *Pindar's Homer*, Nagy gives a wide view of archaic Greek poetry and song, redefining these terms in an innovative way. His vision of the formation of the Homeric poems through panhellenization and their "textual fixation" orally, with all its ramifications, is challenging. The differentiation of the *Iliad* and the *Odessey*, through panhellenization, from the poems of the Cycle, which represent local traditions, is a view worth serious consideration. Most significant, however, is Nagy's concept of the Homer Pindar knew.

These two books, together with *The Best of the Achaeans*, present a rare holistic view of Archaic Greek poetry, including both lyric and epic, and its background in the polis and at the panhellenic festivals.

CHAPTER I

Words Heard and Words Seen

It seems superfluous to remark that in the history of mankind words were heard before they were seen. For the majority of people, as a matter of fact, words still are heard rather than seen, and even those who have learned to visualize words as containing particular letters in a particular sequence continue to operate much of the time with the heard, and hence the spoken, word. In our individual experience we share in varying degrees in both worlds. We have gone in our individual development from orally conceived words, without visible representation, existing within boundaries defined by utterance rather than spelling, to a sense of words with rigid, visual characteristics; cultures, like individuals, moved from one world to another through a series of gradual adaptations. Although the two worlds, the oral and the written, of thought and its expression, exhibit some striking and important differences, they are not really separate worlds.

As my title indicates, I intend to discuss words rather than orality, words in their oral form, as it were, and words in their written form.[1] I

The original form of this paper was read at a conference, "Oral Tradition and Literacy: Changing Visions of the World," held at the University of Natal, Durban, South Africa, July 1985. Selected papers from the conference were published under the same title by the Natal University Oral Documentation and Research Centre, Durban, 1986, edited by R. A. Whitaker and E. R. Sienaert.

[1] A work on oral style that was an early influence on Milman Parry and that he assigned me to read as a student was Marcel Jousse, *Le Style oral rhythmique et mnémotechnique chez les Verbo-Moteurs* (Jousse, 1925 and 1990). For studies of orality from a different point of view see McLuhan, 1962; Havelock, 1963; Bäuml, 1980, 237–265; and Ong, 1982.

want particularly to treat the artistic use of words in what we rightly call literature, and to stress the positive and creative qualities of oral literature, the oldest literature in the human world, and its significance for "written literature."[2]

We use the word "literature" in at least two senses. When the automobile salesman tells us that he will give us the "literature" about a given model of car, he is not using the word in the same sense as the Department of English Literature at a university. When scholars say that they have read all the "literature" on *Beowulf* they are not speaking of belles-lettres. The salesman's "literature" means "something in writing," and the scholars' "literature" indicates "what has been written" on the Old English epic. In this case, scholars and salesman are using the word with the same meaning.[3] The English department, on the other hand, has made a qualitative judgment on part of the vast amount of written documents. Some people, stressing the etymology of the word "literature," make a distinction between the written and the nonwritten, thus viewing all literatures as written, by definition, as the origin of the word implies. At the same time, the same people might hesitate to subscribe to the idea that everything that is written is literature, although that is the automobile salesman's attitude. They would insist that literature means belles-lettres. This is a well-attested use of the word. Surely you have heard someone say that a given piece of writing is not "literature." Sometimes writings that contain many obscenities are condemned because they are *not* literature, and sometimes they are defended because they *are* literature. Whichever side may be in the right, they are both speaking about the quality of what is written, not whether it is written or not. In that use of the word "literature," therefore, we make a distinction of quality among various expressions in words. It is to that meaning of literature that I turn, for under it we can speak of both an oral and a written literature, products of verbal expression of high artistic quality. In sum, words heard, when set in the forms of art, are oral literature; words seen, when set in the forms of art, are written literature.

---

[2] See Ong, 1982, 56–57. "To assume that oral peoples are essentially unintelligent, that their mental processes are 'crude,' is the kind of thinking that for centuries brought scholars to assume falsely that because the Homeric poems are so skillful, they must be basically written compositions" (p. 57).

[3] Robert Alter decries the leveling of literature with all other kinds of discourse; Alter, 1989, 13 and 25.

These considerations lead us to the question of what the role of writing is in literature. Written literature is dependent on writing. That sounds axiomatic, but the type of literature that I think of as "written literature" par excellence, historically, was created in writing and was impossible without writing. Let me illustrate by way of explanation. Can you imagine James Joyce's *Ulysses* being created without writing? Or a poem of e.e. cummings, whose very name must be seen to be recognized? Or a short, graphic example from Ezra Pound's *Canto LXXVI*:

> nothing matters but the quality
> of the affection—
> in the end—that has carved the trace in the mind
> dove sta memoria.[4]

This is visual poetry; its very placement on the written or printed page indicates a phrasing and emphasis in meaning; and its lack of punctuation is a purposeful element put there by the author to convey a message. You must see it to understand it fully. The Italian quotation was taken from Guido Cavalcanti's *Donna mi prega*.[5] This is real borrowing from a thirteenth-century poet, impossible without a written text. This kind of poetry requires writing. These words have to be seen.

Even such lines as the following from Yeats's "The Wanderings of Oisin," which exhibit some of the characteristics of oral literature, are inconceivable without writing:

> Like sooty fingers, many a tree
> Rose ever out of the warm sea;
> And they were trembling ceaselessly,
> As though they all were beating time,
> Upon the centre of the sun,
> To that low laughing woodland rhyme.
> And, now our wandering hours were done,
> We cantered to the shore, and knew
> The reason of the trembling trees;
> Round every branch the song-birds flew,

[4] Pound, 1970, 457.
[5] I am indebted to Jonathan F. McKeage for the passage from Pound and for the reference to Cavalcanti's *Donna me prega*. See Cavalcanti, 1967, 47. For other uses of *dove sta memoria* in Pound's *Cantos* see Edwards and Vasse, 1957, 54.

> Or clung thereon like swarming bees;
> While round the shore a million stood
> Like drops of frozen rainbow light,
> And pondered in a soft vain mood
> Upon their shadows in the tide,
> And told the purple deep their pride,
> And murmured snatches of delight;
> And on the shores were many boats
> With bending sterns and bending bows,
> And carven figures on their prows
> Of bitterns, and fish-eating stoats,
> And swans with their exultant throats.[6]

In spite of the adding style of this lovely passage—balanced as it is, nevertheless, with necessary enjambements—this poetry must be seen as well as heard, so that one may go over it again and again to appreciate its subtleties. If Yeats's lines were *really* oral-traditional lines, and if you were in the traditional audience or its equivalent, you would not need to go back over them to savor them. The traditional diction would be familiar, known, understood, and appreciated on first hearing, because words and word-clusters or configurations like them had been heard before. They were "just right." On the other hand, the phrase "sooty fingers" has no traditional resonances, and the same can be said for the sentence "many a tree rose out of the warm sea." This is neither traditional diction nor traditional imagery. It is individualistic in an individualist's milieu. Its particular style, its striking choice of words and ideas and poetic combinations are purely Yeats. Song-birds cling to every branch "like swarming bees," which just might be traditional, but a million of them stand on the shore "like drops of frozen rainbow light," which I wager was not. These delights are in a tradition of *written* poetry, but are not in an oral *traditional* Hiberno-English poetry. The technique here, indeed, is to seek a striking nontraditional image.

Few cultures with which I am acquainted have developed writing from within their own society. For many of them writing was brought to them from outside, from a "more advanced" culture, or at least from a culture with writing. But writing does not always imply written literature. The ancient Greeks first presumably devised a script called Linear B, probably adapted from one called Linear A, in the second

---

[6] Yeats, 1983, lines 172–192, pp. 359–360.

millennium B.C.; and in the eighth century B.C. they borrowed and modified the Phoenician alphabet for writing the Greek language. One of the noteworthy facts about Linear B is that it seems not to have been used for writing down Mycenaean oral-traditional literature or even for creating a written Mycenaean literature. Mycenaean literacy served the interests of trade or religion. In Mycenaean times, to be literate had practical mercantile or cult implications but none concerning the culture of literature.

The Greeks themselves then developed a literary culture from within their own ranks. There may have been outside models from ancient Near Eastern cultures with writing *and* with a literature in writing, be it written down or primary, which influenced the Greeks in that development. I have often wondered whence the idea came to someone in the eighth century B.C. to write down the Homeric poems, since whatever had been written up to that point had been aimed to further commerce or admininstration. There is the possibility that the writing of the earliest Hebrew scriptures, or the terracotta tablets of other Near and Middle Eastern peoples, may have become known to the Greeks from their contacts with the Near East and that they may have given the Greeks the idea of writing down their own myths.

Greek literature was already formed when it was first written down. The earliest written texts, such as the Homeric poems, could not be transitional, because oral literature was highly developed and so far as we know, written literature, as *written* literature, was nonexistent when they were recorded. It might be said that on the basis of the oral-traditional Homeric poems and other archaic Greek poetry ancient Greek written literature was created. The oral period must have lasted for a long time and true written literature must have been worked out very gradually; oral literature satisfied all requirements.[7]

Writing did however, provide an opportunity for Homer to dictate—or write, if you wish, although I find the idea incongruous—a song, or songs, longer than a normal performance.[8] It took away one set of time

---

[7] See Nagy, G., 1990, 17–18. "From this vantage point we should not even be talking about oral poetry, for example, as distinct from poetry but rather about written poetry as possibly distinct from poetry; in other words, written poetry is the marked member of the opposition, and the poetry that we call oral is the unmarked." Nagy continues, "From the vantage point of our own times, however, *poetry* is by definition written poetry, and what we need to do first is to broaden our concept of poetry. Aside from questions of oral poetry and written poetry, the very word *poetry* becomes a source of confusion, in that it excludes dimensions normally included in the word *song*."

[8] See Lord, A., 1953, Chapter 2 in this volume.

limits, that of performance before an audience, the circumstances under which the traditional epic was usually sung. It imposed another set of time limits, more flexible, but artificial and probably difficult for the poet/singer without the accustomed type of audience. Yet the flexible time limits held great potential for more prolonged composing than occasion usually afforded, a different kind of performance, as it were. At this stage, that potential was for greater *length*, for more of the same, nothing else.

The case of the Germanic peoples is in part much the same as that of the Greeks. They had a runic alphabet with a restricted and nonliterary use.[9] Like the Mycenaeans, they did not have a literature written in that, their own, alphabet. Like the Mycenaeans, too, they had an oral-traditional literature. That it was highly developed we know, because when it eventually came to be written down, it was revealed to be of a complexity in its structure that argued a formative period of generations before writing recorded it. Words heard were sufficient for literature, for ritual utterances, for the recounting of myths, and for the telling and singing of tales, just as words heard were sufficient for everyday communication. Literary language, oral or written, after all, differs from everyday language in its function, particularly in its association with the sacred world. It was characterized by repetitions of sounds, and by parallelisms of structure, for example, which had the function of rendering magic utterances more powerful and hence more surely effective. Writing was not needed for those devices. In fact, when you come to think of it, the written word becomes operable as sound only when spoken aloud! Many basic rhetorical devices of written literature do not depend on words being seen, but come to life only when they are words heard.

In the case of the Germanic tribes in continental Germany, Scandinavia, Iceland, and England, writing was not used to record and eventually really to write literature, until the peoples were converted to Christianity. The Church, moreover, brought these tribes not only an alphabet, but a developed literature in a hieratical language. The alphabet that came with Latin was used to write down some of the oral literature. Since that literature was pagan—non-Christian—in its sacred ambience, however, the Christian Latin texts were translated or paraphrased in the vulgar tongue so that the teachings could be understood by those who did not know Latin. And the pagan oral-traditional literature of the people was sometimes adapted, when possible, to Christian ideology. And thus gradually a new phase began in those literatures and a real written literature in those languages began to appear. It was an amalgam of two cultures, the vernacular with its own developed oral-traditional literary style and the new Christian Latin culture. The first effect of the latter was on ideas, on content, rather than on style, because, especially in poetry, Latin written style was not easy to reproduce in the metrical and alliterative schemes of Germanic verse. The oral-traditional vernacular style continued for some time to be the backbone of the new vernacular written literatures. Only then among the Teutonic peoples did words heard become literally words seen. Yet, except for a certain small and limited group of people, the literate—not only those who could read and write, but, more specifically, those who actually *read* literature—the vision of the world of orality changed not one iota.

Latin brought with it not only religious writings and the works of the Church Fathers such as Augustine, but it also made available the great writers of ancient Rome, such as Vergil and Ovid, and the new non-religious Latin literature. All these writings eventually played a decisive role in the development of the new literature in the vernacular. And a new secular Latin literature appeared, which for a while dominated the learned world as well as producing a medieval Latin literature of great distinction.

Oral literature did not need writing to become literature, and it continued long after writing was invented. Walter J. Ong has given us a useful term, "oral residue," referring to the characteristics of orality which remain in the world of literacy after the introduction of writing. The term applies very well to literature. But his "characteristics of orality," given in his book *Orality and Literacy*, were really intended to cover many other areas than literature.[10] Accordingly, they apply more widely than "words heard and words seen," to encompass a psychology of the "oral mind" and many facets of the world of the unlettered, including their literature and its interaction with the written word.

At this point it would be helpful to distinguish oral literature from oral history and also to place oral literature in respect to that vague but useful term "oral tradition."[11] Sometimes that term is synonymous with oral literature; it may be another way of saying "oral-traditional litera-

---

[10] Ong, 1982, especially 36–57.
[11] See Vansina, 1965.

ture." For example, one may hear, or read, that a particular story is found in "oral tradition." More often, the term is used to designate oral report, which shades into oral history. Oral tradition in that case covers what one hears of what has happened in the past, distant or recent. Although it can exist in a casual form, when it takes on a formal aspect it is oral history. Literacy has little or no effect on oral history, except that eventually, when literacy becomes widespread and begins to be used for recording, and finally for writing, literature, the *writing* of history is an important part of that larger development.

Oral literature is varied. It includes a number of genres, and each has its own role. In it, stories are told, songs are sung, riddles are posed, proverbs are wisely expounded, and in Africa praises are "performed." Stories and songs entertain and instruct, as do also the more humble, shorter forms of proverbs and riddles. Each has its time and place. Certain genres of wisdom literature—proverbs and riddles—sometimes, in fact quite frequently, are contained within stories and songs. Genres are not watertight compartments.

Among the shorter forms of song is a group that includes ritual songs of several kinds, such as lullabies, wedding songs, laments, and keenings at funerals. Here, too, belong the praise poems for which Africa is justly famous.[12] Laments and praises tend to be pure improvisations. Literacy has little effect on the shorter forms of oral literature. Except for an occasional collector, no one would think it useful to write down proverbs, riddles, or sayings, and, by definition, improvisations do not require writing.

Prose stories in oral-traditional literature, that is, anecdotes or more complex folktales, do not have set texts, except that there are "more or less stable" introductory formulas, such as "once upon a time," and concluding words, as well as some short set "runs," for frequently recurring passages.

Excellent examples of such runs can be found in Irish storytelling. In his relating of the long hero story *Eochair Mac Ri in Eirinn*, Eamon Bourke used the following run whenever the hero came to a giant's castle and "struck the challenge pole."

> And when he came to the giant's house, he struck the challenge pole. He did not leave foal in mare, lamb in sheep, child in woman, a kid in goat

[12]For praise poetry see Kunene, 1971; Cope, 1968; and Opland, 1983. For epic in Africa see especially Biebuyck and Mateene, 1969; Biebuyck, 1978; Johnson, 1986; Okpewho, 1979; and Innes, 1974. Finnegan, 1970, is also useful.

that he did not turn nine times in its mother's belly and from there back again; he did not leave the old castle unbroken, the new castle unbent; the old tree unbroken and the new tree unbent; and it said upon his sword that there was not a fighting man under the ground or over the ground fit to beat him. The herald came out and asked what he wanted.[13]

Another run in the same story—there are many of them—is a description of the beheading of a giant:

And he came to him and struck him, and took the head off him on the eighth day. When he did the head was whistling as it went up and humming as it went down in hope of coming upon the same body again. But Mac Ri in Eirinn made no mistake: he struck it a blow of his right topboot, he sent the head a ridge and seven acres from him.

"Well for you!" says the head, says he. "If I came on the same body again, half the Fianna would not take me down!"

"Well, assuredly, says Mac Ri in Eirinn, "weakling, it was not to let your head up that I took it down, but to keep it here below!"[14]

Here is another example of the same run from Myles Dillon's translation of a text of "The Giant of the Mighty Blows" that he recorded by dictograph from Joe Flaherty in County Galway in 1932.

And he struck him where his head joined his neck, and sent his head into the air. The head was singing as it came down, but he leaped up, and as it turned to go back onto its body, he gave it a kick and a shove that sent it over seven ridges and seven rows out onto the green lea.

"You did well!" said the giant. "If I had got back onto my body, half the Fenians would not have cut me off again!"

"Oh," said the King of Ireland's Son, "you may tell that to someone else."[15]

These last two quotations illustrate individual variants of the same common "theme." The storyteller may vary the run a little or not, or he or she may omit it, but in individual practice it is comparatively stable, although not actually memorized as fixed. When writing comes, these set passages tend to disappear, because in written literary style variety, rather than repetition, is sought after. Yet the stories, as narratives, remain the same, though the written style of them changes.

[13] O'Nolan, 1982, 97.
[14] Ibid., 145.
[15] Dillon, 1971, 63.

The storytellers continue to tell their stories as before. Even when they become literate, this is true. It is what the literate person *other than* the storyteller—usually a collector from either within or outside of the traditional community—does with the tale, that brings about a real change. Through such persons a written literary folktale genre is created.[16] The tales in it are often compilations of elements belonging to several traditional tales, told in written literary style. The literacy in the community and the presence of an already developed literature create a new genre, which lives its life in literary circles, parallel to the continuing oral-traditional stories in their usual setting, as long as that setting itself remains unchanged.

The case of oral-traditional poetry, specifically epic song, is somewhat different, because with it we are dealing with stories in long poems in verse, or rhythmic periods of some sort. The question then arises: What is the impact on the individual singer of the introduction of writing into the oral epic poet's community? If the singer did not personally learn to read or write, it had no direct effect at all, of course. There might, however, be indirect effects. Someone might read a song to the singer from a printed or written source. Other than possibly bringing him an epic tale which he might otherwise not have known, this reading would not trouble the waters of his oral-traditional literary world.

As printed material increases in the community and more and more people learn to read and write, and to read literature, prestige may become attached to the literate, and literary, members of the society, and consequently the unlettered may lose prestige. As a result, their cultural activities, such as singing traditional songs and telling traditional stories, may also lose prestige and eventually be lost. There would be pressures, of course, for the unlettered traditional singer to join the prestigious group of the literate. This would not necessarily mean at first that he would immediately become a person knowledgeable in written literature. If he succumbs to the pressure, nothing may happen to him or to the songs or stories, provided the society continues to foster the traditional culture as well as the newer written culture, to listen to and to sing and tell traditional tales and songs.

If the traditional singer/poet is composing in that special oral formulaic style which came into being to make rapid composition in performance possible, and which he has learned from previous generations

---

[16] For the typical case of the brothers Grimm see Ellis, 1983, and Tatar, 1987.

of singer/poets, he does not need writing to compose lines and tell stories. But in a literate, more particularly a literary, society, a singer might get the idea of writing down an epic song from his repertory in the words and manner in which he usually sang it. This would be the same as if someone else wrote it down from his dictation. If, however, a singer made changes in the way in which he wrote from the way in which he sang, then his knowledge of writing would have played a role in the composing of his text. If, for example, he uses some new, non-traditional, phrases or constructions, nevertheless still keeping mostly to the traditional diction, he would be moving in the direction of written literature. It could be argued that he is already a practitioner of written literature or that he is writing in a transitional style. Such a singer's text, therefore, could be considered legitimately as either a written literary text or a transitional one. One must, however, be cautious. Not every "new" word used necessarily constitutes a breaking of the traditional formulaic style, for some new words quite normally find their place in the traditional formulaic systems. The singer without the pen, including the beginner at one end of the scale, the highly gifted singer at the other end, and the unskilled singer in between, breaks the system from time to time, making unmetrical or inept lines, or even lapsing into prose. These are the aberrations of performance, be it before a live audience or in dictating to a scribe. The breaking of the new structure of the *formulaic systems* themselves is more important than are new words. Donald Fry was right in stressing the system in his definition of the formula in Old English.[17] As long as the systems continue, it does not matter whether the singer composes with or without writing. In fact, the "oral residue" expressed in the systems, themselves formed in orality, would persist in the world of literacy, in the usage of the literate traditional singer until such time as the nontraditional-minded writer with a pen in his hand should rearrange the words and traditional patterns in the basic systems. Thus would a written literature be born from an oral literature.

How can one distinguish an oral-traditional text from one of written literature? It must be said at the beginning that one must know something—the more the better—about the tradition in question to which a singer belongs as well as his own habits of composition in order to make the judgment. By that I mean that one must know what the specific characteristics of a given tradition are in order to tell whether they are

[17] Fry, 1967, 193–204.

present or not in the text under consideration. One needs, also, as many texts of a singer or storyteller as possible.

Milman Parry distinguished three stylistic characteristics of oral style: (1) the presence of a large number of formulas; (2) the presence of "themes"; and (3) the presence of many cases of unperiodic enjambement.[18] During his lifetime he wrote much about formulas, something about enjambement, and very little about "themes." Enjambement is useful as a rule-of-thumb measurement if other characteristics are also present, but is not in itself decisive as a criterion of orality. It is a manifestation of the adding style. That style is a sign of oral-traditional composition, but it is easily imitated.

Formula density, the presence of a substantial number of true formulas in a text, is still a reliable criterion for oral composition under certain circumstances which need further review. Formula density should, however, be tempered by an additional investigation of the specific formulas used in a given work vis-à-vis the traditional formulas as they are known.

Let me give two examples that may help in determining whether a given poem is an oral composition, or, more specifically, was composed in the oral-traditional style. The first is the poetry of Peter II, Petrović Njegoš, Prince-Bishop of Montenegro in the first half of the nineteenth century.[19] He was brought up as an (oral) traditional singer of epic, but after his education he became a well-known written literary poet. One can trace in his early *written* poems his gradual departure from the style in which he was brought up. One can note phrases and patterns that were not "traditional," and thus one can document in his case the moving away from tradition, even while keeping the traditional meter. The formula count, in such a case, would in the course of time naturally reflect the emerging written literary style of the author. In addition, an

---

[18] In the second stylistic characteristic, I put "theme" in quotation marks to indicate that the word is used in a special sense of a "repeated passage with a fair degree of verbal or formula repetition from one occurrence to the next," rather than simply as meaning "subject" or "topic." Some scholars use the term "formula" to designate this "theme," but I continue to use it in the sense in which Parry used it, thus differentiating theme from "formula," which is "a group of words which is regularly employed under the same metrical conditions to express a given essential idea" (Parry, M., 1930, 80). For unperiodic enjambement see Parry, 1929, and Lord, A., 1948a. Parry described unperiodic enjambement as follows: "The verse can end with a word group in such a way that the sentence, at the verse end, already gives a complete thought, although it goes on in the next verse, adding free ideas by new word groups."

[19] For more on Njegoš and transitional texts see Lord, A., 1986.

analysis of specific phrases and structures would show marked differences from his known tradition.

The other case is of an author, a poet, brought up in an educated milieu as a Franciscan monk in the eighteenth century. Andrija Kačić-Miošić became so immersed in the traditional style that he could write poems which were, to the uninitiated, indistinguishable from the real thing. In other words, he used well-known traditional formulas. He sought no new stylistic effects. Occasionally, as in expressing a date, he broke the tradition, not only with new words but with new structures. Thus his style betrayed the writer. But he could also write, still in the traditional *meter*, poems, which by content and even genre (e.g., an epistolary genre from the written literary tradition in which he was brought up) were clearly not oral-traditional compositions. If one were to analyze all his work together, the formula density would be fairly high. It is necessary, however, to analyze each song separately, or to segregate those which are clearly written literature from those "in the style of" oral-traditional poetry. His chief and most influential work was a history in prose and "popular" verse of the South Slavs, written in a manner which they could readily understand.[20] He could *write* in both oral and written styles.

The "theme" in oral-traditional epic, a repeated *passage*, is as characteristic of oral-traditional composition as is the formula and for the same reason, its usefulness in composition.[21] There are several important things to note about the "theme." First, it is not *simply* a repeated subject, such as a council, a feast, a battle, or a description of horse, hero, or heroine. It is that, but it is more than that. All those subjects occur repeatedly in written literature as well. The "theme" in oral literature is distinctive because its content is expressed in more or less the same words every time the singer or storyteller uses it. It is a repeated *passage* rather than a repeated subject.

Second, the degree of variation of text and of detailed content among occurrences of a "theme" in the usage of a single singer or storyteller differs considerably from individual to individual and from "theme" to "theme." In general it is clear that a "theme" which he or she uses frequently tends to be more stable in its text, as well as in its content than one used infrequently. It is also true that a short "theme" is more

---

[20] Kačić-Miošić, 1967.
[21] See note 8 above. For more on "theme" see, among others, Lord, A., 1951; 1953; 127–128 (Chapter 2 in this volume); 1960, chap. 4; 1974, especially 19–24.

stable than a long one. One singer I have known had the opening scene of his favorite song down pretty much word for word—not quite, but the text for ten or fifteen lines was fairly stable. This comparative fixity of text in a "theme" is not a mark of a written text. The singer involved, Djemail Zogić of Novi Pazar, was illiterate; he had not consciously memorized those lines.[22] He simply remembered them. Here are the pertinent lines from his dictated version of July 1934 (on the left) and his sung version of November 1934 (on the right). The lines common to both versions are printed in the center column.

No. 25		No. 24
Jedno jutro tek je osamnulo,		Jedno jutro kad je zora bila,
Studena je rosa osamnula,		Studena je rosa udarila,
	Zelena je bašća beherala,	
	Leskovina mlada prelistala,	
A svakoja pilad zapevala,		He svakoja pilad prepevala,
Sve pevahu, a jedna kukaše.		Sve pevahu, jedan zakukaše.
	To ne beše tica lastavica,	
	No to beše sinja kukavica,	
	Kukavica Alibegovica.	
		Kroz kukanju vako govoraše:
		—Hala njojzi do Bora jednoga,
		Bez nikoga desna ni s' lijeva,
		Kukajući dvanajes godina!—
Kroz kukanje Bosnu proklinjaše:		Sve proklinje Bosnu cip cijelu:
"Ravna Bosna kugom pomorena!		"Hala Bosno, kugom pomorena!
		A po Bosni lajale lisice,
		E sve žene ostale udovice,
	Što nemade Bosna kahrimana,	
Da okahri moga dušmanina!"		Da zakahri našeg dušmanina!"
One morning had just dawned,		One morning when it was dawn,
The cold dew (dawned),		The cold dew settled,
	The green garden blossomed,	
	The young hazelwood sent forth leaves,	

---

[22]Parry, 1953, "Bojičić Alija izbavi djecu Alibegovu," by Djemail Zogić, no. 24, sung for the records, November 22, 1934, lines 7–25, and no. 25, dictated to Nikola Vujnović, July 24, 1934, lines 5–18.

And every bird began to sing,	And every bird started to sing,
All were singing, but one lamented.	All were singing, one lamented.

That was not a swallow,
But it was a cuckoo-bird,
A cuckoo-bird, the wife of Alibeg.

In her singing she spoke thus:
—Her lot was hard, by God!
With no one at her right or left,
Lamenting for twelve years!—

In her lamenting she cursed Bosnia: "May level Bosnia be struck by the plague!	Ever did she curse all Bosnia: "By God, Bosnia, may you be struck by the plague! May the foxes bark in Bosnia, And all the women remain widows,

Since Bosnia has no champion,

To challenge my enemy!"	To challenge our enemy!"

"Osamnula" in the second line, wrongly repeating the verb of the preceding line, is a slip of the tongue (or of the recording pen) for "udarila." In the fifth line the only difference is in the prefix of the verb, namely, "zapevala" and "prepevala." In the last line, in addition to the difference in prefixes in "okahri" and "zakahri," there is the difference between "moga" (mine) and "našeg" (our). The main differences between the two versions are the expansions in the singing of the second version.

As further evidence that the lines were not memorized, I present the pertinent lines from Zogić's version sung for the tape-recorder in the summer of 1962, nearly twenty-eight years later.[23]

Jedno jutro kad je zora bila,	One morning when it was dawn,

[23] Unpublished text from the Lord and Bynum Collection, transcribed by Dr. Z. Čolaković. During the sixties David E. Bynum and I collected epics in some of the same centers in Yugoslavia in which Milman Parry had gathered songs in the 1930s, especially Novi Pazar, Gacko, Stolac, and Bihać. Working out of Senica and Duga Poljana, we also went into the heart of the Pešter region in South Serbia at Karajukići Bunari; a number of Parry's singers had come from that area. This collection is presently housed with the Parry Collection in Widener Library at Harvard University.

A ne beše sinja kukavica,	It was not a cuckoo-bird,
No to beše Alibegovica	But it was the wife of Alibeg
Od Udbine, od turske Krajine.	Of Udbina, of the Turkish Border.
A kukaše na dimir kapiju,	She was lamenting at the iron gate,
A preklinje Bosnu cip cijelu:	And she cursed all Bosnia:
"Ravna Bosno, kugom pomorena!	"Level Bosnia, may you be struck by the plague!
I po Bosni lajale lisice,	May the foxes bark in Bosnia,
A sve žene 'tale udovice! . . ."	And all the women remain widows! . . ."

There is a popular misconception that oral literature is crude, form-less, unstructured, and that without writing one cannot create intricate structures of verbal expression. A corollary to this belief is the idea that any work of literature with a complex structure must be a product of the written word, the word seen, rather than the word heard. Those inti-mately acquainted with an oral-traditional literature, however, are cog-nizant of the fact that this is a false impression, arising from a lack of experience with that type of literature.

Cope and Opland have demonstrated the stylistic and artistic excel-lence of Zulu praise poems and folktales and of Xhosa praise poetry, respectively.[24] Douglas Mzolo has done the same for Zulu clan praises, and Daniel Kunene has been especially painstaking in analysis and elo-quent in describing the heroic poetry of the Basotho.[25]

For an illustration of larger orchestration in a long epic song by a talented South Slavic singer I offer here a brief sketch of ring-composition at the beginning of Avdo Međedović's 12,311-line song, "The Wedding of Smailagić Meho," collected by Milman Parry in 1935 and written down by Nikola Vujnović from Avdo's dictation.[26]

The song opens with an assembly of the nobles with Hasan pasha Tiro at their head. He notices that young Meho, son of Smailaga, is unhappy, and he sends Meho's uncle, Cifrić Hasanaga, to inquire the reason for his sadness. Meho responds that he is sad because his elders

[24] See inter alia, Cope, 1978, and Opland, 1975.

[25] Mzolo, 1978; Kunene, 1971.

[26] Međedović, 1974a. Vol. 4 contains the Serbo-Croatian text. For further analysis of rings in this text see Lord, A., 1986.

will not allow him to engage in warfare. He plans to rebel and go over to the enemy. His uncle tells him that he has been the darling of all, that they have been waiting for him to grow up so that he may assume his father's and uncle's position as leader of the Border warriors. The pasha agrees to send Meho to Buda to receive his credentials from the vizier there. The nobles sign the petition and say farewell to Meho.

This opening council scene—a typical "theme," by the way—is a good example of ring-composition. Here is the scheme:

(1) Description and listing of *nobles* with Hasan pasha Tiro at their head.
(2) The intervention of *Hasan pasha Tiro*.
(3) *Cifrić Hasanaga's* speech to Meho.
(4) *Meho's* response.
(3) *Cifrić Hasanaga's* response to Meho.
(2) *Hasan pasha Tiro* has the petition prepared and gives his blessings.
(1) Listing of *nobles* as they sign the petition and say farewell to Meho.
1. Nobles; 2. Pasha; 3. Uncle; 4. Meho; 3. Uncle; 2. Pasha; 1. Nobles.

This is a perfectly acceptable ring. Its pattern is inherent in the narrative itself, and its focus, the speech of Meho to the assembly, is significant in the story; for in it is contained the background for the whole plot. The dramatic confrontation between uncle and nephew with its centerpiece of the nephew's angry speech, which is to provide motivation for the entire poem, is framed in a setting of hierarchical social organization and a statement of heroic values.

After a brief linking theme which takes Meho and his uncle back to Smailaga's house to report what has happened in the assembly, of which the father had as yet no knowledge, the scene for the next ring begins. It extends from the report of Meho's uncle to his brother Smail to the completion of preparations for the departure of Meho and his companion Osman for Buda. The first ring is the conversation between the brothers. The second circle of the ring is the scene between mother and son. This is a scene of elaborate ritual adornment of Meho prior to his appearance before his father. The center of the ring is that appearance. Moving outward in the circle we find a ceremonial preparation of the hero's companion, Osman. This balances the ceremonial preparation of Meho himself. The outermost circle reveals Meho, Osman, and their alter egos, their horses, also ceremonially prepared. Schematized, the ring looks like this:

(1) Meho with father and uncle.
(2) Meho with mother—ritual preparation of Meho.
(3) Meho appears before father and receives his approval.
(2) Meho with father and Osman—ritual preparation of Osman.
(1) Meho with Osman and horses—ritual preparation of horses.
(Meho has passed from father and uncle to Osman and the horses.)

There is not space to follow the intricate structure of rings for the whole poem. Suffice it to say at the moment that each scene can be analyzed in this way, as well as the whole narrative, in terms of rings or chiastic constructions, resembling Cedric Whitman's analysis of Homer's *Iliad*.[27] Some would doubt that oral-traditional poets would have the ability to construct their scenes, and perhaps even an entire poem of some length, in this manner. Here is proof that they not only *can* do but actually *do* just that.

There is a tendency for us in the European tradition to forget how extensive and how basic our literary heritage from the world of orality has been, and there is a corresponding tendency to believe that the world of literacy invented some of the characteristics of literature, which in reality originated in oral literature. Among them is a sense of form and structure, as I have just illustrated, and many devices, later termed "rhetorical" and attributed to the schools, actually were created in the crucible of the oral world. The world of orality gave us anaphora, the use of the same word at the beginning of each series of lines, epiphora, the use of the same word at the end of each of a series of lines, alliteration, assonance, rhyme, both internal, medial, and final, and the sense of balanced structure as typified by parallelisms in sentences and other forms of parataxis. In short, our poetics is derived from the world of orality, with some later additions and modifications introduced by the world of literacy.

Consider as an example of anaphora, alliteration, and parataxis the following passage from one of the South Slavic epics from the Milman Parry Collection collected in 1935. The setting is an assembly of leaders of the Border. All are boasting except one who keeps his head down (my translation reflects the structures of the original).[28]

[27] Whitman, 1958.
[28] Međedović, 1980. The text here quoted is from Međedović's sung version of "Ženidba Vlahinjić Alije," pp. 73–74, lines 51–77, Parry Text no. 12,375, recorded in Bijelo Polje, July 14–15, 1935.

Počeše se falit' kraješnici,	The Borderers began to boast,
Šta je koji bolje učinijo,	What each had done better,
Ko je više dobijo mejdana,	Who had won more duels,
Ko l' njemačkog roba porobijo,	Who had taken a German captive,
Ko l' je carski hudut raširijo;	Who had broadened the imperial Border;
Ko l' je boljeg konja podhranijo,	Who had reared the better horse,
Ko l' je boljeg sina podnivijo,	Who had nurtured the better son,
Ko l' je bolju ćerku podgojijo.	Who had raised the better daughter.
Egleniše šta ko begeniše.	Each said what he wished to.
Neko sebe, neko konja fali,	One praises himself, another his horse,
Neko sina, a neko sinovca.	One his son, and another his nephew.
Neko fali svoju milu šćerku,	One praises his dear daughter,
Neko šćerku, neko milu seku.	One his daughter, another his dear sister.
Neko fali od brata devojku.	One praises his brother's girl.
E, sve age fale na izredu.	E, All the nobles boast in turn.

Note that after two lines of introduction, there are six lines beginning with "ko" (who), followed by a summary line. The six lines are paratactic, in addition to their alliteration and anaphora. Moreover, the next five lines, this time beginning with "neko" (someone), are in parataxis with the preceding group of five lines, and they too end in a "coda." They repeat in substance the previous group, but with a slightly different construction, both grammatically and alliteratively, the "neko" appearing not only at the beginning of the line, but also, in three lines, after the caesura.

The play of "ko" and "neko," which is joined by the neuter "nešto" (something, or somewhat) continues in the scene in the negative. The text goes on then with a rhyming couplet:

Svak se šenli des'jo i vesejo.	Each was joyous and happy.
Jedan im je junak nevesijo,	One hero was unhappy,

Pa nit' vina pije ni rakije,	He drinks neither wine nor brandy,
Ni duhanske tegli tumbećije,	Nor does he draw on his pipe.
No mu mrke objesijo brke,	But he let droop his dusky moustaches,
A ponisko podpušćijo glavu.	And hung his head low.

Note the internal rhyme "pije"/"rakije", "mrke"/"brke," and the alliterations "tegli tumbećije", and "ponisko podpušćijo."

The next couplet ends the first part of the scene and at the same time introduces the second:

Bože mili, ko je junak bijo?	Dear God, who was that hero?
To je Hrnja sa Kladuše Mujo.	It was Mujo Hrnjica of Kladuša.

In the next two couplets we return to the negatives:

Pa serdara niko ne pitaše	But nobody asked the sirdar
Što je nešto Mujo nevesijo.	Why Mujo was not happy.
Neko neće, neko ne vidaše,	One would not, another did not see,
A neko ga pitat' ne smijaše.	And some dared not ask him.

And the passage continues to weave its way binding couplets together into quatrains and other configurations with sound and syntax. This is oral-traditional poetic composition at its most typical.

As many have remarked, the Finnish *Kalevala* makes abundant use of parallelism and repetition, and in his translation of it Francis Peabody Magoun, Jr. has preserved those elements of the style. For example, here is a passage near the beginning of Poem 33:

> He uttered a word as he went along
> kept saying while walking:
> "Woe is me, poor lad,
> woe the unfortunate lad.
> Now I have got into something,
> got into the futile occupation
> of being the herdsman of a steer's tail,
> a tender of calves . . . "

Another compositional device in the *Kalevala* is the repetition of the end of one line at the beginning of the next, as in the following:

> "With what shall I now pay back the woman's mockery,
> the woman's mockery, the girl's derision?"

Note that the second half of the second line is parallel to the first half. In the next example the fourth line is also parallel to the second:

> In this way Kullervo, son of Kalervo,
> took vengeance on the girl's ridicule,
> on the girl's ridicule, the woman's derision,
> paid the bad wife her wages.[29]

Such repetitions are common in Slavic oral-traditional epic as well. In commenting on similar devices in Irish traditional poetry Daniel Melia remarked that they are not primarily mnemonic, but compositional and structural.[30] They are basic to oral-traditional style and characteristic of it.

One is inclined to ask whether written literature would tolerate the kind of poetics that makes frequent use of these and other similar devices. It is well known that most oral-traditional texts are heavily "edited" before they are published. This was especially true in the nineteenth century but such practices still exist today. The Grimm brothers are classic examples for the European folktale, but their case is by no means isolated.[31] What would a well-intentioned editor with a literary bent try to do with passages such as those just quoted to make them accord more with his own feeling for style? He would do what even the most careful translator of Homer does. Where Homer uses the same epithet for a god or hero many times, the translator varies the epithets, because English style (or written literary style in general) avoids repetitions as much as possible. In the editing practice of the person who prepared for publication the songs collected by one of the best of the nineteenth-century Croatian scholars, Luka Marjanović, of the Matica Hrvatska in Zagreb, when the end of a line is repeated at the beginning of the next, the repetition is frequently—though not always—omitted

---

[29] Lönnrot, 1963, p. 236, lines 7–12; p. 237, lines 44–48; p. 239, lines 219–222.
[30] Melia, 1977, 285–300.
[31] See Ellis, 1983, and Tatar, 1987.

and the lines are reformed. In short, the published texts do not reproduce what the singer said, but what the editor thought that the singer should have said, or intended to say. It is for this reason that Milman Parry made his own collection of field recordings of epic so that he could have reliable material for meaningful research; and it is with this in mind that the texts in his collection are published exactly as the singers sang or dictated them.

In addition to balanced structures and poetical devices, we have also inherited from the oral period the great myths from the past of most cultures of the human race, myths telling of the formation of the universe, of the beginning of all things. They were both believed and believed in, and they have had very profound influence on the history of mankind. Yet they, too, belonged originally in the world of orality, until they were written down. Here are to be found the accounts of the lives of gods, or heroes, saints, or legendary rulers. In them the birth of a god or hero was important, because it explained his special powers and characteristics. Narratives of his childhood deeds gave early evidence of his extraordinary personality and strength, proving his divine, or at least "different," origin. And the story in many cultures of a hero's acquisition of a horse and special weapons provided him with the means of accomplishing his mission in the world. One of his earliest deeds, after initiation and often associated with it, is his acquiring of a bride, in order to assure the continuity of quality in future generations.

In some cultures in many parts of the world the biographical scheme in oral-traditional literature plays a very large role, second only to their creation myths and sometimes intertwined with them. The miraculously born and magically equipped god or hero creates order from chaos, thus establishing the cosmos, and he also overcomes monsters that would destroy the universe and return humanity to chaos and death.

This is the mythic side of oral literature; its basic and oldest message evolved through the ages in the minds of the people who created it, perfected its forms, and continued it over time. The battles of gods and demigods, and those of heroes, provided the patterns, the fundamental vocabulary of words and themes, heard, not seen, so that in the course of time, when myth was secularized, or, whichever the case may be, when secular narratives arose side by side with myth, they found ready-made patterns in the forms of literature for recounting history. History has played a significant role in African praise poetry, as well as in African oral literature in general. Both tribal and personal history have contributed to the praises of chiefs. Topical compositions, too, like the odes of Pindar, may on occasion make reference to past events as well as to the present subject.[32] A people's history and the fundamental values of its legal and social structures are expressed in its traditional literature.

In some societies oral literature, as such, has given way to a large extent to written literature. But the form and the content of much of our written literature were created before writing was invented. The fact of the matter remains that, without overtly realizing it, when we read the Homeric poems, the *Gilgamesh* epic, most of the chansons de geste, and many other "literary" works, we are reading in essence the masterpieces of oral literature, which evolved in the oral period, but became set in that of literacy. Like the oral literatures of Africa, of the Balkans, of Central Asia, of all those regions of the world where oral-traditional literature has been recorded, they too were once written down. They are older than writing.

From an intimate acquaintance with the oral background of its past one gains a perspective on one's own culture, a knowledge of its age and depth, of what it held dear in the generations long gone, as well as some insight into why one still holds it dear in the present.

[32] See Nagy, G., 1990.

CHAPTER 2

Homer's Originality:
Oral Dictated Texts

In his impressive book *Heroic Poetry*, Sir Cecil M. Bowra places Homer "in the middle of an important change produced by the introduction of writing." "Behind him [Homer] lie centuries of oral performance, largely improvised, with all its wealth of formulae adapted to an exacting metre; these he knows and uses fully. But if he also knows writing and is able to commit his poems to it, he is enabled to give a far greater precision and care to what he says than any improvising poet ever can." Bowra concludes, "Since it is almost impossible to believe that the *Iliad* and *Odyssey* were ever improvised, and the richness of their poetry suggests some reliance on writing, we may see in them examples of what happens when writing comes to the help of the oral bard. He continues to compose in the same manner as before, but with far greater care and effectiveness."[1]

These are the latest words in Homeric scholarship and they demand our attention. Bowra has ranged widely in the field of oral epic, realizing full well the importance of the comparative method in scholarship. He has focused our studies now on the period of transition from oral to written technique, and he is right. It was inevitable that a solution to the question of whether or not Homer was an oral poet would be sought in a compromise that would make him both; that is to say, an oral poet

This paper was first read at the annual meeting of the American Philological Association in 1952 and published in *TAPA* 94 (1953), 124–134. Although it is somewhat dated, I have chosen to leave it essentially unchanged except for minor editorial differences. I have added an occasional comment in the notes.
[1] Bowra, 1952, 240–241.

who wrote. The motivating force behind this solution is the reluctance to associate the greatness of Homer's poetry, the unity of his poems, his originality, or individuality, with unlettered oral song.

The feeling seems to be growing that the work of Milman Parry in the 1930s was an attack on the citadel of Homer's creative greatness. This feeling is far less apparent in Bowra's book than in H. T. Wade-Gery's *The Poet of the Iliad* (1952), which is more typical of this increasing sentiment.[2] Wade-Gery also accepts the fact that Homer used the oral technique of composition, but he too stumbles on the stone of creative genius. For him Homer was an oral poet who had the ambition to make a poem that is beyond the limits of oral composition.[3] "The *Iliad* is what it is because of the impact upon an oral technique of a brand-new literacy invented by the Greeks themselves." "It was the *Iliad* which for its scale and its organic structure demanded this new device." To him the *Iliad* "is not a traditional book, but a great poem by a great poet." It is distinguished "from the common run of heroic poetry" by "the tragic unity of its theme and the dramatic intensity of its characters."[4] In other words, a traditional book cannot be "a great poem," cannot have "tragic unity" or "dramatic intensity" of character. If we can show that a poem is "great" and has "tragic unity" and "dramatic intensity" of character, we can prove that it is not a traditional book, according to Wade-Gery.

On the surface Bowra's and Wade-Gery's positions may appear to be the same. To both Homer is an oral poet who writes. Yet in Bowra the Homeric poems become what they are artistically with the help of writing; whereas in Wade-Gery the grand concept of the poems precedes their actual creation and demands the alphabet for its expression.[5]

At this point three questions present themselves as tests of this com-

---

[2] Wade-Gery, 1952. L. A. Post, in his Sather Classical Lectures, similarly misinterprets Parry's writings on oral technique and accuses Parry and myself of a non sequitur: "To conclude that, because the technique of modern Yugoslav epic is comparable to that of the Homeric poems, therefore no Homeric poet existed who was very different in capacity and achievement from modern oral poets, is a *non sequitur*" (Post, 1951, 274–275, n. 13). Neither Parry nor I has ever denied the greatness of Homer, or ever made any statement that would imply that there are no grades of distinction among oral poets. We have nowhere said or written that there could have been no Homer because "most or even all modern oral poets are comparatively unoriginal." Our experiences on the contrary have shown us, as this present article indicates, that the capacities and achievements of oral poets, ancient or modern, have been unjustly minimized and misunderstood.

[3] Wade-Gery, 1952, 13–14.

[4] Ibid., 39, 40, 17.

[5] Unfortunately, versions of these views are current in some quarters even today.

promise solution. Does the oral technique exclude originality, and if not, how can oral poets be "original" or "individual" or "great"? What do we know about the period of transition from oral to written technique? What occurs in the process of writing down an oral poem?

Wade-Gery terms Parry "the Darwin of Homeric studies" and explains: "As Darwin seemed to many to have removed the finger of God from the creation of the world and of man, so Milman Parry has seemed to some to remove the creative poet from the *Iliad* and *Odyssey*." He quotes part of a sentence of Parry's, published in 1930, that has been fastened upon by Parry's critics as denying originality to oral poets in general and to Homer in particular. Wade-Gery calls it "Parry's paradox about the epic poet, that [and here he quotes Parry] 'at no time is he [the oral poet] seeking words for an idea which has never before found expression.'"[6]

Parry wrote this before he had had any experience of oral singers, at a time when he was arguing deductively from his analysis of style. In his second article on the same subject, published in 1932, written before his Yugoslav trips, he made use of evidence from other poetries and from the reports of collectors.[7] It was because he was dissatisfied with both of these methods that he decided to conduct his own investigations of oral poetry. It is truly amazing that most of his conclusions in these early papers have proved to be completely accurate by field observation and experiment. If one places the controversial sentence quoted by Wade-Gery in the full context of the two articles, Parry's meaning is put in perspective and not distorted. What he says in essence is that the question of originality of style means nothing to the oral poet, because he has at his command ready-made phrases which have been built up by generations of poets to express all the ideas needed in the poetry. In order for the tradition to have come into being and to have continued to exist, one must suppose that singers made changes from time to time, but these changes would have been slight and new formulas would have been modeled on the old ones. In Parry's words, "An oral style is thus highly conservative; yet the causes for change are there, and sooner or later must come into play. These causes for change have nothing to do with any wish on the part of the single poet for what is new or striking in style."[8]

[6] Wade-Gery 35–39, 41.
[7] Parry, M., 1930 and 1932.
[8] Parry, M., 1932, 9.

These statements have been checked by field experiments. They still hold true, but they should be elaborated in two directions. First, we have learned in Yugoslavia that there are differences between the text of a song as actually sung and the text of a song that was taken down from dictation. Previously evidence about oral technique had come from texts that had been written down from the singers' dictation and then edited.[9] A certain amount of normalizing occurs during both the dictating and editing processes, so that the published song does not by any means exactly reproduce the formulaic style of the sung performance. A study of actual sung texts, however, indicates considerable formula deviation. We know now that creation and re-creation occur on the formula level much more actively than Parry had at first thought. Each singer has a group of formulas that forms the basis of his style. These change but seldom; on them he patterns others. They represent, of course, the most common narrative or descriptive ideas of his poems. All other formulas vary greatly in their susceptibility to change at the hands of a single singer. As Parry noted, the changes follow the patterns of the stable formulas, because the singer thinks in those patterns. Nevertheless, the singer has freedom to create new phrases and he does so.

Thus the singer has scope for his creative powers on the formula level. And because the basic core of formulas is not necessarily the same even for singers from the same district or who have learned from the same man, these experiments provide us with a means of distinguishing individual styles among singers. We should eventually by this means be able to come to some reasonable answer to the question of whether the *Iliad* and the *Odyssey* are by the same poet.

The second direction in which Parry's statements should be elaborated leads to a field about which he had actually written but little, that which I choose to call "the epic technique of oral song-making." I spoke about this at the 1950 American Philological Association meetings in a paper titled "Composition by Theme in Homer and Southslavic Epos."[10] The themes of oral poetry are the repeated narrative or descriptive elements, and they function in building songs in much the same way in which the formulas function in building lines. The formula content of a theme is variable depending on the wishes of the singer to lengthen or shorten his song. Some themes in turn are purely ornamental, and they may be included or eliminated according to the wishes of the singer.

[9] E.g., Karadžić, 1932–36.
[10] Lord, A., 1951.

Moreover, the themes vary in stability, both as to formula content and as to place in any given song, in accordance with the frequency of their use. Themes that are basic to many songs and are hence used very often tend to be fairly stable, like the basic core of formulas.

Since songs are, therefore, only relatively stable in their content, they readily combine. They may be added to one another without difficulty, one being sung as a continuation of another. They may be easily inter-twined. In Yugoslav tradition there are songs that tell of a son setting out to find a lost father, and there are songs recounting the return of a hero from captivity after many years to find his wife about to marry again. These two stories are combined in the *Odyssey*. By studying the combination and separation and recombination of themes and songs in the Yugoslav tradition we are learning the principles that these processes follow; we know that the processes are not merely haphazard. But what we need to point out for the present purpose is that the oral poet has a great degree of freedom in the construction of his song, if he wishes to be creative and to make use of that freedom. How else could new songs enter the tradition? Homer obviously used that freedom of combination in the *Iliad* and *Odyssey*.

On both the formulaic and the thematic level, then, the oral technique not only allows freedom for change and creation but aids in providing the means by which the singer may exercise his creative imagination if he so desires. His medium is not so restrictive that he is stifled by his tradition. An oral poet can be creative to whatever degree his inspiration moves him and his mastery of technique permits. A singer will show originality both in new phrases and in new combinations of themes, perhaps even in new themes. Even lesser oral poets than a Homer are original, particularly at that point when they first sing a song which they learned from another singer. Unwittingly perhaps, they recombine themes, or add and eliminate themes, using their own individual for-mulaic techniques.

In the Yugoslav laboratory we can determine, after working long with a single singer and with other singers in his district, in exactly what points any given singer is original. For Homer we simply do not have anywhere nearly sufficient material, and we must heed F. Combellack's sage words in his excellent article, "Contemporary Unitarians and Ho-meric Originality," warning us not to be too specific in claiming origi-nality for any given passage.[11] Yet even here I believe that with time we

[11] Combellack, 1950.

can arrive at an appreciation of the ways in which Homer shows his superiority to all other oral epic poets.

Homer, then, I am certain, did not need writing to be a creative poet in his tradition. But it must be true that he lived in an age when writing existed and was developed to such a point that the *Iliad* could be written down. It was probably the age of transition from oral to written technique in literature. Our second question is, What do we know about this transition?

Wade-Gery presents us not with a transition but with a lightning-like metamorphosis. Bowra is infinitely more realistic. He is aware that the transition from oral to written literature does not occur overnight. Indeed, in the passage from his book that I quoted earlier, he has described the process very accurately, I believe. The oral artist comes to realize the possibilities that the leisure of the new medium permits for careful composition and for calculated changes different from the rapid changes forced by the speed of oral performance. To telescope the change from expert oral technique to a sophisticated use of literary technique into the lifetime of one individual, even granting that the singer is a genius, is, I am sure, not consistent with the facts.

There are in Yugoslavia a number of oral poets who can write. Their first attempts at writing were mere recordings of the songs that they knew. When they go beyond this and begin to break the formula patterns in which they have thought poetically all their lives, the results are not felicitous. They abandon such imaginative introductions as "Once in the days of old, when Sulejman held empire," for such prosaic beginnings as "In the bloody year of 1914, on the sixth day of the month of August, Austria and all Germany were greatly worried." They become wordy and stilted to the point of being unconsciously mock heroic. The natural dignity of the traditional expressions is lost and what remains is a caricature. The literary technique takes several generations to mature. I cannot conceive of the author of the *Iliad* as semiliterate. The poem is too great, is done with far too much assurance, to be the first hesitating steps in a new technique. It seems to me rather that it is the product of a great oral poet in a rich oral tradition. The poems of a semiliterate oral poet are awkward in construction because they mix two techniques, one of which has not yet had time to develop, and the other of which the poet already disdains.

There is a further difficulty in the compromise solution of a literate oral poet that needs to be answered. Why should oral poets take to writing down their songs? Since the oral technique does not hamper in any way those who practice it well, since in Homer's period I do not believe that we can posit a highly developed literary technique that would make them dissatisfied with the older one, I cannot see why oral poets should even think of turning to writing. The rich possibilities of the literary technique are not apparent at its inception, especially to those who already have a technique that is rich in known possibilities.

Someone may suggest that it would be a mnemonic device, but this too is unrealistic. The singer has no need of a mnemonic device in a manner of singing that was designed to fill his needs without such written aids. A mnemonic device implies a fixed text to be memorized, a concept unknown to the oral poet. A written text would be useful to the reciter or rhapsode of a later period who is no longer an oral poet, but simply a mouthpiece.

Another suggestion might be that the singer wishes to preserve his song for posterity. This too is invalid. His song will be handed down to younger generations, even as he received it and other songs from his elders. It would never occur to the singer that his song would be lost. That is why he sings, that the glories of the past might not be lost to memory. Perhaps the singer wanted to have his song preserved in the exact words and form in which he sang it. But we must reject this also; for one must remember that in the oral manner the singer has no idea of a fixed, word-for-word form of a song.

It would seem, then, that the idea to write down an oral song must come from an outside source, not from the singers themselves. A question of prime importance for the dating of Homer must ask when the idea of writing down epic songs arose and under what circumstances. Possibly there was an early period of collecting from which only these two songs have survived and about which we have no other reference or record. We know from other traditions that writing has really arrived at that moment when it is used for artistic purposes; the first things written are the songs of the people. It seems to me that this is the question to which we should be turning our attention, because when we can answer it, we shall know when Homer lived and when the poems were composed. For they are unmistakably the product of the collecting of oral poetry. To this extent writing is indispensable to the composition of the *Iliad* and the *Odyssey*.

But this is not the only extent, I believe, to which writing is indispensable to the Homeric poems as we have them. Bowra has stated that "it is almost impossible to believe that the *Iliad* and *Odyssey* were ever improvised, and the richness of their poetry suggests some reliance on writing." This statement is properly cautious. Allow me to rephrase it more precisely. It is impossible to believe that the *Iliad* and *Odyssey* as we have them represent exactly the songs as actually sung in normal performance by Homer; their length and consequent richness of content, the perfection of their lines, suggest some reliance on writing. We must now elaborate and explain this rephrasing.

The Homeric poems belong to the period of transition from an oral to a literary technique, a transition that takes at least several generations before it is completed, yet they are oral poems as their style indicates. Homer, then, was an oral poet living in an age of writing. Oral songs can be collected either by phonograph apparatus, which is obviously out of the question here; or by dictation to a scribe; or by a literate oral poet who has been asked to write down his song for someone else who, for some reason, wants it in writing. The last of these possibilities is highly unlikely, because the oral poet, if he is at all literate, can have only a smattering of writing, if he is to remain an oral poet. Had he enough facility in writing to record 21,000 lines of text, his style could not be that of an oral technique, which Homer's demonstrably is. In my own mind there remains no doubt that Homer dictated the *Iliad* to someone else who wrote it down, because the Homeric poems have all the ear-marks of dictated texts of oral epic songs. They are not the text of normal oral-traditional performance; without recording apparatus it is impossible to obtain such texts. They are not texts produced by written technique of composition, because such a technique had not been developed, and they do not show signs of a break in the formulaic tradition. They are not semiliterate texts in the sense of texts that occur at the beginning of the development of written technique, because they are too good. But they are oral dictated texts, a completely separate category that represents, from the point of view of the oral singer, an "ideal" text. To understand this we must look very closely at the moment of their composition; we must examine what occurs when the singer dictates his song to a scribe.

This moment has hitherto been ignored by Homeric scholars because they have not thought it worth their while to undertake field collecting. Milman Parry realized that the experience of being in the field was

necessary, that he could not simply read oral epics that had been collected by others and the accounts that those collectors had written. He
had to relive the experience. Fortunately he collected songs from dictation as well as songs sung for the recording apparatus. I myself have
written down songs from dictation, a process that I learned from a true
master. To the best of my knowledge the only other Homerist to have
the temerity to leave the comfort of his study and enter the field is J. N.
Notopoulos.

An oral poet who is asked to dictate a song for someone to write finds
himself in an unusual and abnormal position. He is accustomed to composing rapidly to the accompaniment of a musical instrument, which
sets the rhythm and tempo of his performance. For the first time he is
without this rhythmic assistance, and at the beginning he finds it difficult to make his lines. He can easily learn to do this, however, and he
sets up a certain rhythm in his mind. He is also somewhat annoyed by
having to wait between lines for the scribe to write. His mind moves
ahead more rapidly than does the writer's pen. This technique he can
also learn, particularly if the scribe is alert and helpful. The singer is also
accustomed to the stimulus of an audience, but again an intelligent
scribe and a small group of onlookers can provide this stimulus. These
are the disadvantages of the dictating technique, but they are not insur-
mountable. When they are surmounted, the singer discovers the advantages of the technique and proceeds to profit by them, as long as the
scribe can mitigate the boredom of slow performance, and maintain the
singer's interest.

The chief advantage to the singer of this manner of composition is
that it affords him time to think of his lines and of his song. His small
audience is stable. This is an opportunity for the singer to show his best,
not as a performer, but as a storyteller and poet. He can ornament his
song as fully as he is capable; he can develop his tale with completeness,
he can dwell lovingly on passages that in normal performance he would
often be forced to shorten because of the pressure of time or because of
the restlessness of the audience. The very length of the Homeric poems
is the best proof that they are products of the moment of dictation rather
than that of singing. The leisureliness of their tempo, the fullness of
their telling, are also indications of this method. The poetic moments of
the tradition, used perhaps sparingly in normal performance, accumulate to provide that richness of poetry which Bowra feels suggests writing. To the method of dictation one can also attribute the piling up of

similes in Homer and the extended simile. It is not that Homer goes beyond the bounds of the oral technique, but that he uses it to the full. It is interesting that when Parry asked singers when they had finished dictating songs for him whether they thought that sung songs were better than dictated ones or vice versa, their answers invariably were: "Sung songs are truer, dictated songs are finer!" I would paraphrase this as: "Sung songs are closer to what we have heard from others, but we can be better poets in dictated song!"[12] That dictated songs are indeed superior to sung texts can be seen in the first volume of the Parry Collection.[13]

There is a certain amount of originality in each performance of an oral epic. It has never been sung exactly the same way before, even by the same singer; it will never be sung exactly the same way again. It is unique. If each performance under normal conditions can be original, then the dictated performance allows for the greatest originality. It is, moreover, the kind of originality that still remains within the tradition, because the tradition is but the sum total of the singers and their songs. The oral poet constantly combines and recombines and adds and subtracts from what he has heard. And this combining and recombining, adding and subtracting, is the tradition. When a singer makes a new song, he is following the tradition.

The Homeric poems are what they are because they are the products of an oral technique with its abundant opportunities for freedom of creation, recorded by a method and under circumstances that bring to the fore the very best that an inspired poet can instill into them. Even as the moment of singing is the normal moment of creation of oral epic, so the moment of dictating is the moment of creation of our texts from the past. The more we know about that moment, the greater will be our understanding of those texts.

Addendum 1990

As I reconsidered very recently the stylization of a passage from Salih Ugljanin's "Song of Bagdad" that was found in a dictated version but not in two sung texts, I was suddenly aware of the experience of listen-

12 Cf. Parry, M., 1954, 263 and 416, n. 1.
13 Parry, M., 1954.

ing to Salih dictate. In my memory I could envisage a room in Novi
Pazar on a series of rainy days, where I could see him sitting at the table
at which Nikola Vujnović was writing and hear him speak the lines
rapidly but with a deliberate tempo; a line, a pause, then another line, as
he watched Nikola set it down on the paper. But the pause interrupted
neither Salih's thought nor his syntax. The measured delivery made the
parallelisms in the following lines of the passage I just referred to almost
inevitable:

> Kad tatarin pod Kajnidu dođe,
> Pa eto ga uz čaršiju prođe,
>
> When the messenger came to Kajniđa,
> Then he passed along through the market place.
> When . . . to Kajniđa he came,
> Then . . . along the market place he passed.

This kind of construction may emerge more clearly in the mannered
dictating than in the necessary flexibility of composition in the hurly-
burly of the live singing performance.

One might think that dictating gave Salih the leisure to plan his words
and their placing in the line, that the parallelism was due to his careful
thinking out of the structure. First of all, however, dictating is not a
leisurely process; neither the singer nor the scribe has the patience for
long pauses for deliberation. The hours pass and the lines accumulate as
the song is set down. But more especially, a mood and a tempo, as I
have suggested, are established that produce the balanced utterances of
the poet. Not conscious planning but the rhythm of that particular
process of composition calls forth the structures. I might add that not all
singers can dictate successfully. As I have said elsewhere, some singers
can never be happy without the *gusle* accompaniment to set the rhythm
of the singing performance.

CHAPTER 3

Homeric Echoes in Bihać

In the Milman Parry Collection of Oral-Traditional Literature in the Harvard University Library are a number of texts that tell of the return of a hero after a long captivity to find his wife about to marry again.[1] This basic Odyssean tale attracted Parry because of its similarity to the Homeric poem and he collected by dictation and by phonographic recording as many versions of it as he could. Some of those have been summarized in the appendixes of *The Singer of Tales.*[2] One of them contains an incident very like an episode in the *Odyssey* of Homer. The song, "The Captivity of Šarac Mehmedaga," was dictated to Nikola Vujnović by Franje Vuković on March 15, 1935, in Bihać in northern Bosnia.[3] The singer was a Christian, but the song and its hero are Moslem. The story goes as follows:

Uskok Radovan, in a German disguise, set out from Udbina on his black horse to find his blood-brother, Šarac Mehmedaga. A mist fell and Radovan lost his way. When he came to the well of Mitrović Ilija, he dismounted to rest. Ilija's servants saw him and reported his presence to Ilija, who looked at him through his spy-glass and recognized him. Ilija sent his servants to capture Radovan alive, and after a struggle they

Published in *Zbornik za narodni život i običaje*, vol. 40 (Zagreb: Jugoslavenska akademija znanosti i umjetnosti, 1962), 313–320.
[1] For details of the Parry Collection see Parry, M., 1954, 3–45.
[2] Lord, A., 1960, 243–265.
[3] Parry Text no. 1905, Milman Parry Collection, Widener Library, Harvard University, Cambridge, Mass.

succeeded. Radovan told Ilija that he was searching for his blood-brother who had been missing for twelve years. He had set out for Kotari but in the fog had wandered to Ilija's well in the coastland. Ilija sent Radovan to Gavran Kapetan, who in turn sent him to the governor of Zadar, who put him in prison.

In the prison Radovan found thirty captives from the Lika and Udbina. They all greeted him except one who was sitting on a stone, playing a mother-of-pearl *šargija* (a kind of stringed instrument) and singing. When he had finished his song he went over to Radovan. It was Šarac, who asked him if anyone knew that they were in prison and how long ago he had left Udbina. Radovan told him the whole story of his capture, after which Šarac asked him a series of questions about Šarac's tower at home, his horse, his servant Bilaver, his mother, his wife, his pistols, and his mother-of-pearl *tambura*.[4] Radovan replied that Šarac's tower was unscathed as was his servant also; his horse had not been out of the stable for twelve years; his mother had been weeping constantly; his sword and pistols and *tambura* were safe; but his wife was about to marry Hrnjičić Halil. Radovan advised Šarac to shout in prison to get attention. For three days and four nights he shouted and greatly disturbed the governor, his wife, and his little child in the cradle. The governor sent the jailer to ask the prisoner what was wrong. Šarac replied that he would like to go before the governor to tell him his troubles. He promised the jailer to give him a horse and a sword if the governor would talk to him and let him go home to Udbina. The jailer reported to the governor, who agreed to talk with Šarac. Šarac told him about his wife and asked that he be sent to Udbina to collect ransom. The governor first refused but at the intercession of his wife he agreed to release him for a ransom of one hundred ducats.

Šarac was given a haircut, but a collar was put around his neck to indicate that he was a prisoner. The governor gave him a little money for the journey, and, after thanking the governor's wife, Šarac set out for home. When he came to Mount Vučjak he rested and then took a shortcut to the top of the mountain whence it was possible to see Udbina. His eyes, however, had been dimmed from long imprisonment, and he could not make out the houses, so he came down and continued until he reached Mount Komić, whence he could at last see Udbina. He addressed his own tower, wondering whether he would find his mother

---

[4] A *šargija* is a kind of *tambura*, a strummed musical instrument with two metal strings.

there. Then he went down the mountain and across the meadow until he came to the River Crvać and to a well where he stopped for the late afternoon prayer.

Soon the gates of Udbina opened; thirty maidens emerged and went to the well to fetch water. When Šarac saw them, he fled into the reedy grass. After the girls had drawn the water, they began to dance the *kolo*. Šarac came out of the grass, approached and gave them greeting; and they asked whence he came and whither he was going. He told them that he had been in prison in Zadar and that he was the only son of Omeraga of Mostar. His father was dead, he said, and his mother was dying. He had asked the governor to release him to visit his mother. He told them of the ransom. The girls asked if he had seen Šarac in Zadar, and he replied that Šarac had died in prison. He said that Šarac had asked him, if he was ever released, to go to Udbina to tell his wife to marry again. The girls told Šarac that they would reward him for this news, and he received sixty ducats. They told him that Šarac's wife was about to marry again and that the wedding guests had arrived. Then the girls picked up their pails and went into Udbina. Šarac finished his prayers, took up his staff, and set out for town.

There were many wedding guests in the courtyard of his tower, but Šarac went straight to the stable where he found his horse and the servant Bilaver. He asked permission to touch the horse, but Bilaver told him that the horse would not allow him to do so. Šarac, however, embraced the horse, and Bilaver also recognized his master. Šarac asked Bilaver not to tell anyone that he had been in the stable; he was going to see whether his mother would recognize him. In the tower he found the wedding guests, and they made room for him at their table. Mujo, the brother of Halil the prospective bridegroom, and the commander in chief of the armies of the Border, asked him who he was, whence he had come, and whither he was going, and Šarac told him the deceptive story that he had told the girls at the well. Mujo also asked about Šarac and was told of Šarac's death and request for the stranger to visit his family and to tell his wife to marry again. Mujo gave him a good gift as did the others, and he collected another sixty ducats.

Šarac asked permission to go to see his mother and the permission was granted. He told her that he had no news from her son because he was dead; it was he who had buried him in the cold sea. His mother screamed and then gave him a gift. Šarac returned to Mujo and asked permission to go to see his wife. He put his pistols in his pocket and went to her room, saying to himself that if he found her merry, he would shoot her, if not, he would not do anything. In the harem he asked which of the women was Šarac's wife, and when told, he repeated to her the same story about Šarac's death and request that he tell his wife to marry again. His wife screamed and also gave him a gift. Šarac then went to his own room, hung up his pistols, and returned to Mujo and the wedding guests, who again made room for him at the table.

After a bit of drinking, Mujo asked Šarac if he would like to enter a race with a prize of thirty ducats. Šarac agreed and they went out onto the field for the footrace. There were twenty entries. When they reached mid-field Šarac struck Halil, who was in front, and challenged him for the "widow." Halil was about to shoot Šarac, when Mujo stopped him, saying that if he killed the governor's prisoner, the governor would challenge him.

They all returned to the tower and Šarac went to his room, where he picked up his *tambura* and began to sing, saying that he did not wonder at his horse's recognizing him, but he did wonder that the mother who had borne him had not. When his mother heard that, she came to his room and they embraced. When his wife heard that, she came to his room and they embraced. When the wedding guests heard that, they came to his room and they embraced. He dismissed the wedding guests, who returned home to Kladuša, with the exception of Mujo.

The next day, Mujo and Šarac, dressed as young officers, said good-bye to Šarac's mother and set our for Zadar. Šarac returned to prison, but Mujo managed to capture the governor's son and to escape with him to Kladuša. In return for the release of his son, the governor agreed to release Šarac and the other prisoners, to give them new clothes and horses. The prisoners were exchanged at the border.

There are clearly many points in this song that are reminiscent of episodes in Homer's *Odyssey*. The most striking of these is surely the encounter of the hero with the girls who have come to draw water at the well outside Udbina. The incident reminds one of the scene in Book 6 of the *Odyssey* when Nausicaa and her maidens come to the river to wash clothes and Odysseus hides from them. He comes out of hiding only when the girls have begun to dance or play. This theme is not a common one in the Serbo-Croatian return songs, but it is found in a modified form in the texts of "Marko Kraljević and Mina of Kostur" which

Parry collected from Petar Vidić in Stolac.[5] In these texts Marko's wife has been captured by Nina and taken to his tower in Koštun, where Nina plans to marry her. Returning from war in Arabia where he had heard of his wife's captivity, Marko, dressed as a monk with some companions also disguised as monks, meets his wife and either twelve women or his sister washing clothes at a spring near Koštun.[6] Marko's wife recognizes his horse and asks Marko about the horse's master. Marko tells of Marko's death and says that the horse had been given to him as payment for burying Marko.

The episode in "Marko and Nina" contributes at least one new Homeric touch, namely the washing of clothes. In both Homer and "Marko and Nina" the lady in question is either about to be married (Marko's wife) or has thoughts of marriage (Nausicaa). There are, of course, dissimilarities as well. For example, Marko arrives with companions, whereas Odysseus at this point is alone, all of his comrades having perished; Marko comes upon the women, whereas the women come upon Odysseus; Marko does not hide, but Odysseus does. None of these details seems to be especially significant. In the tale of Marko the deceptive story is used in this episode, but it is not found in the encounter with Nausicaa in the *Odyssey*. In Vidić's text recognition of Marko's horse by his wife and deceptive story come in this scene: Marko's wife actually does not recognize him until just before the marriage scene. There is no deceptive story in the Nausicaa episode and it is not until Book 9 of the *Odyssey* that Odysseus reveals his identity to Arete and Alcinous, just before he tells the tale of his wanderings.

If we compare the events in "The Captivity of Šarac Mehmedaga" with those in the Nausicaa episode in the *Odyssey*, we may note the following correspondences:

1. The hero is on his way home after a long absence.
2. The hero arrives at a spring or other body of water.
3. The hero has prayed or is in the process of praying.
4. A group of women comes to draw water or to wash clothes.
5. The hero hides or is hidden when the women arrive.

[5] "Marko Kraljević and Nina of Koštun," Parry Text nos. 6, 804, 805, 846. See Lord, A., 1960, Appendix II, for parallel analyses. The classical version of this song is no. 61 in Karadžić, 1958.
[6] In Parry Text no. 804 the spring occurs at a different point in the story, and Marko's wife sees him from the window as he enters the courtyard.

6. The women dance or play when they have finished their work.
7. The hero emerges from cover and talks with the women.
8. The women return to town first and the hero follows later.

The similarity is very striking. It is also striking that the element of deceptive story, which plays an important role in "The Captivity of Šarac Mehmedaga," is missing, as I mentioned before, in the Nausicaa episode in the *Odyssey*. In the South Slavic song the deceptive story has two parts: in the first the hero tells a false story about his own identity, and in the second he tells about the death of the hero (himself, of course) and how he had buried him and been given certain tasks to perform. Recognition takes place in the Phaeacian episode when Odysseus weeps at the bard's singing in the court of Alcinous about the fall of Troy, and, on questioning, reveals his identity to Arete and Alcinous. The main recognitions and especially those coupled with deceptive stories occur in Ithaca, not in Phaeacia, where the beginning of the episode in "The Captivity of Šarac Mehmedaga" led us first.

Deceptive stories are, of course, abundant in the *Odyssey*! We might do well, as a matter of fact, to examine the series of deceptive stories and of recognition in both "The Captivity of Šarac Mehmedaga" and the *Odyssey*.

Although it may seem that the first deceptive story and recognition in the *Odyssey* occur in the hut of Eumaeus, there is a very provocative episode that takes place between the Phaeacian adventures and the deceptive story to Eumaeus, which turns out then not to be the first deceptive story after the hero's return to his island home! Odysseus has been put ashore by the Phaeacians in Ithaca at the harbor near an olive tree sacred to Athena and a cave sacred to the nymphs, where there are ever flowing springs (Book 13). He sees a youth approaching dressed as a shepherd (Athena in disguise), and Odysseus asks where he is; for Ithaca also has been disguised and he does not recognize the island. Athena tells him where he is but not who she is, and then he launches into his first deceptive yarn. She announces that his deception is useless with her, and she reveals herself. They plan together his future action, and she disguises him as a beggar. In this episode in the *Odyssey* we have the chief ingredients of the episode in "The Captivity of Šarac Mehmedaga," namely, the hero meets and converses with women at a spring or other body of water, and in the course of the conversation the hero tells a deceptive story, receives information about what is going on in town, and recognition is somehow or other involved. Athena in Ithaca completes Nausicaa and Arete in Phaeacia by adding the element of the deceptive story, which was absent from the Phaeacian episodes. With the recognition by Athena—who, of course, knew him all the time—Odysseus is back in the human world. She had not been in the world of fantasy where he had been. She is the first to encounter him in the real world.

The next complex of deceptive story and recognition occurs in the hut of Eumaeus, where Odysseus tells the swineherd his deceptive story, and later, after Telemachus has arrived, Telemachus recognizes his father with the help of Athena, who reveals Odysseus to him. I have discussed elsewhere the possibility that a recognition scene with Eumaeus himself may in some versions have occurred before the recognition by Telemachus.[7] If I am right in regard to that passage, the recognition by Telemachus has interrupted and taken the place of the recognition by Eumaeus, which is delayed until much later in the story. The second recognition in the *Odyssey* is by the dog Argos, and it is to be noted that Eumaeus is present at that time with Odysseus, although he has not yet recognized his master, nor does he do so because of the recognition by Argos, since he does not appear to have seen the dog's wagging tail. After the poet mentions the death of the dog, the camera immediately turns to Telemachus; again an almost-recognition by Eumaeus is interrupted by the part of the story concerned with Odysseus's son. But for the purposes of studying the episode under consideration, it should be pointed out that the deceptive story told to Eumaeus is followed by the recognition by the beloved animal of the returning hero. This is also the case of Šarac, whose deceptive story told to the women at the well is followed by a going to town and recognition by the hero's beloved animal, his horse. In the *Odyssey* Telemachus interrupts the pattern here, as he does elsewhere. The next recognition in the *Odyssey*, after that by Argos, is by the faithful servant Eumaeus. In both tales the deceptive story is told first outside of town, but the recognitions (except for the intrusive Telemachus) are in town. In the conversation with Eumaeus, moreover, at the time of the deceptive story, Odysseus tells the swineherd about having met Odysseus during his travels and he prophesies that the wanderer will soon be home. Eumaeus tells Odysseus about the suitors at the palace. In "The Captivity of Šarac Mehme-

---

[7] See Lord, A., 1960, 180–183.

daga" Šarac also tells about meeting the hero, although in this case he falsely reports his death. The women at the well tell him about the wedding guests at his tower. The basic correspondences between the series of events in the two songs, always excepting the Telemachus interruptions, are astonishing.

The episode which we have found most arresting in its similarity to the *Odyssey* is not the only part of the story of Šarac that is reminiscent of Homer. For example, Šarac the returned hero, either not yet identified or in disguise, is challenged to a footrace, the prize to the winner being the hand of the hero's wife. This episode recalls two in the *Odyssey*: the challenge to Odysseus in Phaeacia by Euryalos and the final challenge by the suitors in Ithaca. The double parallel is significant, because Phaeacia is a transitional station between the "other" world and reality, and events on that island are "duplicated" on Ithaca. Wedding is in the air in Phaeacia as it is in Ithaca, and the question of identity arises in both scenes of challenging. The footrace in "The Captivity of Šarac Mehmedaga" is reminiscent of the contests in Books 8 and 21 of the *Odyssey*. But the entire song, as well as others of the same narrative content, should be analysed in relation to the *Odyssey*.

Certainly, on the basis of the episodes on which we have concentrated here, one can legitimately ask whether it is possible that the oral tradition of the return of the hero from long absence has been continuous in the Balkans since Homeric times. The evidence in this song of a Moslem hero by a Christian singer from Bihać in northern Bosnia would seem to suggest an affirmative answer. Stories, or their narrative essences, cling tenaciously together and pass easily from language to language, providing only that there is a singing tradition on both sides of the language "boundary." I like to think that in "The Captivity of Šarac Mehmedaga" and in other similar songs in the South Slavic tradition one is hearing the *Odyssey*, or ancient songs like it, still alive on the lips of men, ever new, yet ever the same.

CHAPTER 4

Avdo Međedović, *Guslar*

Demodocus, I praise you beyond all mortal men, whether your teacher
was the muse, the child of Zeus, or was Apollo.
—Homer, *Odyssey* 8.487–488

Avdo Međedović of the village of Obrov, a half-hour's walk from
Bijelo Polje in eastern Montenegro, died sometime during 1955 at the
approximate age of eighty-five. It may well be that he was the last of the
truly great epic *guslari* of the Balkan Slavic tradition of oral narrative
song. The texts of some of his songs that were recorded for the enlight-
enment of the scholarly world have been published, but his real fame is
still a thing of the future.[1] Yet his passing must not go unmarked by the
scholars who have benefited much already by his remarkable talents.

Avdo was Moslem, as is clear from his given name, Abdullah; but by
blood he was Slavic. In centuries past his family had been Serbian Orthodox and had come from central Montenegro; they were related to the
Rovčani and came from Nikšić.[2] Avdo knew neither when nor why
they had embraced Islam.

Published in the *Journal of American Folklore* 69 (1956), 320–330. Reprinted by permission of the American Anthropological Association. Not for further reproduction.

[1] Međedović, 1974a, 1974b, and 1980.
[2] The information concerning Avdo's life comes from the following recorded conversations in the Milman Parry Collection, Text nos. 12,436 and 12,443, Widener Library,
Harvard University, Cambridge, Mass. These conversations are also a source for our
knowledge of the singers from whom he learned his songs. For more on Avdo see David
E. Bynum's translation of conversations concerning "The Singer's Life and Times" in
Međedović, 1974a, 37–78; the original texts were published in Međedović, 1974b, 1–54.

During the first half of his life Avdo was a Turkish subject; for up to the First World War Bijelo Polje belonged to the Sandžak of Novi Pazar in the Turkish Empire. Here he was born and here he lived and died. His father and grandfather were butchers in the town, and in his mid-teens Avdo began to learn their trade. After some two years of apprenticeship he went into the army as "a still beardless youth," and when he returned seven years later his father did not recognize him.

In the army he spent three years in Kriva Palanka on the Bulgarian border. For another year he fought with Šemsi Pasha in Albania, and then after six months in Kumanovo near Skopje in Macedonia he was sent to a school for noncommissioned officers in Salonica, where, according to his own account, he "rotted for a year and emerged a sergeant." He then passed another year in Kriva Palanka drilling others in the tactics he had learned under "Alamani" (German) officers in Salonica, after which he was on guard duty for six months at a post on the Bulgarian frontier "under the skies, high in the mountains." When he returned to headquarters his discharge came.

It is characteristic of Avdo that the only time that he was disciplined in the army was after he struck an "Anatolian" with the butt of his rifle for cursing the faith (din). Ordinarily a peaceful man, he was stirred deeply by the religious laxity of the Anatolian Turks, whom he called "unbelievers." He was himself devout and conservative, a person of lofty principles, yet unostentatious. All this is reflected in his poems.

Although Avdo learned to speak and understand Turkish in the army, he was never able to read or write any language. In those days there were only Turkish language schools, and his father had never sent him to them. During his lifetime he saw the growth of literacy in younger generations and shared both the feeling of inferiority and the pride of accomplishment of those illiterates who had led successful lives. It was "stupid" he thought, in retrospect, that he had never learned to read and write; and yet, in spite of that, he had been a good tradesman because he was honest. He had the respect and confidence of his fellow merchants. One of the greatest shocks of his life had come when the son to whom he had given over his business and all his capital, so that Avdo himself might retire peacefully to the farm, had squandered everything in riotous living. There was bitter disillusionment in his voice as he told of it. He had been brought up to honor and obey his father and to believe that "as a man sows, so shall he reap." Having been a good son, he felt that he deserved to have a good son.

In Avdo's song, "The Wedding of Meho, Son of Smail," there is a deep personal ring in the words of young Mehmed when asked whether the old men are better than the young. "Opinions are divided," he said, "but mine shall ever be that the old men are better than the young." His questioner replied: "Bravo, my dear son! If God grants, you will be an honor to us." Avdo was singing of a past age, the ideals of which were his own, tried and not found wanting in the acid of his own experience.

After serving in the army Avdo returned to his trade with his father, but later he was called up again as a border guard, this time on the Montenegrin frontier, where he stayed for a year and a half. He was wounded in the Balkan wars; his right arm was broken by a bullet. With some epic exaggeration he told of how the doctor in Bijelo Polje could not stop the blood for four days and finally had to put him on a horse and send him with two soldiers to Senica. Here the doctor did not dare even to inspect his wound but sent him on to Novi Pazar. Four doctors looked him over, saw the danger, and sent him to Mitrovica, where twelve doctors consulted together about his case and then sent him post haste by train to Salonica. There he lay in the hospital forty-five days. One bullet was extracted, but another remained in his arm for the rest of his life.

Two years after returning from the army he was married, when, according to his reckoning, he was twenty-nine years old. It was at this time that he acquired the little farm in Obrov. His friends had praised a girl in that village to him, and he married her, as the custom was, without ever setting eyes on her or she on him. He lived through the terror of the First World War and somehow managed to keep his butcher shop. His descriptions of the lot of the Moslems in Bijelo Polje during the few months immediately following the downfall of Turkey are graphic. Until the new law and government were set up, for a period of about three months, the Moslems were plundered and killed by their former Christian subjects, the *raja*. Avdo was among those who survived; his family had never been rich, they had never been "aghas."

He watched the world around him torn to shreds once more by the Second World War. During these later years of his life he had the satisfaction that as father and patriarch he felt was his right. One son had disappointed him, but two other sons stayed by him and cared for him. He had daughters-in-law to help his wife and a grandson to dandle on his knee. He was a quiet family man in a disturbed and brutal world. The high moral tone of his songs is genuine. His pride in tales of the glories of the Turkish Empire in the days of Sulejman, when it was at its height and when "Bosnia was its lock and its golden key," was poignantly sincere without ever being militant or chauvinistic. That empire was dead, and Avdo knew it, because he had been there to hear its death rattle. But it had once been great in spite of the corruption of the imperial nobility surrounding the sultan. To Avdo its greatness was in the moral fiber and loyal dedication of the Bosnian heroes of the past even more than in the strength of their arms. These characteristics of Avdo's poems, as well as a truly amazing sensitivity for the feelings of other human beings, spring from within the singer himself. Avdo believed with conviction in the tradition that he exemplified.

Milman Parry of Harvard University's Department of Classics collected epic songs from Avdo during the months of July and August 1935. Avdo had a repertory of fifty-eight epics; Parry recorded nine of these on phonograph discs and Nikola Vujnović, Parry's assistant, wrote down four others from Avdo's dictation.

RECORDED

"The Death of Mustajbey of the Lika" (Parry Text no. 6807, Rec. nos. 5146–5180, June 28, 1935, 2,436 lines).

"Hrnjica Mujo Avenges the Death of Mustajbey of the Lika" (Text no. 6810, Rec. nos. 5181–5278, June 29–30, 1935, 6,290 lines).

"The Wedding of Vlahinjić Alija" (Text no. 12,375, Rec. nos. 5459–5552, July 14–15, 1935, 6,042 lines; there is also a dictated version of this song from Avdo, Text no. 6841, July 16, 24, 25, 1935, 5,883 lines. Both texts were published in Međedović, 1980.).

"The Heroism of Ðerđelez Alija" (Text no. 12,379, Rec. nos. 5595–5635, July 15–16, 1935, 2,624 lines).

"Osmanbey Delibegović and Pavičević Luka" (Texts nos. 12,389 and 12,441, Rec. nos. 5712–5817, 6471–6561, July 17–20, August 1–3, 1935, 13,331 lines; text published, Međedović, 1980).

"Sultan Selim Captures Kandija" (Text no. 12,447, Rec. nos. 6677–6763, August 4, 5, 8, 1935, 5,919 lines).

"The Illness of Emperor Dušan in Prizren" (Text no. 12,463, Rec. nos. 6848–6857, August 8, 1935, 645 lines).

"The Captivity of Kara Omeragha" (Text no. 12,465, Rec. nos. 6888–6906, August 9, 1935, 1,302 lines).

"Bećiragić Meho" (Text no. 12,471, Rec. nos. 7015–7108, August 10–11, 1935, 6,313 lines).

DICTATED

"The Arrival of the Vizier in Travnik" (Text no. 6802, June 29–30, July 4–5, 1935, 7,621 lines).

"The Wedding of Meho, Son of Smail" (Text no. 6840, July 5–12, 1935, 12,311 lines; text published Međedović, 1974b, translation published Međedović, 1974a.).

"Gavran Harambaša and Sirdar Mujo" (Text no. 12,427, July 26, 1935, 4,088 lines).

"The Captivity of Tale of Orašac in Ozim" (Text no. 12,428, July 30, 1935, 3,738 lines, unfinished).

The mere bulk of these epic songs is astonishing: 637 record sides, or 319 twelve-inch phonograph discs recorded on both sides; 44,902 lines sung on discs, and 33,653 lines written from dictation. His longest song on records contains 13,331 lines and fills 199 record sides, or 100 twelve-inch discs recorded on both sides. If one reckons five minutes of singing on one side of a record, then this song represents more than sixteen hours of singing time. The total singing time for all the recorded material listed here is approximately fifty-three hours.

To these songs must be added the conversations with Avdo that were recorded on discs. These conversations cover 180 twelve-inch records recorded on both sides. In other words, the total recorded songs and conversations from this single singer fill 499 discs on both sides, or nearly one-seventh of the 3,584 twelve-inch records in the entire Parry Collection from the 1930s. The conversations contain the story of his life, a lengthy discussion of the singers from whom he learned his songs, and a running commentary from questions prepared beforehand by Parry to two of his texts, "The Arrival of the Vizier in Travnik" and "The Wedding of Meho, Son of Smail."

It was my privilege to return to Bijelo Polje in 1950 and 1951, where I had been with Parry as a student in 1935, and to find Avdo still ready, in spite of poor health, to sing and recite epic songs. At that time I recorded on wire the following texts, partly sung, partly recited:

"Osmanbey Delilbegović and Pavičević Luka" (Lord Text no. 33; 23, 24, May 26, 1950, 6,119 lines).

"The Wedding of Meho, Son of Smail" (Lord Text no. 35; May 23, 1950, 8,488 lines).

"Bećiragić Meho" (Lord Text no. 202, August 16, 1951, 3,561 lines).

These additional 18,168 lines bring the total lines of epic from Avdo Međedović to 96,723.

The statistics alone are an indication of the value that Milman Parry placed on Avdo as a singer and tell at a glance one of the reasons for this high regard. Avdo could sing songs of about the length of Homer's *Odyssey*. An illiterate butcher in a small town of the central Balkans was equaling Homer's feat, at least in regard to length of song. Parry had actually seen and heard two long epics produced in a tradition of oral epic.

In the case of two of Avdo's songs, "The Wedding of Meho, Son of Smail" and "Bećiragić Meho," we had the exact original from which Avdo had learned them and we knew the circumstances under which he acquired them. A friend of his had read "The Wedding of Meho" to him five or six times from a published version.[3] It had been written down in 1885 by F. S. Krauss from an eighty-five-year old singer named Ahmed Isakov Šemić in Rotimlje, Hercegovina, and had been published in Dubrovnik in 1886. It was later reprinted, with minor changes in dialect, in cheap paper editions in Sarajevo, without notes and introduction. In this form it was read to Avdo. Krauss's text has 2,160 lines; Avdo's in 1935 had 12,323 lines and in 1950, 8,488 lines.

Avdo's singing of this or any other song was always longer than anyone else's performance, because he belonged in a tradition of singers who habitually "ornamented" their songs by richness of description, and because he had himself always had a fondness for this "ornamentation." His technique, and that of his fellows, was expansion from within by the addition of detail and by fullness of narrative. Catalogues are extended and also amplified by description of men and horses; journeys are described in detail; assemblies abound in speeches.

Avdo culled his "ornaments," as he himself called them, from all the singers whom he heard. But he did not stop there. He admitted that he thought up some of them himself; and this is true. He told me once that he "saw in his mind every piece of trapping that he put on a horse." He visualized the scene or the action, and from that mental image formed a verbal reflection in his song. Avdo's songs are living proof that the best of oral epic singers are original poets working within the tradition in the

---

[3] For details of the reading of the poem to Avdo see the text of the conversation with Hivzo Džafić who did the reading (Međedović, 1974b, 51–54; English translation in Međedović, 1974a, 76–78).

traditional manner. These texts provide priceless evidence for the theorists in comparative epic studies.

It is impossible here to do more than hint at illustrating this singer's technique of amplification. The opening scene of "The Wedding of Meho, Son of Smail" is an assembly of the lords of the Turkish Border in the city of Kanidža. In Krauss's published version this assembly occupies 141 lines; Avdo's text has 1,053 lines. The essence of the assembly is that all the lords are merry except young Meho. The head of the assembly asks him why he is sad, and he replies that he alone of all of them has nothing of which to boast. He has been pampered by his father and uncle and not allowed to engage in raids across the border. He will desert to the enemy, he declares. The lords then decide that they will send him to Budapest, there to be invested by the vizier with the position of authority which his uncle has held up to this moment. The uncle is old and agrees that the time has come to give over his authority to his nephew. The lords prepare a petition to the vizier, deliver it to Meho, and the assembly is dissolved. All this is in the songbook version published by Krauss.

Avdo gains length by adding much description such as the following:

As you cast your eyes about the gathering to see which hero is the best, one stands out above them all, even Mehmed, the young son of Smailaga. What a countenance has this falcon! He is a youth of not yet twenty years, and one would say and swear by Allah and the Rosary that the radiance from his two cheeks is like sunshine and that from his brow like unto the light of the moon. The black queue that covered his white neck was like a raven that had perched there. He was the only child his mother had borne; she had cared lovingly for his queue and bound his locks over his forehead, and her son's thick dark locks curled around his fez. His mother had strung them with pearls, which completely covered the strands. His eyes were black as a falcon's, his teeth fine as a demon's. His forehead was like a good-luck charm, his eyebrows thick as leeches. His eyelashes were so long that they covered his two cheeks even as swallows' wings. Beard had he none, nor yet moustache. One would say that he was a fair mountain spirit. The boy's raiment was of Venetian stuff; his blouse of choice silk embroidered with gold. There was, indeed, more gold than silken fabric. His doublet was neither woven nor forged, but was hand embroidered with pure gold. The seams of his cloak were covered with richly embroidered gold, and golden branches were twined around his right sleeve. The young man's arm was as thick as any other fine hero's slender waist. The youth's breeches were of white Venetian velvet, embroidered with pure gold, with braided snakes on the thighs. The whole glistened like the moon. He wore two Tripolitan sashes about his waist and over them the belt of arms of Venetian gold. In the belt were two small Venetian pistols which fire without flint, all plated with gold. Their sights were of precious stones, and the handles were inlaid with pearl. His Persian sword with hilt of yellow ducats was at his left side in its scabbard inlaid with pearls. Its blade was deadly steel. As the sword lay thrown across the youth's thighs one would say a serpent was sleeping there. A golden breastplate embraced the young hero, two-pieced, reaching to his white neck. Each half of the breastplate contained an even half pound of gold, and on them both was the same inscription. That breastplate had been sent by the sultan to the alajbey, Smail the Pilgrim, and to his true son; for that house had held the alajbeyship for full forty-seven years by charter of Sulejman the Magnificent, by his imperial charter and appointment.

Avdo also adds new action to the assembly, action that indicates that not only is the singer's eye observing the scene but that his mind and sensitivity to heroic feelings penetrate within the hearts of the men depicted on this animated tapestry. For example, the head of the assembly, Hasan pasha Tiro, notices that the young man is sad, and the pasha is disturbed.

He could not bear to see the young man's sadness, nor could he ask the lad before all the beys to speak out the cause of his sorrow. So Hasan pasha leaped to his feet and called Cifrić Hasanaga: "Come here with me a moment, Hasanaga, that I may have a word with you!" Hasanaga went to Hasan pasha and sat beside him. Then Hasan pasha whispered to Hasanaga: "Hasanaga, golden plume, my heart breaks within my breast to see your brother's son, Mehmedaga, son of Smail the Pilgrim. All the rest are merry. He alone is sad. You go and sit beside him. Do not question him immediately, lest he notice that I called you to me for that purpose and be angry at me."

Then Hasanaga obeyed the pasha and took his seat beside Meho, the son of Smail the Pilgrim. The cursed cups flew around, and the aghas drank; for they had no cares, and no one noticed that that hero was unhappy. Since he has all he wants, why should the young man be sad? A half hour passed. Then Cifrić Hasanaga leaped to his feet. "O pasha, and all you beys, have patience a moment!" They all stopped and looked at the agha. Cifrić Hasanaga knelt and then asked his brother's son Mehmed: "My Mehmed, honor of our house! Why do you sit there so sad in the company of the imperial Hasan pasha Tiro and the fifty warriors of the sultan?"

This little play between the pasha and Meho's uncle is original with Avdo; I have found it nowhere else. And it is a stroke of real genius. Only a poet who lived what he was telling would have thought of it. Avdo was the kind of person who would have done just what the pasha did. Such additions do much more, of course, then add length to the song; they make the characters in the story, in this case a usually stiff and stereotyped chief of the assembly, feeling, breathing human beings. Such touches are Homeric.

Another technique that Avdo uses very effectively in gaining length, breadth, and depth of song is the time-honored "flashback." We have seen something of it in the comment on the breastplate of Meho that had been sent by the sultan to Smail and to his son. Avdo develops this theme later in the long speech of Meho's uncle to the youth after the boy has said that he will run away to the enemy.

When you were born, your head rested on a pillowed couch, your brow fell upon gold, and your locks were strewn with pearls. My dear son, when you were born from the pearly lap of your mother, in every city up and down the Border, in Bosnia, Hercegovina, and Hungary, cannon roared and beys and aghas held festive gatherings in honor of your father Smail and me, your uncle. . . . They sent word to the sultan, and the sultan sent a firman to your father and to me, your uncle: "I congratulate you both on the birth of your son! May his life be long and honorable, and may the alajbeyship fall to him as it did to his father and to his uncle Hasan!" Nor, my son, did we pick a name for you at random, but we gave you the name of imperial Mehdija, Mehdija, the imperial pontiff. That you might live longer, we brought in three women besides your mother to nurse you, in order that you might receive more nourishment, grow more in a short time and attain greater strength. We could scarcely wait for you to grow up, so four nurses gave you suck, first your mother and then the other three.

Day followed day, and after four years had passed, my son, you had grown well, in God's faith, and were as large as any other lad of eight years. Then we began your schooling and brought the imam to your feet. We could not bear to send you away from home to school, and the imam taught you at our own house. You studied until you were eight years old, my son, and if you had studied yet another year, you would have been a hafiz. Then we took you from school.

When you were twelve, another firman came from Stambol asking me and your father, Smailaga, "Smailaga, how is the boy? Will he be like his father and his uncle Hasan?" And we boasted about you to the sultan: "O sovereign, most humble greetings! It is likely that the boy will be good; he will not fall much short of us."

When your thirteenth year dawned, my son, the imperial chamberlain came from the halls of Sultan Sulejman, bringing an Egyptian chestnut horse for you, one that had been bought from the Shah of Egypt. Golden-winged, its mane reached to its hoofs. Then a two-year-old, it was like a horse of seven. The trappings were fashioned in Afghanistan especially for the chestnut steed when it grew up. The saddle was decorated with coral; the upper portion was woven of pure gold. . . .

It is now nineteen years, my dear son, since that day when you were born, and this is the ninth year since the chestnut steed with its trappings came to you as a gift. . . . We hid the horse from you and made a special stall for him in the side of the stable. There is no other horse with him. Two servants are in the stable and four torches burn the whole night long beside your horse. They exercise him within the stable. They groom him four times every twenty-four hours; not as any other horse is groomed, but with a scarf of silk. You should see how well-nourished the horse is, even though he has seen neither sun nor moon, my dear son, for nine years. . . .

Among the clothes which have come for you is a breastplate covered with pearls; its silk is from Damascus. . . . And a Persian sword was sent, which had been forged especially for you, my son, of fiery Persian steel tempered in angry poison, which cuts fierce armor. Its scabbard is deco-rated with pearls and its hilt with diamonds. When it was finished, they sent the sword to Mecca by an Arab messenger, who delivered it to the sheikh of the Kaaba. The sheikh inscribed it with a passage from the Sacred Book and then blessed it. No ill can befall him who wields it. The common ranks will flee in terror before him. In Mecca, with the imperial blessing, they named the sword "The Persian Pilgrim," because it was made for you in Persia and taken on a pilgrimage to Mecca. Woe to him who stands in its way! On its hilt are three imperial seals and the two seals of the sheikh of Mecca, my son.

Upon the fur cap which was sent to you, my son, there are twelve plumes. Neither your father nor I has such a cap; how then would any other, except you to whom the sultan presented it! . . .

Were you to gather all these treasures together, they would be worth a good Bosnian city![4]

I have quoted at some length not only to illustrate Avdo's use of a Homeric type of flashback, but also to emphasize the various attributes

[4] Međedović, 1974a, 81–82, 1974b, lines 177–250; 1974a, 83, 1974b, lines 292–332; 1974a, 89–91, 1974b, lines 727–881.

which he has given his hero, young Mehmed. They are not bestowed upon him in any other version of this song that I have found; they seem to me to be Avdo's gift to Meho. Not, of course, that Avdo invented the precocious childhood, the magic horse, the wonder-working sword, and the protective breastplate and cap. These are perhaps in their essences inheritances from Slavic tradition, later reinforced by Byzantine and Ottoman influences. The glitter and elegance remind one of Byzantium and the Sublime Porte. They can be found in the songs of other poets, although Avdo, it must be admitted, describes them more fully than I have seen elsewhere.

The wonder of this passage, however, does not rest merely in its ornamentation. It rests also in the fact that Avdo has thought fit to add these particular attributes to Mehmed. For these are the qualities and possessions of the magic hero who slays dragons and saves maidens, who rights wrongs and destroys evil. Mehmed is, indeed, that kind of hero. He kills the treacherous vizier and the vizier's henchmen; he saves a maiden; he restores law and order in Budapest, and brings exiles back from Persia. Avdo unwittingly, or by a sure instinct for the richness of the tradition in which he was steeped, has chosen the proper attributes for the proper hero. He has related Meho to Digenis Akritas and to the basic epic theme of the divine, or divinely inspired, hero who is a savior of mankind.[5] Somehow or other, Avdo Međedović, the butcher from Bijelo Polje, had acquired a deep and unerring sense of the well-springs of epic.

Avdo belonged to a tradition that had been in the hands of fine singers for many generations. Without such a tradition behind and around him he could not have had the materials of song. He learned his art from skilled men; first and of most lasting importance from his father. Avdo's father had been deeply influenced by a singer of his generation whose reputation seems to have been prodigious, Ćor Huso Husein of Kolašin. We know something of this singer not only from Avdo, who heard about him from his father, but also from other singers in Bijelo Polje and Novi Pazar who learned songs from Ćor Huso. From the material in the Parry Collection we shall some day be able to reconstruct part of his repertory, at least; and probably also his handling of specific themes. His most distinctive characteristic as a singer was his ability to "ornament" a song. Of this we are told by all who knew him. Avdo was a worthy student of the school of Ćor Huso.

[5] See Mavrogordato, 1956. Avdo's song of Smailagić Meho should be carefully studied in its relationship to medieval Greek epic in general and to *Digenis Akritas* in particular.

With Avdo the song, the story itself and the telling of it, was paramount. He had exceptional powers of endurance, but his voice was not especially good. He was hoarse, and the goiter on the left side of his neck could not have helped. Nor was his playing of the *gusle* in any way of virtuoso quality. He told Parry that he learned the songs first and then the musical accompaniment. His singing ran ahead of his fingers on the instrument; thoughts and words rushed to his mind for expression, and there were times when he simply ran the bow slowly back and forth over the strings while he poured forth the tale in what seemed to be prose of lightning-like rapidity but was actually verse. He was not a musician, but a poet and singer of tales.

Parry in 1935 made trial of Avdo's ability to learn a song that he had never heard before. Among the singers from whom Parry collected while Avdo was dictating or resting was Mumin Vlahovljak of Plevlje. Parry arranged that Avdo was present and listening while Mumin sang "Bećiragić Meho," a song that Parry had adroitly determined was unknown to Avdo. Mumin was a good singer and his song was a fine one, running to 2,294 lines. When it was over, Parry turned to Avdo and asked him if he could now sing the same song, perhaps even sing it better than Mumin, who accepted the contest good-naturedly and sat by in his turn to listen. Avdo, indeed, addressed himself in his song to his "colleague" (*kolega*) Muminaga. And the pupil's version of the tale reached to 6,313 lines, nearly three times the length of his "original," on the first singing!

Avdo used the same technique of expansion from within in ornamenting "Bećiragić Meho" that he used in "Smailagić Meho." This song also opens with an assembly of the lords of the Border. Bećiragić Meho leaves the assembly at line 1,320 in Mumin's version, at line 3,977 in Avdo's. There are similarities between the gathering at the beginning of "Smailagić Meho" and that which begins "Bećiragić Meho." In the midst of the lords in both instances is a young man who is unhappy. But the head of the assembly in "Bećiragić Meho," Mustajbey of the Lika, unlike Hasan pasha Tiro, is a proud and overbearing man; and Bećiragić Meho himself is at the foot of the assembly, poor, despised. As we should expect, Avdo's telling is distinguished by richness of description and by such similes as, referring to the unhappy Meho, "His heart was wilted like a rose in the hands of a rude bachelor." But when a messenger arrives with a letter for Meho and Meho has to announce his own presence, because Mustajbey is ashamed to acknowledge him, Meho lashes out at the head of the assembly in moral indignation; and Avdo "ornaments" the theme of Meho's reproach far beyond Mumin's telling of it. Avdo has Meho remind Mustajbey that he has riches and power now, but everything comes in time; time builds towers and time destroys them. Meho said that he, too, had once been of a well-to-do family, but time and destiny had deprived him of all. Avdo's earnestness, his philosophizing and moralizing, have a personal note. As we said earlier, Avdo had seen the Turkish Empire fall; and just before our arrival in Bijelo Polje, his own house had been burned to the ground. His ornamentation is not mere prettiness, nor trite sayings, but words of wisdom from personal experience.

Avdo has made two minor changes in the action of the song up to this point that are worth noting as characteristic of his artistry. His sense of the dramatic has caused him to withhold Bećiragić Meho's identity— even though, of course, the audience is perfectly aware from the start who the unidentified young man is—until Meho himself rises to reproach Mustajbey. Even more interesting, however, is the way in which Avdo has prepared us for Mustajbey's attitude. In Mumin's version the messenger arrives, inquires if he is in Udbina, asks to have Mustajbey pointed out to him, does obeisance to the bey and then speaks. Avdo's handling of the arrival of the messenger is somewhat different. The messenger is seen from afar; Mustajbey sends his standard-bearers to meet him; they bring him before the aghas and beys and he asks if he is in Kanidža (Avdo has changed the place). Mustajbey, rather than Halil in Mumin's version, answers, and the messenger, noting that Mustajbey is the most honored man in the assembly, asks his name and rank. Mustajbey replies with his name and a list of all the places over which he rules. The messenger then does obeisance and speaks, beginning with flattery of Mustajbey, praising his fame. This is typical ornamentation on Avdo's part, and yet it emphasizes Mustajbey's vainglory.

These are but samples of Avdo's methods in changing and expanding the songs that he has heard. He does not, one should stress, gain length by adding one song to another. His long songs provide no solace to the theorists who have held that long epics are made of shorter ballads strung together. Avdo's technique is similar to Homer's. It is true that some singers, when pressed to sing a long song, add one song to another and mix and combine songs in various ways. This is, however, a process that good singers look down upon and do not practice.

Avdo in 1935, when he was already sixty years of age, maintained that he had been at the height of his powers when he was in his forties. We have seen a glimpse of the quality of this talented singer in his sixties and can only guess at his excellence twenty years earlier. We should do well not to minimize the extraordinary feat that he performed when he was in his eighties. For at least ten years he had sung very little. He was weak and ill in 1950 and 1951, and, alas, the circumstances of collecting were far from ideal. I had very little time, and working with a singer like Avdo requires leisure. Yet, even under adverse conditions, he sang and recited two long songs totaling more than 14,000 lines in about a week's time! When he finished the song of "Osmanbey Delibegović and Pavičević Luka," he apologized that it was shorter; he had cut down some of the description of the army. He was indeed unwell, and we took him to the doctor, who was very kind. Six thousand lines is still a sizable song. And the 8,000 and more lines of his "Smailagić Meho" in 1950 was a prodigious undertaking which few, if any, younger men could have accomplished.

His description of young Meho was shorter than that quoted earlier, but the flashback to the birth of Meho, his precocious childhood, and the gifts of the sultan, the horse, helmet, breastplate, and pilgrim sword were not forgotten. They were not in the same place in the song, however. Avdo now put them into the mouth of Meho's father after the boy had returned with his uncle to their home to inform Smail of what had happened. As Smail is about to send Meho to his mother to prepare for the journey to Budapest, Smail tells him about the horse and weapons and clothes which have been kept for him. It is a fitting place for the theme.

Perhaps the most astonishing of Avdo's accomplishments was the reciting of the song of "Bećiragić Meho" (not to be confused with Smailagić Meho) in 1951. I have already described the circumstance under which he learned and first sang this song in 1935. He assured me that he had not sung it since that time, nor had he heard it in the intervening years. Sixteen years and five days exactly had passed. There is some confusion toward the beginning of the 1951 text; one can feel Avdo probing his memory. He was straining to prove himself; but most of all, I believe, he sang it for Milman Parry and Nikola Vujnović, in memory of a peaceful, sunny day so many years before. Before reciting the tale he recalled how Parry had asked him to sing the song; how he had asked to be excused, because he did not wish to take honor away from Mumin. Avdo knew that his song would be longer and more ornate. "The professor said, 'whatever is not a sin is not shameful,' so I found Mumin, and embraced him and took his hand 'You will not be hurt, because my song will be much, much longer?' 'No, Avdo, I beg you as my son—he was older than I—I will not be hurt.' And the professor listened, like this professor, and Mumin sat there, and I sang." Then Avdo remembered and added "Muminaga and the professor told me that he had learned that song from Ćor Husein [Ćor Huso]; and Ćor Husein was an excellent singer in these parts."

From the past the song was unwound and the tale emerged. Its essence, however, was from a time long before Avdo and Mumin and Ćor Huso; for more than half of this song takes place in the assembly with which it opens, as Bećiragić Meho tells of his wanderings and adventures, his trials and sufferings which have brought him to his present sorry state. To those who have ears to hear, Homer is singing of Odysseus in the court of Alcinous, recounting his wanderings and the misfortunes which had brought him to the shores of Phaeacia.

On May 21, 1939, in Cambridge, Massachusetts, Nikola Vujnović completed his review of his transcription from the records of the words of Avdo's song "Sultan Selim Captures Kandija." He wrote this note at the bottom of the page: "Onda kad ne bude Avda među živima, neće se naći niko ko bi bio ovakav za pjevanje"; "When Avdo is no longer among the living, there will be no one like him in singing." He has left behind him, however, songs that will be remembered in days to come.

CHAPTER 5

Homer as an
Oral-Traditional Poet

Some misconceptions have arisen about the "oral theory" and about the quality of the Serbo-Croatian oral-traditional epic and its possible relevance to an understanding of the Homeric poems. They are the subject of this paper. Much of its burden is to demonstrate to the Homerist how the superb singer in the South Slavic tradition can make clear the relationship of the gifted individual to the other singers in the tradition. By observing what he does, we can learn the ways in which his songs are superior to those of his fellows, because his thought is on a higher level than theirs, even as Homer's surpassed the songs of lesser bards for the same reason.

It is discouraging at this late date still to find references to a body of formulas, fixed phrases, "memorized by all singers" and to which singers were restricted. It is sometimes said that this is a situation "implied" by Milman Parry or by the "oral theory." In *Archery at the Dark of the Moon* Norman Austin wrote:

> Parry's theory of the traditional formulas assumes memorization, not of fixed texts to be sure, but of vast quantities of epithets and fixed metrical units from the common stock. We must assume in oral poets an admirable unanimity in restricting themselves to formulas already created and in constant use by all their competitors. Some time after a formula such as "Achilles swift of foot" was created, poets must have voluntarily aban-

The original form of this paper was read at a Homer symposium at the University of Pennsylvania, March 22–23, 1984. It has not been published before.

doned any other metrical equivalent in order to perpetuate the new coinage through the centuries.[1]

The theory assumes no such thing. There is no body of formulas to which all singers are restricted. Singers remember phrases they have heard and lines they have used, but they do not "memorize" set formulas.

On the other hand, there is a peculiar depth to some oral-traditional epithets—for certain of them have their own histories—which stems from a combination of metrical thrift and special meaning. Take "swift-footed Achilles" for example.

In 1963 M. W. M. Pope stated that Homer uses ὠκὺς Ἀχιλλεύς (swift Achilles) five times (actually six times) as against πόδας ὠκὺς Ἀχιλλεύς (swift-footed Achilles) fifty-four times, and that ὠκὺς Ἀχιλλεύς is the metrical equivalent of δῖος Ἀχιλλεύς (godlike Achilles).[2] I was relieved to find that Homer was not as mechanical as exaggeratedly thought. The author also pointed out that five (that is, six) cases were found only in the last four books of the *Iliad* (actually in five of the last six books—it is used in Book 19 but not in Book 20). Lest it be implied that Homer uses ὠκὺς Ἀχιλλεύς and only it in those books, I hasten to add that he also uses πόδας ὠκὺς Ἀχιλλεύς in Books 19, 21, 22, 23, and 24.

If one looks at the usage a little differently, one might say that Homer had three ways of saying "swift-footed Achilles"; πόδας ὠκὺς Ἀχιλλεύς, ὠκὺς Ἀχιλλεύς, and ποδάρκης δῖος Ἀχιλλεύς (swift-footed, godlike Achilles). These noun-epithet combinations around the idea of "swift-footed" may be fraught with meaning from ancient traditional stories of childhood deeds, as Gregory Nagy has pointed out in *The Best of the Achaeans*, on the basis of Pindar's "Nemean 3."[3] In other words, viewed in this way, ὠκὺς Ἀχιλλεύς is not an alternative for δῖος, although metrically equivalent to it, but for πόδας ὠκὺς Ἀχιλλεύς and ποδάρκης δῖος Ἀχιλλεύς, its equivalent in sense. I might point out that M. W. M. Pope failed to see this equivalence, because he was tied too closely to metrics. The fact that there are three ways of saying "swift-footed Achilles" argues that there is, or was at one time, a value to the meaning of the epithet significant enough to

[1] Austin, 1975, 17–18.
[2] Pope, 1963, 12.
[3] Nagy, G., 1979, 325–326.

74 Epic Singers and Oral Tradition

warrant the invention over time of three different ways of expressing it
metrically. Metrics are important. Vivante's book on epithets in Homer
proceeds as if Homer's works might just as well have been written in
prose.[4] But there are other values as well as metrics, as, for example, the
kind of meaning indicated by Gregory Nagy and developed further by
Joseph Nagy in his book on the childhood deeds of the Irish hero Finn
MacCumail.[5]

Criticism like that of Austin (quoted earlier) entirely ignores formula
systems, although the systems were highly important in Parry's work
with formulas. It is rather unfortunate that this criticism of the general
theory continues to persist even after the work of H. Hoekstra in 1964 in
Homeric Modifications of Formulaic Prototypes, of J. B. Hainsworth in *The
Flexibility of the Homeric Formula* in 1968, and of Richard Janko in
"Equivalent Formulae in Greek Epos," in 1981.[6] The theory has been
explained and deepened and modified constructively by a number of
distinguished hands, not least of all in respect to formulas.

In *The Singer of Tales* in 1960 I wrote:

> I believe that we are justified in considering that the creating of phrases is
> the true art of the singer on the level of line formation, and it is this facility
> rather than his memory of relatively fixed formulas that marks him as a
> skillful singer in performance.[7]

In 1975 I elaborated on that statement:

> Because, however, of the restrictions of the verse, there emerges a num-
> ber of more or less fixed phrases, lines, or groups of lines, i.e. the for-
> mulas and the formulaic expressions of the poetry. *Both* these elements
> (formulas and formulaic expressions) are characteristic of this style. It has
> already been noted by others who were seeking to define the formula that
> the complex substitution systems that appear in an in-depth formulaic
> analysis are really equally significant, if not more so, than the exactly
> repeated formulas.[8]

Even though there are South Slavic singers whose style may seem
mechanical (and there probably were ancient Greek singers of that cali-

[4] Vivante, 1982.
[5] Nagy, J., 1985.
[6] Hoekstra, 1964; Hainsworth, 1968; Janko, 1981.
[7] Lord, A., 1960, 43–44.
[8] Lord, A., 1975.

ber also) a look at Avdo Međedović's formulaic style easily disproves that statement. There is nothing mechanical in his composition of lines. The process just described is only one aspect of the oral-traditional formulaic style. There are other elements and devices of composition in which repetition occurs that are also characteristic of that style. One of these is the repeated gnomic type of line or couplet. By the "couplet" in this case I mean two lines that are always (or almost always) found together. They are an extension of the kind of single line that always has two parts seen together, for example, "San je laža, a Bog je istina" (Dream is a lie, but God is truth). "Dušmani ti pod nogama bili, ka' doratu klinci i potkovi" (May your enemies be beneath your feet, as the nails and shoes beneath your chestnut horse).[9]

The repeated couplets do not have to be gnomic in content, but may express any oft-repeated idea that can be expressed in two lines. Indeed the couplet is frequently expanded by a line or two. The main thing is that there be a more or less stable block of lines that is frequently repeated and plays an important role in oral-traditional composition.

There are instances of repeated couplets in the Homeric poems as in Serbo-Croatian epic. Take, for example, *Iliad* 8.66–67 and *Iliad* 11.84–85:

ὄφρα μὲν ἠὼς ἦν καὶ ἀέξετο ἱερὸν ἦμαρ,
τόφρα μάλ' ἀμφοτέρων βέλε' ἥπτετο, πῖπτε δὲ λαός.

So long as it was early morning and the sacred daylight
increasing, so long the thrown weapons of both took hold
and men dropped under them. [Lattimore translation].

Or compare *Odyssey* 19.600:

19.600 ὣς εἰποῦσ' ἀνέβαιν' ὑπερώϊα σιγαλόεντα,
19.601 οὐκ οἴη, ἅμα τῇ γε καὶ ἀμφίπολοι κίον ἄλλαι.
So she spoke, and went back up to her shining chamber,
not alone, since others, her women, went to attend her. [Lattimore]

and

18.206 ὣς φαμένη κατέβαιν' ὑπερώϊα σιγαλόεντα,
18.207 οὐκ οἴη, ἅμα τῇ γε καὶ ἀμφίπολοι δύ' ἕποντο.

[9] Ramo Babić, "Ženidba Smailagić Meha," "The Wedding of Smailagić Meho," Lord Text no. 8, lines 191–192, housed with the Milman Parry Collection, Widener Library, Harvard University, Cambridge, Mass.

So she spoke, and made her descent from her shining
chamber, not all alone, since two handmaidens went to attend her.
[Lattimore]

George Goold lists this as a fixed repeated couplet, which it obviously is
not.[10] This case is like those in Serbo-Croatian of similar lines rather
than of exact repetitions; I have christened them "multiformed couplets." They are an excellent example of Homeric compositions as oral-
traditional composition!

Such lines and couplets form a special group of repeated lines. Just as
the formulas come to the singer's lips by conditioned reflex without
conscious remembering, it may be correct to say that the multiformed
couplets too are unconsciously remembered whole; they are certainly
not memorized.

The use of the term "improvisation" in referring to the method of
composition of the South Slavic oral-traditional epic has caused some
misunderstandings. The *Oxford English Dictionary* defines improvising
as making up a song or words "on the spur of the moment," "extempore." It quotes Tobias George Smollett in *Travels Through France and
Italy*, who mentions "improvisatori, the greatest curiosities, unique
within Italy, individuals who have the surprising talent of reciting verses
extempore on any subject you propose." The OED in its discussion also
uses the word "unpremeditated" and defines improvisation as "the production or execution of anything off hand." This is a far cry from the
technique of composition of oral-traditional epic.

My own preferred term for that type of composition is "composition
by formula and theme." "Composition in performance" or possibly
"recomposition in performance" are satisfactory terms as long as one
does not equate them with improvisation, which, to my mind, means to
make up a new nontraditional song from predominantly nontraditional
elements.

There is considerable confusion on the difference between improvisation and the creation of new songs in an oral tradition of singing narrative songs. It is a complex problem, but this much may be said at
present. New songs in a living tradition of epic are forged from traditional formulas and themes and deal with traditional subjects. A new

[10]Goold, 1977, 31.

song in this genre has new names, but almost everything else in it has appeared before in the tradition in one form or another. The improvising of shorter topical songs "on any subject" "on the spur of the moment" is a very different matter, especially since the subjects may be, and usually are, nontraditional, thus requiring a new vocabulary.

Milman Parry asked an epic singer in Nevesinje, Hercegovina, if he could compose a song about him. Milovan Vojičić did so, and it has been published in *The Singer of Tales*.[11] Parry asked a wrong question. Milovan was not an "improvisatore," and the resulting song was an anomaly, a tour de force. Jeff Opland noted when he collected praise poems among the Xhosa in South Africa that their praise poems about chiefs used many formulas, but when one of them made up—at Opland's request—a song about an automobile accident that Opland had told him about, the song had fewer formulas. The first were traditional praise poems; the second a nontraditional improvisation.[12]

The outsider misunderstands, when he is told that singers can make up songs "on any subject," and asks for subjects outside the tradition. The result is a curiosity that proves nothing except that the singer normally does not compose a song extempore about "any subject," but only about certain kinds of subjects, for which he has the materials in his experience.

Ramon Menendez Pidal, in commenting on *The Singer of Tales*, expressed polite shock that I had, allegedly, said or implied that the *Iliad* and the *Odyssey* were "improvised" by Homer.[13] I would share his shock, were I to hear anyone say that. To repeat, "composition in performance" does not imply "improvisation." It can, and in my usage it does, mean "composition by formula and theme."

In *The Singer of Tales* I described how a singer learns to sing by listening to singers and gradually absorbing—learning, if you will, but not memorizing—the often used phrases, lines, or even couplets and small blocks, which he hears. I believe that this is what we do when we learn to speak a language. Although some of the phrases may be comparatively stable, because they express the often used thoughts of the poetry, they are not irrevocably fixed. There are several ways of saying the same thing. They emerge from usage and are not imposed by the

---

[11] Lord, A., 1960, 272–275.
[12] Opland, 1983.
[13] Menendez Pidal, 1967, 201.

"tradition" on the singer. There are phrases that singers use because they help in saying what they want to say and in forming lines. They do not have to use them, yet they feel no compunction about doing so. They do not avoid them; many of them are necessary for making lines, but there are other ways and sometimes singers in the natural way of singing use those other ways.

Some singers do not vary the common phrases (formulas) much, others do. Some singers use many well-known expressions, others use fewer. Neologisms are not unknown. In short, singers in practice may vary a great deal in their use of the common phrases according to their individual ability and sense of "style," if I may use that term. Each singer in a tradition is an individual and his style is discernible as his. The "tradition" is not a rigid monolith outside the singer, but as dynamic as the singers who operate in it, who form and constantly reform it. Homer's originality is within the tradition, not in the sense of being within limits but in the sense of being within potentials that can be realized by superior individuals. The tradition includes individuality. If one can understand the processes one can see the potentialities being expressed.

It is as important, if not more so, to understand what is meant by "tradition" as it is to appreciate the flexibility and complexity of individual idiosyncrasies within it. A tradition is easy to define but not easy to know. It is the sum of all its parts, by which I mean that it consists of all the singers of epic, good and bad, and all the performances, also good or bad, of all the songs, likewise of variable quality, in the course of the life of a culture. There is cohesiveness within a tradition, because singers learn from other singers both the songs and the technique of making them. A golden thread of family relationships runs through the tradition vertically and horizontally. Some elements in a tradition are fleeting and others long-lasting. We generally think of the latter as marking a tradition, and correctly so, but the transitory elements should be recognized as well, because they represent the momentary response of the individual poet to an idea. Here belong the neologisms and the hapax legomena. Avdo depicts one of the chief men of the northern Border, Tale of Orašac (who is sometimes a crude character on the surface, but a very complex one), as addressing the commander of the armies of the Border as "an old ox" (*bivolice stari*).[14] Tale asks him "Have you recently fallen

---

[14] At *Iliad* 1.159, Achilles calls his commander in chief, Agamemnon, κυνῶπα, "dog-eyed," "having the looks of a dog."

ill?" (*Jesi li se freško obolijo?*). The question is a little like saying, "What's wrong with you?" *Freško* (freshly!) is clearly a neologism and quite possibly also a hapax legomenon. Avdo likes such words, and frequently enlivens his songs with "colloquialisms," or borrowings. Another example is *kolega*, "colleague," in the phrase, referring to one of the nobles in the assembly, *moj dobri kolega*, "my good colleague!" Although such usages may not have permanency, inasmuch as they are created by a traditional poet operating within a tradition, they are part of the fabric of the tradition.

One should not suppose that a traditional singer can quickly become an Ezra Pound or a T. S. Eliot, although he may already be a Homer. If he is good enough, if he too is a genius, within the bounds of his tradition he can be a Homer. But he can never be a Pound or an Eliot. There is nothing that Homer, or any traditional singer, does that *requires writing*, contrary to what has frequently been said. On the other hand, Pound and Eliot are inconceivable without writing. They choose their words, they construct a "fixed" text, although they may later shift the position of some words or substitute others. The very self-conscious way in which that is done argues an attitude toward a text that is not part of the mentality, or "mind-set," of oral-traditional poets. The nontraditional poet uses a variety of references, often very individualistic and, except to a given few, obscure. The singer of oral-traditional epic cannot do all that for several reasons, and the act of writing itself is probably the least important of them. What Pound and Eliot—and many others, of course—did was the result of a long period of historical development of literature from many times and places. Theirs is a style that belongs primarily to short, for the most part non-narrative poetic forms, but it is not limited to them. The style is the result of a long period during which there was a seeking for new and different forms and effects, not merely an individual style within a traditional framework, but a style so totally different that no one else could have created it. This type of poetics is not that of oral-traditional poetry. It is ludicrous to say that there is no difference between oral-traditional poetics and written literary nontraditional poetics! Homer should not be treated as if he were writing like Pound or Eliot.

Take the final stanza of Eliot's *The Waste Land*:

London Bridge is falling down falling down falling down
Poi s'ascose nel foco che gli affina
Quando fiam uti chelidon—O swallow swallow

Le Prince d'Aquitaine à la tour abolie
These fragments I have shored against my ruins
Why then Ile fit you. Hieronymo's mad againe.
Datta.   Dayadhvam.   Damyata.
    Shantih   shantih   shantih

This is *written* poetry! Here, placed together, are a well-known game song, line 148 from Dante's *Purgatorio* 26, another from *Pervigilium Veneris*, then one from Gerard de Nerval's "Sonnet El Desdichado," and after a line by the poet himself, T. S. Eliot (speaking, however, in the persona of the Fisher King from the Grail Romance, about which Eliot had been reading in Jessie Weston's *From Ritual to Romance*), we find a quotation from *The Spanish Tragedy* by Thomas Kyd, and the final commands are from the *Brihadaranyaka Upanishad*. Of "Shantih" Eliot noted: "Repeated as here, a formal ending to an Upanishad. 'The peace which passeth understanding' is our equivalent to this word" (p. 54).[15]

In a review of a new edition of W. B. Yeats's poems Seamus Heaney wrote (*New York Times Book Review*, March 18, 1984, p. 1): "Stone-work, facing and planing the blocks, the deliberate exercise of strength, the exclusive intent of the craftsman absorbed in this task—it all fits with what we know of Yeats as an artist in verse. He would work long at shaping a poem, handling and testing a line until it pressed down with the greatest semantic density and conducted the right musical strain from the lines before and after. The evidence is in the manuscripts, but it is also there in the perfect feel of the individual stanzas." The oral-traditional singer of epic, composing in performance, even in a dictated performance with a scribe, does not, indeed cannot, compose in this way.

The singers of oral-traditional epic in Yugoslavia say that they think about songs between singings in "public." They may even practice them to themselves or with a small, intimate group. Such rumination—"practicing" may imply too conscious an activity—should be differentiated from the early period of learning; although it is akin to it, it is less intensive. The process of learning is always going on. Every singing is involved in it to some degree, because the singer always learns in con-

---

[15] My thanks to Jonathan F. McKeage for the quotation from Eliot and for pointing me to Eliot's notes on it. *The Waste Land and Other Poems* (New York: Harcourt, Brace & World, 1934); the text of the poem is on pages 29–46; the lines quoted, the final lines of the poem, are on page 46; the notes to the poem are on pages 47–54.

junction with a song. When the singer is thinking about a song, he is thinking about its story; and when he sings to himself he is thinking about the telling of it in song. To us the song may be inseparable from the text, but to the singer a text emerges from the song at each performance even when the singer sings only to himself.

As he thinks about a song, remembering it, singing it to himself, if he is an Avdo Međedović, he will find himself embellishing his catalogues or envisioning his assemblies and realizing anew his descriptions of heroes and horses. These themes are not composed "on the spur of the moment." Although not textually fixed, they have a kind of stability. It is not merely by chance, for example, that the two scenes of hospitality on the hero's journey to Buda in Avdo's "Smailagić Meho" are differentiated so carefully from one another. In one the sons of the family aid their father, in the other it is the daughters. The conversations are different, too, one comparing the older and the younger generations—a favorite subject of Avdo's—the other disclosing the possible untrustworthiness of the vizier in Buda. Both conversations are significant in the song, presenting ideas and information that serve the overall purposes of the song. They are the result of Avdo's thinking of the story and of its telling. They were not "improvised" extempore.

In the study of a traditional passage one can see some of the traditional poetic values in its structure and sound patternings. The following passage is from Salih Ugljanin's "Song of Bagdad," recorded in Novi Pazar in November 1934.[16] In order to demonstrate the patterning in the passage I have underlined the verbs in it. One should also note the prevalence of alliteration and of rhyme, both internal and final in these lines.

VERSION A

Kud god skita, za Aliju pita.	Wherever he wandered, he asked for Alija.
Kazaše ga u gradu Kajniđu.	He said he was in the city of Kajniđa.
Kad tatarin pod Kajniđu dođe,	When the messenger came to Kajniđa,
Pa eto ga uz čaršiju prođe.	He passed along the main street.
Pa prilazi novom bazdrđanu,	He approached the new shopkeeper,

[16]Parry, M., 1953, no. 2, lines 113–128. See also Lord, A., 1960, 54–57.

Te upita za Alino dvore.	And he asked for Alija's house.
Bazdrđan mu dvore ukazao.	The shopkeeper pointed out the house.
Kad tatarin na kapiju dođe,	When the messenger came to the gate.
Pa zadrma halkom na vratima.	He beat with the knocker on the door.
Zveknu halka, a jeknu kapija.	The knocker rang, the gate resounded.
Doma nema Đerđelez Alije,	Đerđelez Alija was not at home,
Samo stara Alijina majka.	Only Alija's old mother.

Salih Ugljanin actually put those words in those positions, yet he did so subconsciously, following the traditional techniques of his inherited poetic language. The patterns of assonance, alliteration, and line structure, the balancing of words by analogy and antithesis are all part and parcel of the traditional singer's language. In this he is unlike the nontraditional poet who, after considerable thought, consciously chooses the exact words he or she wishes and places them precisely where he or she wants them for particular effect, for nontraditional reasons of which the poet is perfectly aware. Yeats's poetics is his own. Salih's poetic art is not uniquely his; it is inherited and shared by others, valued by his listeners as the proper expression of ideas held in common.

Parry collected three versions of Salih's "Song of Bagdad." The passage just given (version A) is from the earliest of them, dictated to Nikola Vujnović on July 23, 1934. A second version was sung for the records on July 24, 1934, and a third sung on November 22, 1934.[17] The corresponding passages in the later two versions are as follows:

VERSION B	VERSION C
July 24, 1934	November 22, 1934
[lines 131–142]	[lines 113–128]
Kud skitaše, za Aljiju pita,	Kud goj skita za Aljiju pita;
Za gaziju Đerđeljez Aljiju.	
Kazaše ga u gradu Kajniđi.	Kazaše ga u gradu Kajniđu,
	U Kajniđi gradu carevome. [115]

[17] Parry, M., 1954, no. 1, lines 131–142, and no. 3, lines 108–128.

Tera tatar u gradu Kajnidi.
A kad dođe, do u Kajniž siđe, [135]
Ej! traži kulu Đerđeljez Aljije.

Kazaše mu kulu i kapiju.
Tatar brže tera na kapiju,

Pa zatrupa halkom na vratima.

Jeknu halka a goljema vrata. [140]
Nemaše tu Đerđeljez Aljije,
Samo stara do penđera majka.

Kad tatarin pod Kajniđu
dođe,

Pa otide novijem sokakom
Kroz čaršiju od grada
Kajniđe,
Pa upita mlada bozdrđana,
Bozdrđana upita tatarin: [120]
"Kamo dvore Đerđeljez
Alije?"
Bazdrđan mu dvore ukazao.
Ćera tatar novijem sokakom.
Kad Aljiji na kapiju dođe,
Pa zatrupa halkom na
vratima. [125]
Jeknu halka a goljema vrata.
Tu nemaše Đerđeljez Aljije,
Samo stara na odaji majka.

The text in the column on the left was sung the day after Salih had dictated the same song in the first excerpt quoted earlier (version A) and that in the column on the right was sung four months later. The fine pairing and balancing of verbs in the dictated version are not found in either of the sung texts. In dictating Salih got into a kind of rhythm, which manifests itself in this passage by pairing and balancing. The tendency to alliteration, assonance, rhyme, and chiasmus, however, is strong in all three "performances." Such acoustical patterns and arrangements are clearly organizing forces in the structure of groups, or blocks, of lines. To a certain degree, within blocks of lines, they have mnemonic value, but it is clear from these three examples that the singer has not memorized a fixed text. Only one line is common to all three texts, "Kazaše ga u gradu Kajniđu," "He said that he was in the city of Kajniđa," but note that in the July 24 version the name of the city is in the dative, "Kajniđi."

The first two or three lines form a block. The first is built on "za Aliju pita," "he asked for Alija." "Kud god(j) skita," "wherever he wandered," in versions A and C results in internal rhyme. Version B, curiously, breaks that pattern. I would suggest that Salih had in mind, or, better, was possibly influenced by "kazaše," "he said," in line 3 of version B, which is in line 2 of the other texts, with the potential of creating the following two lines:

> Kud skitaše, za Al'ju pitaše,
> Kazaše ga u gradu Kajniđu.

All that is speculation, of course, yet version B is notable for its second line, "za gaziju Đerđelez Aliju," "for the hero Đerđelez Alija," which repeats the internal rhyme of the putative first line and typically elaborates on the content of that line. The structure is not unlike the appositives of Anglo-Saxon poetry. The third line of version B and the second of versions A and C round out the block with the chiasmus of alliterations k-g-g-k. Just as the second line of version B elaborates on the preceding line in that version, so the third line of version C elaborates on its second line, and in so doing it makes a chiastic arrangement of consonants between the two lines:

> Kazaše ga u gradu Kajniđu,
> U Kajniđu gradu carevome.
> K   g   g   K
>   K   g

The B version is the only one of the three to have a line indicating the journey of the sultan's messenger from Stambol to Kajniđa, "tera tatar u gradu Kajniđi," "the messenger rode to the city of Kajniđa." The clause "tera tatar," with its attractive alliteration, is, however, a constant in the passage in the sung texts. Later in version B the messenger goes to Alija's gate, "Tatar brže tera na kapiju," "The messenger quickly rode to the gate," and in version C he goes along the street, "ćera tatar novijem sokakom," "the messenger rode along the new street."

Whatever sense of textuality there may be in the oral formulaic type of composition is to be found in the blocks of lines like those just discussed and the themes that are made up of such blocks. One expects a degree of verbal correspondence among instances of the same theme by the same singer in one or more songs, and it is the subject matter itself and the blocks of lines used to express it that cause that expectation.

A theme is a repeated passage and it is useful in composition because it has a group of lines basic to it which by modification and addition of other lines may be adapted to a particular context.

Here, side by side, are two descriptions of battle from two different poems by Salih Ugljanin in Novi Pazar.[18] I present first the Serbo-Croatian original and then an English translation. The broken underlining indicates words in the right-hand column that are different from those in the left-hand column; lines with asterisks have been adapted to the specific song.

I	II
The Captivity of Đulić Ibrahim	The Wedding of Ćejvanović Meho
[lines 1624–1661]	[lines 663–698]
Kad se dvije sile sastaviše,	Pa se dvije sile sastaviše,
	Sastaviše, pa se smiješaše.
	Dragi, milji, nemila sastanka! [665]
	Bela danka, a vrana sastanka.
Mač se sijeva, krv se prolijeva, [1625]	(same)
Klapusaju od insana glave,	(same)
A mrtve se noge koprcaju.	(same)
A sve ječu ranjenici ljuti.	
Neko ljelje: "Ne gazi me, druže!	Cf. below, lines 674–677.
Neko: "Kuku! Prifati me, druže!" [1630]	
Kad se tako radi po ratama.	
Ljetu konji, binjađija nema.	(same) [670]
	Sve na stranu sedla izkrivilji,
	Sve prosiplju gredom tegezgije.
	Kuburluci krvljem nakićeni.
	Ljuto ječu ranjenici ljuti.
	Neko kaže: "Ne gazi me, druže!" [675]
Cf. above, lines 1628–1630.	Neko: "Kuku! Ne gazi . . . ne pregazi, druže!"
	Neko: "Ljelje! prifati me, druže!"
	Neko kaže: "I otac i majko!"
Sekoše se do po dana ravna.	
Vej planinam' magle zatamiše,	
Zatamiše magle na sve strane. [1635]	

[18] Ibid., nos. 4 and 12.

Sekoše se uz dva dana ravna,
A dva dana a tri noći ravne.

Tako beše magle zapanule,
Pa široko polje ufatila. [680]

Kad četvrto jutro osvanulo,
Maglje tame fataju planinu.
Turci slazu strmom niz planinu.
    [1640]
*Kad sidoše polju zadarskome,
*Jača sila od Zadara stiže,
*Pa sidoše, te him udariše.
Pa se seču poljem zeljenijem;
Sjekoše se cijo dan do podne. [1645]
Magla butum polje pretisnula.
Niko koga poznat' ne mogaše.

Sekoše se tri dana bijela,
Tri dana i noći četiri.
        (same)

Ta put Talje ruke podignuo.
Molji Boga, da mu vetar puhne,
Ej, da vetar sa planine puhne, [1650]
Pa da vidi čije društvo gine
Koje gine a koje dobije.

Talje mače čošku najdaljemu,
Diže ruke, dovu izučijo. [685]

Da mu vetar sa planine puhne,
A da vidi čije društvo gine,
Koje gine a koje dobiva.
Pa sad Talu kabul dova bila.
        (same) [690]

Vetar puhnu, maglu rasturijo.
Kome stati polja pogljedati,
Ravnine se mesa nakitile. [1655]

Kad stade kome pogljedati,
Ravnine se leša nakitile,
A doline krv se proljijeva.

*Vojska sve se vraća ka Zadaru.
A lješina polje pritisnula.
Đe su brda, na tojage glave,
Vej him više ratovanja nema.

A brda su na tojage glave,

*Čadorovi sve su propanuli. [695]
*Sto j' ostalo od Madžara, kaže,
*To je krajem izbežalo.
Stadoše se Turci pokupiti.

Stadoše se pokupiti Turci, [1660]
Skupiše se u polje široko.

I
When the two forces met,

II
Then the two forces met,
Met, and then mingled.

Dear one, a merciless meeting! [665]
A bright day, but a dark meeting!

Sword flashed, blood flowed, [1625]   (same)
Men's heads toppled,   (same)
And dead limbs twitched.   (same)
Ever the badly wounded groaned.
One wailed: "Do not tread on me,   Cf. below, lines 647–676.
    comrade!"
One: "Alas! Take me up comrade!"
    [1630]
Thus is done in wars.
Horses flew by without riders.   (same)
                                           They had twisted the saddles to the
                                               side [670]
                                           And lost their blankets.
                                           The saddle holsters were filled with
                                               blood.
                                           Sorely the badly wounded groaned.
                                           One said: "Do not tread on me,
                                               comrade!"
Cf. above, lines 1629–1630.   One: "Alas! Do not tread . . . do not
                                               tread on me, comrade!" [675]
                                           One: "Woe! Take me up, comrade!"
                                           One said: "Father and mother!"

They fought until midday.
Already the mists had fallen on the
    mountains,
The mist had fallen on all sides.
    [1635]

                                           So the mists had fallen,
                                           And covered the broad plain.

They fought for two full days,
Two days and three full nights.

                                           The fought for three bright days,
                                               [680]
                                           Three days and four nights.
When the fourth morning dawned,   (same)
Dark mists covered the mountains.
The Turks came steeply down the
    mountain. [1640]

*When they came to the plain of
    Zadar,
*A stronger force came from Zadar,
*They descended and attacked them,
And fought on the green plain.
They fought a whole day until noon.
    [1645]
A mist covered the whole plain.
No one could recognize anyone else.
    [1645]

Tale moved to the farthest corner,
Raised his arms, recited a prayer.

Then Tale raised his arms.
He prayed God for a wind to blow.
    [1650]
For a wind to blow from the
    mountain,
To see which side was losing,
Which losing and which winning.
    [1650]
The wind blew, dispersed the mist.
Were anyone to look at the plain,
    [1655]
Flesh adorned the plains.

That a wind blow from the
    mountain, [685]
    (same)
    (same)
Tale's prayer was accepted.
    (same)
    (same) [690]

Corpses adorned the plains.
Blood flowed in the valleys.

*The army returned to Zadar.
The hills held heads on stakes.
For them the fighting was over.

    (same)

*The tents had all collapsed.
*What Hungarians remained
*Had fled. [695]

The Turks began to assemble, [1660]
They assembled on the broad plain.
    (same)

It is clear from these parallel passages of description of battle from
two different songs by the same singer that (1) he has not memorized the
theme, that (2) he repeats blocks of two, three, or four lines more or less
verbatim, that (3) he sometimes alters the order of groups of lines, that
(4) he has a shorter and a longer form of some groups (as in the first lines
of the theme), that (5) there are some groups close in meaning but
different in wording (indicated by the bracketed but joined lines), and

that (6) he has adapted the theme somewhat to the particular battle (indicated by the asterisked lines). This type of composition is very characteristic of oral-traditional formulaic style.

It is crucial for the Homerist to observe in the foregoing parallel texts those lines that are repeated both verbatim and almost verbatim, because Goold has claimed that such repetitions in the Homeric poems are among the evidence that Homer was working with a fixed text and, therefore, that the Homeric poems were products of written, rather than oral-traditional literature.[19] The singer of the lines just quoted, a long-time teller of epic tales in oral tradition, was not proceeding from a fixed text, nor, as the parallel passages demonstrate, had he memorized the lines. As I said earlier, themes in oral-traditional literature—in Parry's sense of the term—are made up of smaller blocks of lines, held together by sense, by syntactic parallelism, by acoustical resonances such as alliteration and various kinds of rhyme, that make the lines memorable, with a core that is more or less stable, some even being on occasion repeated exactly, but, as we have seen, not always so. Verbatim or almost verbatim repetition of small blocks of lines is a regular characteristic of oral-traditional composition and not of written nontraditional literature; the latter would tend to shun them.

The theme—not the subject but the passage—is, indeed, as much a mark of oral-traditional composition as the formula, if not more so. The well-known arming scenes in the *Iliad* are excellent examples of Homer's technique of composition by theme.[20] There are four of them (Paris, 3.330–338; Agamemnon, 11.17–46; Patroclus, 16.131–139; Achilles, 19.369–374) and they consist of three or four basic lines, qualified, elaborated on, and added to.

The arming of Paris begins with lines 3.330–332:

κνημῖδας μὲν πρῶτα περὶ κνήμῃσιν ἔθηκε
καλάς, ἀργυρέοισιν ἐπισφυρίοις ἀραρυίας
δεύτερον αὖ θώρηκα περὶ στήθεσσιν ἔδυνεν.

First he placed along his legs the fair greaves linked with silver fastenings to hold the greaves at the ankles.
Afterwards he girt on about his chest the corselet.[21]

---

[19] Goold, 1977.
[20] See Arend, 1933, 92 ff., J. I. Armstrong's splendid article (1958) on the arming scenes, and Bernard Fenik's treatment of them (Fenik, 1968, 73–74, 78–79, 191).
[21] The translations of the *Iliad* used in this paper are by Richmond Lattimore. See Lattimore, 1951. The Greek text used is that of Thomas W. Allen in the Oxford Classical Texts (*Homeri opera*).

The armings of Agamemnon, Patroclus, and Achilles begin with the same three lines as that of Paris. The first epithet in these lines is καλάς, modifying κνημῖδας in the preceding line, and I would like to suggest that one of the factors in its choice was that it alliterates with the "k's" of that line. The only other epithet in these lines immediately follows καλάς. It is ἀργυρέοισιν, modifying ἐπισφυρίοις, and I should like to suggest in this case also that the choice was in part influenced by the fact that it assonates with the last word in its line, ἀραρυίας, even though it does not modify that word.

The arming of Paris continues with an idea peculiar to that hero's corselet (line 3.333):

οἷο κασιγνήτοιο Λυκάονος ἥρμοσε δ'αὐτῷ.

it belonged to his brother Lykaon, but it fitted him also.

This picks up the "k" alliteration again. After the description of the greaves, the donning of the armor is resumed in lines 3.334–338:

ἀμφὶ δ'ἄρ' ὤμοισιν βάλετο ξίφος ἀργυρόηλον
χάλκεον, αὐτὰρ ἔπειτα σάκος μέγα τε στιβαρόν τε·
κρατὶ· δ' ἐπ' ἰφθίμῳ κυνέην εὔτυκτον ἔθηκεν
ἵππουριν· δεινὸν δὲ λόφος καθύπερθεν ἔνευεν·
εἵλετο δ' ἄλκιμον ἔγχος, ὅ οἱ παλάμηφιν ἀρήρει.

Across his shoulders he slung the sword with the nails of silver,
a bronze sword, and above it the great shield, huge and heavy.
Over his powerful head he set the well-fashioned helmet
with the horse-hair crest, and the plumes nodded terribly above it.
He took up a strong-shafted spear that fitted his hand's grip.

The same lines are used in the arming of Patroclus, and there too they are preceded by a line peculiar to that hero, referring to his breastplate, or corselet:

16.134   ποικίλον ἀστερόεντα ποδώκεος Αἰακίδαο.

elaborate, and starry, of swift-footed Aiakides.

The last line of the run, which mentions the spears, is changed from one spear taken up by Paris to two taken up by Patroclus.

3.338   εἵλετο δ' ἄλκιμον ἔγχος, ὅ οἱ παλάμηφιν ἀρήρει.

He took up *a* powerful spear that fitted his hand's grip.

16.139   εἵλετο δ' ἄλκιμα δοῦρε, τά οἱ παλάμηφιν ἀρήρει.

He took up *two* powerful spears that fitted his hand's grip.

The arming of Paris ends with that line, but that of Patroclus continues with what he did *not* take, Achilles' Pelian ash spear. In other words, the basic lines in each case have been adapted to the hero of the moment, Paris or Patroclus.

But the first three lines we considered were used to introduce the arming of Agamemnon and of Achilles as well. In the case of Agamemnon, lines 11.20–28 describe the special corselet Agamemnon put on:

> τόν ποτέ οἱ Κινύρης δῶκε ξεινήϊον εἶναι.
> πεύθετο γὰρ Κύπρονδε μέγα κλέος, οὕνεκ' Ἀχαιοὶ
> ἐς Τροίην νήεσσιν ἀναπλεύσεσθαι ἔμελλον·
> τοὔνεκά οἱ τὸν δῶκε χαριζόμενος βασιλῆϊ.
> τοῦ δ' ἤτοι δέκα οἶμοι ἔσαν μέλανος κυάνοιο,
> δώδεκα δὲ χρυσοῖο καὶ εἴκοσι κασσιτέροιο·
> κυάνεοι δὲ δράκοντες ὀρωρέχατο προτὶ δειρὴν
> τρεῖς ἑκάτερθ', ἴρισσιν ἐοικότες, ἅς τε Κρονίων
> ἐν νέφεϊ στήριξε, τέρας μερόπων ἀνθρώπων.

<the corselet> that Kinyras had given him once, to be a guest present,
for the great fame and rumour of war had carried to Kypros
how the Achaians were to sail against Troy in their vessels.
Therefore he gave the king as a gift of grace this corselet.
Now there were ten circles of deep cobalt upon it,
and twelve of gold and twenty of tin. And toward the opening
at the throat there were rearing up three serpents of cobalt
on either side, like rainbows, which the son of Kronos
has marked upon the clouds, to be a portent to mortals.

After this special passage the lines in the two other armings (those of Paris and Patroclus) reappear in that of Agamemnon slightly changed in 11.29–31:

> ἀμφὶ δ' ἄρ' ὤμοισιν βάλετο ξίφος· ἐν δέ οἱ ἧλοι
> χρύσειοι πάμφαινον, ἀτὰρ περὶ κουλεὸν ἦεν
> ἀργύρεον, χρυσέοισιν ἀορτήρεσσιν ἀρηρός.

Across his shoulders he slung the sword, and the nails upon it
were golden and glittered, and closing about it the scabbard
was silver, and gold was upon the swordstraps that held it.

Before the first line has ended, the sword's description (29–31) has
begun. That description is followed by that of the shield, a special and
ornate passage that is unparalleled in the other passages (11.32–40).

> ἂν δ' ἕλετ' ἀμφιβρότην πολυδαίδαλον ἀσπίδα θοῦριν,
> καλήν, ἣν πέρι μὲν κύκλοι δέκα χάλκεοι ἦσαν,
> ἐν δέ οἱ ὀμφαλοὶ ἦσαν ἐείκοσι κασσιτέροιο
> λευκοί, ἐν δὲ μέσοισιν ἔην μέλανος κυάνοιο.
> τῇ δ' ἐπὶ μὲν Γοργὼ Βλοσυρῶπις ἐστεφάνωτο
> δεινὸν δερκομένη, περὶ δὲ Δεῖμός τε Φόβος τε.
> τῆς δ' ἐξ ἀργύρεος τελαμὼν ἦν· αὐτὰρ ἐπ' αὐτοῦ
> κυάνεος ἐλέλικτο δράκων, κεφαλαὶ δέ οἱ ἦσαν
> τρεῖς ἀμφιστρεφέες, ἑνὸς αὐχένος ἐκπεφυῖαι.

And he took up the man-enclosing elaborate stark shield,
a thing of splendour. There were ten circles of bronze upon it,
and set about it were twenty knobs of tin, pale-shining,
and in the very centre another knob of dark cobalt.
And circled in the midst of all was the blank-eyed face of the Gorgon
with her stare of horror, and Fear was inscribed upon it, and Terror.
The strap of the shield had silver upon it, and there also on it
was coiled a cobalt snake, and there were three heads upon him
twisted to look backward and grown from a single neck, all three.

The basic lines then reappear for another brief spell, also somewhat
modified in lines 11.41–45:

> κρατὶ δ' ἐπ' <u>ἀμφίφαλον</u> κυνέην θέτο <u>τετραφάληρον</u>
> ἵππουριν δεινὸν δὲ λόφος καθύπερθεν ἔνευεν.
> εἵλετο δ'ἄλκιμα δοῦρε δύω, κεκορυθμένα χαλκῷ
> <u>ὀξέα</u> τῆλε δὲ χαλκὸς ἀπ' αὐτόφιν οὐρανὸν εἴσω
> λάμπ, ·

Upon his head he set the helmet, two-horned, four-sheeted,
with the horse-hair crest, and the plumes nodded terribly above it.
Then he caught up two strong spears edged with sharp bronze
and the brazen heads flashed from him deep into heaven.

In the last passage I have underlined the changes from the "basic lines" of the theme, although one should also note that line 43 has the ἄλκιμα δοῦρε found in the arming of Patroclus in 16.139. The arming of Agamemnon, which ends with line 44 in the passage just quoted, or, more strictly, after the first words of line 45, is a combination of modified basic lines and special passages pertaining to it alone. The preceding examples illustrate admirably the typical thematic structure and composition in the *Iliad*, which are in method of composition so very similar to that in the South Slavic epic.

Milman Parry turned to the Yugoslav tradition, as recommended to him by Matija Murko in Paris in 1929, for an investigation of the processes of composition and transmission of oral-traditional epic song.[22] The Russian tradition would have served his purposes as well, except that its songs were not of any great length, and thus less useful than the South Slavic for the Homerist. As James Notopoulos discovered, there were no oral-traditional epics of any length in twentieth-century Greece. Central Asiatic epic, as indicated by the work of Radloff and many others, would have been useful and would have provided longish songs, but it was not possible to collect freely in the Soviet Union. The Yugoslav epic was readily accessible in the 1930s, and except for the war years, has continued to be so since. It is comparable, particularly the Moslem songs, to the Homeric poems in type of composition and in length. Homerists, prejudices aside, have found one main objection to the Yugoslav analogy, to which one might add a second. In the first place they have felt very uneasy about the "inferior quality" of the South Slavic epic compared with the Homeric. In the second place—and related to the first—the fact that it was sung by peasants and for peasants and not in the courts of the aristocracy turned some class-conscious Homerists from it.

Let me comment very briefly on the second point first. In the Moslem Slavic Balkans the singing of epic was fostered in the courts of the pashas and beys, courts and nobles as rich if not richer and more luxurious than the courts and nobles of medieval Europe. The personages of the epics themselves were nobility of various ranks, witness the assembly in "Smailagić Meho" quoted earlier. These are men "dobroga soja i odžaka," "of good seed and family," as the poetry puts it.

[22]Parry, A., 1971, 439–440.

George Huxley, in the Appendix to his *Greek Epic Poetry*, suggests an Irish analogue as perhaps preferable to the South Slavic, in part because it is aristocratic.[23] Beside the fact that it is no more aristocratic than the Yugoslav epic, there are other reasons for finding the Irish material to be not entirely satisfactory. What information we have about the Irish tradition is not as clear-cut as Huxley would have us think. This is borne out by the more recent scholarship in that area.[24] Every bit of evidence about the writing down and exactness of transmission is debatable and debated. And, finally, and perhaps most telling, the majority of the Irish texts we have are in prose. There are no long poetic epics. This is not to say that there are no ways in which the Irish stories, both medieval and modern, can be of help to the Homerist. The narrative and mythic patterns of the Celtic materials provide useful analogues with Homer and other Indo-European patterns of story, but in the area of composition, recording, and transmission they are unfortunately not as helpful as one might wish.

One might add that in contrast to the lack of information available about the circumstances of composition of the medieval poetry we have an abundance of evidence of the exact way in which the Serbo-Croatian songs in the Parry Collection were recorded. We know that they were collected under rigidly meticulous field conditions, with statements by the singers themselves on the phonograph discs about their lives, what songs they knew, and how and from whom they learned them.

In addition to their concern about a Yugoslav peasant epic, some Homerists have felt that the South Slavic oral-traditional epic is so inferior in quality that it has no relevance to the Homeric poems and should be ignored. As a mild and genuine example of that attitude, and with all due respect to a great scholar, I refer to an article published by Albin Lesky in 1954. In it he wrote:

> We must now have reached the kernel of our problem: the question of the orality or literacy of Homeric composition can be decided only from stylistic analysis. . . . Are the structure and execution of the Homeric narrative such that one can think of them as having come into being in pure orality? Here what Wolfgang Schadewaldt has showed us about the

[23] Huxley, 1969, Appendix, "Some Irish Analogues," 191–196.
[24] I refer to the work of Daniel Melia at the University of California, Berkeley, Joseph Nagy and Patrick Ford at the University of California, Los Angeles, and John Collins at the University of Cork, Ireland.

Iliad has special weight. He not only had made the magnificent plan of the poem impressively visible, but he has demonstrated in detail the techniques of foreshadowing, retarding, and combining, which have made the Homeric poem from a plain traditional type of narrative into a great work of art. . . . Let us be reminded at least of two paradigmatic cases: the decision of Zeus, which the nodding of his head in Book 1 announces as effective, is revealed in Books 8, 11, and 15, bit by bit, through the prophecy of the god. The death of Achilles, which will not be told in the *Iliad*, but nevertheless is included in it with such artistry, emerges ever more and more strikingly before our mind's eye through a series of speeches beginning with the words of Thetis (18.96) and reaching to the words of the dying Hector (22.358). All that these two examples represent is unthinkable in an orally conceived epic. From time to time we feel sure that in many cases an oral composition exhibits a remarkable technique of "conjointure," but when we read the summary of the frequently mentioned epic of Avdo Međedović in Bowra's book [1952], the gap between it and Homeric art leaves a decisive impression. One can scarcely expect that the publication of the complete text will change any of that.[25]

I am acutely aware of the very valuable role played by Lesky in respect to Parry's work in Germany, for which I am enormously grateful. Hence my first reaction to this quotation was astonishment that such a reputable scholar as Albin Lesky would make final judgment—and it is clearly a final judgment—on a 13,000-line song from the two-page summary that I gave Bowra in 1949! Could one make a proper judgment of the *Iliad* from a two-page summary? Would one have noticed from such a summary, intended simply to sketch the narrative, that the plan of Zeus was mentioned with increasing involvement in Books 1, 8, 11, and 15? Would the successive foreshadowings of the death of Achilles have emerged from such a summary? I think not. Something must have fogged Lesky's vision. He seems to have been ready to condemn a work merely on report, without having read it!

Moreover, what is so amazing about the references in Books 8, 11, and 15 to the plan of Zeus initiated in Book 1 of the *Iliad* that it would have required writing? Are oral-traditional singers supposed to forget one of the main threads of their song, if other action intervenes? How absurd! An oral-traditional singer knows his song. Like any storyteller he knows what he has said and he knows what he is going to say. One does not need writing to tell a story well and artfully.

[25] Lesky, 1954, 7–8. Translation my own.

Between Books 1 and 8 of the *Iliad* Homer turns his attention away from the will of Zeus and that eminence's plan. Most explanations attempt to demonstrate that Homer's plan is far superior to that of Zeus. Would an oral-traditional singer have been able to stay away for thousands of lines from one of the main subjects of his song, expressed forcefully and very elaborately near the beginning of his song, and revert to it eventually? I believe that something similar happens in Avdo Međedović's long song, "The Wedding of Smailagić Meho."[26] In it, one of the significant elements brought into the story by Meho's betrothed, Fatima, is the exile of her father to Bagdad by the traitorous vizier in Buda. For thousands of lines no mention is made of this and one begins to wonder whether Avdo will ever resolve Zajim Alibeg's complication in the story, or whether he has simply forgotten it. Eventually, however, after several oblique references to it, Avdo returns to the question of Fatima's father and brings him back from exile. The story of the exiled Zajimbeg was not in Avdo's source. This is Avdo's addition to the version he heard, and he does not forget it, in spite of much intervening action. But Zajim's return is important to Avdo's concept of this epic. The fate of Zajim, whose family and succession have been threatened and virtually destroyed by the vizier, is compared with the fate of Meho's father Smail, old and impotent, the future of whose line was also threatened by the same enemy. Both houses are involved, and Avdo tells fully his meaningful tale of succession and loyalty. Fatima's family is a counterpoint to Meho's, as Agamemnon's return in the *Odyssey* is a counterpoint to the return of Odysseus. Avdo has kept complete control of his narrative, even as we feel that Homer has of his. Had Lesky read the South Slavic song with the same perspicacity with which he read the *Iliad*, I am sure that he would have noted this.

One of the main subjects of the Moslem traditional epics in Bosnia is the depiction of the sultan as surrounded by traitors in the pay of the Christian kings, who try to eliminate the great leaders of Bosnia who are loyal to the sultan. There is a series of songs in which the sultan seeks the head of a Bosnian leader for whom the chiefs of the Border substitute someone else, often a blood-brother, who is sacrificed for the leader. One of the leaders whose head is sought thus in song is Đerđelez

[26] Međedović, 1974a and 1974b.

Alija, the nominal hero of "The Song of Bagdad."[27] The song "The Seven Kings Seek the Head of Đerđelez Alija"[28] was known to Salih's audience as well as to himself, and when Alija asks the messenger whether the firman he carries is a "katal ferman," a "decree of death," that song and all others like it come immediately to their minds. Every song in oral tradition has a complex traditional history of its own and is related in tradition to a number of other songs. Alija's question is not an idle one. The audience is as aware as Alija was that decrees of execution have been issued by the sultan against Đerđelez. An oblique reference to those songs is inherent in Alija's query. Songs in tradition are by definition never isolated and must be understood as being surrounded by other traditional songs.

In "The Wedding of Smailagić Meho" Avdo's skill in building suspense and in genuine use of irony is worthy of attention, because that song too concerns the loyalty of Bosnians and the treachery of the vizier in Buda, influenced in this case not by the "seven kings" but by the Christian enemy, General Peter, and traitors around the sultan. When Smailaga gives Polonius-like instructions to his son Meho before the young man's departure for Buda, he stresses that the vizier is their true friend and that Meho and Osman must act accordingly. Avdo and the audience know the irony of this and Avdo plays it to the hilt. When Meho and Osman return from Buda and report to Smail that the vizier is a traitor, Smail even threatens to kill his son for such a traitorous statement. The audience is on edge as to what will happen, even though they know that eventually the old man will be persuaded of the truth.

At the close of his article Lesky concludes, in spite of "the knowledge contributed by comparative literature, important though it be, that the poet [Homer] had formed his work in writing." Lesky continues, "But writing was something new, hitherto unheard of. It enabled a great poet (the author of our *Iliad* whom that of the *Odyssey* followed) to shape from a vast fullness of orally transmitted epic material the gigantic architectonic structure of his great epic, which could be attained only in

[27] Parry, M., 1953 and 1954, nos. 1–3.
[28] There is a synopsis of this song, Parry Text no. 677 in Parry, M., 1954, Synopsis IX, 285–288, with notes on page 428.

this way."[29] Is the implication here that when Homer saw writing he became Wolfgang Schadewaldt?

Most of the characteristics assigned by Lesky to the world of literacy were forged in the world of orality. Homer's skill did not come from writing, although writing provided the opportunity for the poet of the *Iliad* and the *Odyssey* to compose those poems in the form we have them for someone to write them down. Had he not the skill before the writing, had the tradition not afforded him not only the "epic material" but also the conceptual and stylistic potential to create those masterpieces, the occasion would have availed him nothing. So much for writing, either from dictation—which still seems to me to be the only normal way in Homer's time—or by the singer-poet himself. In the 1930s the writing of a scribe to the dictation of the singer provided an opportunity to Avdo Međedović for a 12,311-line version of the song of "Smailagić Meho." But he did not need anybody's writing to produce the 13,326-line version of "Osmanbeg Delibegović i Pavičević Luka" which he *sang* for the phonograph records shortly afterward. No writing was involved in it. If Avdo seized the chance offered by a stable audience, with or without a scribe, to tell his song to his fullest, then Homer too could have done the same. In fact they both did!

It would be appropriate to see what Avdo could do without writing when he was singing at 18–20 decasyllabic lines a minute, not singing a memorized text, but one whose lines he composed as he went along. Analysis of that song from its full text, rather than a judgment from a summary, will eventually demonstrate its qualities. David Bynum's account of the circumstances of the singing of it and the dictating of "The Wedding of Vlahinjić Alija" is instructive:

> Avdo Međedović began to dictate the *Ženidba Vlahinjić Alije* on the twelfth of July, 1935, the same day on which he finished dictating *The Wedding of Smailagić Meho*. Having already that day dictated the final 255 verses of the previous composition, he composed also the first 1,290 lines of the new story. The dictation continued through verse 2,979 on the thirteenth of July. The next day, 14 July, Parry intervened to defer the dictating work then in progress and have Avdo start the *Wedding of Ali Vlahinjić* all over again from the beginning, singing it this time for the recording microphone. That day and the next, 15 July, sufficed to complete the singing of the epic, and on 16 July the dictation of the same

[29]Lesky, 1954, 8.

story, interrupted two days earlier, was resumed and carried forward a few hundred lines to verse 3,292.

Parry then again interrupted the dictation to have Avdo sing the rather different epic of *Osmanbeg Delibegović i Pavičević Luka*. This continued without interruption for four days, 17–20 July, and yielded 7,132 verses of text on the phonograph records. Except for a single day of rest (2 July), Avdo had by this time been dictating and singing between one and two thousand epic verses every day for twenty-three days, and Parry gave him a well-earned vacation on 21–23 July. When Avdo returned to composing poetry on 24 July, he resumed the dictation of the *Wedding of Vlahinjić Alija*, which he had left off in a slightly less than half-finished state a week ago. On 25 July he finally completed that tale, having been given every opportunity that distraction, fatigue, or the lapse of time could contribute to induce him to forget or to change the elements of the Vlahinjić Alija story, or to confuse it with other epics.

Bynum notes that the same process of interruption and distraction occurred when Avdo sang *Osmanbeg Delibegović i Pavičević Luka*. Three other epics (*Ženidba Vlahinjić Alije, Gavran Harambaša i Sirdar Mujo*, and *Robovanje Tala u Ozimu*) intervened, along with "three further days of rest (27–29 July)." Moreover, "many hours of conversations before the microphone about still other epics and the events in Avdo's own life (Parry Texts *12436, 12443,* and *12445*) were introduced between the day (20 July) when Avdo left off singing *Osmanbeg Delibegović i Pavičević Luka* at verse 7,132 and his completion of the epic for the phonograph records on 1–3 August." As Bynum points out,

> Thus, the three texts in this book are not only evidence of the most fluent and most extensive oral traditional epic composition collected from any one man in Europe since Homer, but also of the exact relationship among different complex epics in the mind of a great oral poet at a given "moment" of intensive poetic activity in his tradition. For whereas Avdo's dictation of *The Wedding of Smailagić Meho* [published in vols. 3 and 4 of *Serbo-Croatian Heroic Songs*] took place under virtually ideal circumstances without interruption or distraction over the eight days from 5–12 July, 1935, Parry deliberately made Avdo's dictation and singing of the texts set forth in the present volume to interrupt and interfere with each other so as to test the distinctions among different epic stories and to learn all he could about the "chemistry" of their possible derivations and their narrative dependencies one upon another.[30]

[30] Međedović, 1980, x–xi.

The ability of the great oral-traditional singer to produce an intricate and artistic structure extending over many lines is illustrated dramatically in the songs of Avdo Međedović. The first episode of "Osmanbeg Delibegović" contains an example of ring-composition. It goes like this:

(1) Osmanbeg, an old man of great dignity and importance, rises early and his wife prepares strong coffee for him, and gives him his cape and pipe. (*Agrli*, "strong, bitter," appears only in this passage in the song.)

(2) In sadness he goes with his steward to the ramparts of the city.

(3) He settles there where the cannon are and looks over the plain of Osek, whence a rider appears, who is described at length as he approaches.

(4a) Osmanbeg inquires who he is, apologizing for breaking custom.

(4b) Silić Jusuf identifies himself. He has learned from his widowed mother that he has a maternal uncle, Osmanbeg. He asks why Osmanbeg has never visited his sister.

(4c) Osmanbeg replies that he was so saddened by his son-in-law Mahmut Pasha's death that he had retired and not gone anywhere. He did not know of the birth of his nephew.

(3) Osmanbeg orders the cannon to be fired to summon the lords of Osek.

(2) With Jusuf he returns to his house rejoicing.

(1) The lords arrive. There is feasting, and congratulations are offered to Osmanbeg. The lords spend the night at Osmanbeg's house at his insistence.

The center of the ring is the meeting of Osmanbeg and Jusuf, and especially the discovery of family relationship, uncle and nephew, that will form one of the most significant elements in the song. Continuing the story, we find a duplication of pattern with marked differences amid similarities.

The lords of Osek have spent the night with Osmanbeg. The next morning *they* arise early—as did *he* in the opening scene of the song— and the sun rises over the mountains. They have their morning drinks. Osmanbeg goes to the window and looks out over the plain. A rider appears, a Christian general, who is described as fully as Silić Jusuf was, actually even more fully. Osmanbeg calls his lords to look at the wondrous sight and gives orders that the new arrival be brought to him, but that the general should leave his weapons at the door. He speculates on why a Christian general has sought him out.

The contrast between the two scenes is dramatic. The tired, sad, discouraged Osmanbeg at the beginning of the first episode, alone except for wife and servant, drinking his strong and bitter coffee, is contrasted with the ebullient Osmanbeg of the second episode, surrounded by the lords of Osek, drinking their morning drinks—no stark and bitter coffee here.

Instead of the rider speaking from his horse to Osman on the ramparts, we have a formal and boisterous meeting with the newcomer, a representative of the enemy camp, magnificent, but perhaps deadly.

As we go further into the song, the rings multiply and spread, and there is an intensification of dramatic contrast with the first episode which carries the story forward.

In Avdo's song of "Smailagić Meho" there are two levels, or interwoven strands, the manner of which is typical also of Homer. As touched upon earlier, there is a contrast between the situation of two families, both of which are loyal to the sovereign. One of these, of which the hero Meho is the scion and fond hope for the future, is favored by the ruling power, in direct contact with it, in a region of the state that is a model of loyalty. The whole point of the story is the contrast with the fate of the other loyal family, whose seat is outside of that region, and whose patriarch is in exile. He and his daughter, Meho's betrothed, are separated by traitors. Their family will die out. In one case we have a family solid and assured of a future great destiny—in the other, a split family destined to extinction. The balance and contrast are clear. What good is loyalty, when the ruler is surrounded by traitors? Where is justice to be found and how is it to be attained? The hero is the intermediary, because he momentarily flirted with the idea of treachery, which gives him the right to be the avenging hand of justice against the traitor.

Another level in the song is the personal and mythic one of the initiatory hero. This is ancient, but in Avdo's story two or even three stages of growth are combined: the proving of the hero's worth as a man in battle, his gaining of a bride, and eventually the assumption of his father's position of leadership.

It seems that the processes of oral-traditional narrative patterns overlap in time and in the course of generations, layers of story coalesce. The result is a fabric of great complexity and richness, when the weaver is sensitive to the nuances of his inherited material and the full possibilities of its poetic art.

Up to this point I have discussed Homer's traditional art on the level of formula and theme. I wish to conclude with the role of tradition in the larger view of Homer's songs. In the last years of my teaching I found myself lecturing on the *Iliad* and then the *Odyssey* to a class that had already read Genesis 1–39, the *Enuma Elish*, the Gilgamesh epic, and Hesiod's *Theogony*. On the assumption that narratives of this sort were current in tradition in ancient Greece and the Near East and were likely to have been known in one form or another to the Greek traditional bards and to Homer among them, I began to view Homer's poems from the standpoint of these, for the most part traditional, stories. On the well-established principle that in oral-traditional narrative significant elements are repeated under a variety of forms, or multiforms, I related Achilles and Sarpedon to other semidivine heroes such as Heracles and Gilgamesh and numerous others. It seemed to me that the section of the *Theogony* that catalogues the heroes who came after Zeus was relevant to the *Iliad*, which gives honored reference to Heracles. These semidivine creatures had problems because of their semihumanity, and through them mythic thought, expressing itself in anthropomorphic imagery, struggled with the dilemma of mortal immortals, and that of their progenitors who found it difficult to accept their children's mortality. One of the oral-traditional ways to understand Achilles and Thetis is through the multiforms of Zeus and Sarpedon or Ares and his son Askalaphos, to say nothing of their counterparts in Aeneas and Aphrodite. Tradition and the traditional singers understood the dilemmas in the traditional stories of gods and mortals which we call myths and which came into being to help bridge the inconsistencies in human life, and Homer set them forth with all the poignancy and pathos and sense of tragic inevitability at his command. The traditional narratives taught the singers that it all started when—to quote Genesis 6—"the sons of god mingled with the daughters of men." The special breed of semidivine heroes explained the divine part of human beings, but paradoxically it also showed how mortality touched even those glorious ones. That surely is one of the main threads of the *Iliad*.

Another key to an understanding of the gods in Homer may be found in the War of the Gods in the *Theogony* and elsewhere (for example, in the *Enuma Elish*), a generational war, a war for power. The *Theogony* echoes traditional myths that relate the rise to power of Zeus. It has occurred to me that the *Iliad* reflects the struggle by Zeus to maintain his power, his sovereignty, with some gods on his side, others precariously opposing him, or wishing they could, and squabbling among themselves. Much more than Troy or an Achaean victory or even the wrath of Achilles was at stake, although the relationship of Thetis to Zeus, and the favor he owed her, were part of the struggle of the gods. The divine conflict was nicely interwoven with the theme of mortality of the semidivines, possibly by Homer himself, but probably by the generations before him. Book 5, Diomedes' book, prepares us for the full diapason of Book 21, when even the rivers join in the battle and Achilles is nearly swamped by gigantic forces, a magnificent figure striking out against a cosmos enraged at his rage and excess in heroically challenging his fate. The cosmic forces, even as they themselves strove together, were disrupted by the hero. The gods had *allowed* Diomedes for a brief spell to discern on the battlefield who were gods and who men, but Achilles took on the cosmos itself in his anguish after the death of his substitute Patroclus, a pawn in the plan of Zeus, and in his fight for glory in a short life. Traditional narratives hold in their many folds, in numerous forms, deep meanings on Life and Death. Homer learned these as a traditional singer, and with the mastery of genius he retold them in traditional form in the *Iliad* and the *Odyssey*.

CHAPTER 6

The *Kalevala*, the South Slavic Epics, and Homer

The differences among the three epic traditions represented in this chapter are great. The *Kalevala* is the last of a series of compilations made by Elias Lönnrot of shorter songs collected by himself and others from epic singers in various parts of Finland. The oral-traditional epics of the South Slavs are independent, individual songs, both short and long, ranging from several hundred lines to 3,000, 5,000, and even up to 10,000 lines. In respect to length some of them are close to the Homeric poems. The Homeric poems, that is, the *Iliad* and the *Odyssey* of Homer, are also independent, individual songs, but their lengths are more than 10,000 lines each.

The *Kalevala* emerged in the period when the *Liedertheorie* was in fashion as a means of understanding the composition of both the Middle High German *Nibelungenlied* and the Homeric poems, when the prevalent opinion was that these great poems were stitched together from shorter songs. That theory is no longer widely held. The classicist Milman Parry believed that the Homeric poems were composed in the same manner as the longer songs in the South Slavic tradition, and that each was the unified work of a single traditional singer.

In this paper I wish to discuss first the various kinds of relationships

The original form of this paper was read at the International Folk Epic Conference at University College, Dublin, Ireland, September 2–6, 1985, and published in the proceedings of that conference, *The Heroic Process: Form, Function and Fantasy in Folk Epic*, edited by Bo Almquist, Séamus Ó Catháin, and Pádraig Ó Héalá (Dublin: Glendale Press, 1987).

among the three epic traditions of the title; second, the techniques of composition and transmission in the three traditions, Finnish, South Slavic, and ancient Greek; and third, some of the shared epic subjects and narrative patterns among the three areas.

Part I

The idea of concatenating Karelo-Finnish traditional songs into an epiclike whole was first advanced by Kaarle Akseli Gottlund in 1817: "if one should desire to collect the old traditional songs [*National-sångerna*] and from these make a systematic whole, there might come from them an epic, a drama, or whatever, so that from this a new Homer, Ossian, or *Nibelungenlied* might come into being."[1] In the Preface to the *Old Kalevala* Lönnrot wrote:

> Already while reading the songs previously collected, particularly those collected by Ganander, I at least wondered whether one might not possibly find songs about Väinämöinen, Ilmarinen, and Lemminkainen and other memorable forebears of ours until from these had been got longer accounts, too, just as we see that the Greeks [in the Homeric poems] and the Icelanders [in the *Poetic* or *Elder Edda*] and others got songs of their forebears.[2]

What Lönnrot created was in at least one respect closer to the Old Icelandic Eddic poems than to the Homeric because the individual shorter poems from which the *Kalevala* was made are visible in the final work. Lönnrot succeeded, however, in producing a "national epic" for the Finns, which had never existed before. He did not realize, of course, that the *Iliad* and the *Odyssey* were not really "national epics" for the ancient Greeks, any more than the *Elder Edda* was a "national epic" for the Icelanders.

Although all, or almost all, of its ingredients were oral-traditional songs, the *Kalevala* itself is not one. Domenico Comparetti pointed this out in 1898 in his extraordinary book, *The Traditional Poetry of the Finns*:

[1] Quoted from Lönnrot, 1963, Appendix I, *Materials for the Study of the Kalevala*, B, *The Kalevala*, 350.

[2] Lönnrot, 1963, Appendix I, D, *Lönnrot's Prefaces to the Kalevala*, II, *Preface (1835) to the Old Kalevala*, 366.

That a whole popular, traditional poetry, living and bringing forth for centuries, should come to furnish the material for one single poem is a strange and abnormal phenomenon. Confronted with such a fact we have the right of doubting whether the poem can be defined as a popular production, collective and not individual; as is without doubt the poetry from which the poem was composed.[3]

The *Kalevala* was created by a collector, and it is unique. There are no variants other than the two that Lönnrot himself composed in the process of reaching the final version, created in the same way in which he composed it. They are not the natural variants formed in the normal processes of a living tradition. Lönnrot's material was traditional, but he altered it, and he devised the sequences of songs of different genres, which were usually sung singly and on different occasions. He believed himself to be a traditional singer, since he was thoroughly conversant with the traditional style.[4]

Yet Lönnrot was not really a traditional singer, in the strictest sense of the words, because he was not brought up in a traditional community and did not inherit the specific traditional songs of a specific group. He was an outsider, but, I hasten to add, he was a very special kind of outsider. He could, and did, create poems, and a poem, in an oral-traditional style. Formulaic analysis would surely show a very high percentage of formulas and formulaic expressions. In spite of the fact that everything in the *Kalevala* is traditional, the poem itself, as a whole, is an individual construct by a nontraditional person, a song that did not come into being, as Comparetti noted, under the normal circumstances of the tradition. Lönnrot was a man of some education, acquainted with books. He merged variants of songs from different regions, using his knowledge of many parts of the country, a knowledge no traditional singer of the "old days," or even of his own, would have had.

It is necessary to emphasize that it was not only Lönnrot's knowledge of the world of books that made him an outsider, but he also had access to manuscript collections containing variants of songs from various regions, as just outlined, and he chose elements from those variants. Both the availability of those variants and his manner of using them distinguished him from the traditional singer. Theoretically, a traditional singer could have traveled all over Finland and acquired acquaintance with the songs and variants of many regions, picking up what he heard

[3]Comparetti, 1898, 328.
[4]Lönnrot, 1963, and see Appendixes 1 and 2 of this paper.

as he journeyed and keeping what he found to his liking. His sources in that case would have been live songs heard in living circumstances; they would not have been set down in manuscripts from which he might cull his favorites at leisure. He would have assimilated them under the normal associative processes of the tradition of which he was a part. Moreover, with his education, there is a possibility, even a probability, that Lönnrot's criteria for choice of elements would not be those dictated by the traditional, subconscious association of ideas and phrases, but by those inculcated by written literature.

It is remarkable that a number of other long epics are also, in reality, compilations of short narrative songs. Alexandra David-Neel collected Tibetan songs about Gesar of Ling and constructed an epic from them.[5] Daniel Biebuyck did the same for the Mwindo Epic of Zaire, the former Belgian Congo.[6] The Kara-Kirghiz epics of Manas and of Er Töshtük were formed from individual shorter songs.[7] In all these cases, the real epic songs were the shorter ones which were put together in sequence. In this respect, the *Kalevala* is quite different from either the South Slavic or the Homeric oral-traditional epics, which correspond rather, in spite of differences of length, to the single narrative songs of the Finnish tradition rather than to the *Kalevala*. On this subject also Comparetti is enlightening:

> The *Kalevala* is a poem inferred and put together by Lönnrot from the whole of the popular, traditional poetry of the Finns. . . . Hence the poem is unique; a fact which does not repeat itself in the poetry of any other people. . . . The Homeric poetry, the Nibelungen, the Chanson de Roland are not unique. They have their places in a period of production of numerous large poems, or in one in which national poetry has already elaborated and matured much material for such poems. . . . The epic songs of other peoples who never reached the point of having large poems, as, for instance, the Russians, Servians, Kelts, Siberian Tatars, ancient Scandinavians and others, do not converge towards one poem; but if ever they reached or should reach the maturity of large compositions they would give many poems of different subjects.[8]

[5] David-Neel and Lama Yongden, 1933.
[6] *Mwindo*, 1969; and Biebuyck, 1978.
[7] Examples of the "short" songs—some have more than 2,000 lines—about these two heroes can be found in German translation in Radloff, 1885. A composite epic of Manas can be seen in Russian translation in *Manas*, 1946, and one of Er Töshtük in French translation with introduction and notes in Boratav and Bazin, 1965.
[8] Comparetti, 1898, 327–328.

It is necessary to add that the Serbian tradition to which Comparetti refers actually did produce songs of several thousands of lines, comparable, for example, to the length of those in the Old French tradition. Most of these Serbo-Croatian epics of such length belong to the Moslem singers in South Serbia, Bosnia, and Hercegovina, and until recently were not so well known as the shorter Christian songs. Curiously enough, the first publications of the Moslem songs were by Kosta Hörmann in 1888–89, and then by Luka Marjanović in 1898–99, at the very time when Comparetti was writing. The longest song published by Hörmann, however, had only 1,878 lines and the longest published by Marjanović had 1,862 lines.[9] The longest songs in the Milman Parry Collection at Harvard have 12,311 and 13,326 lines. These lengths are exceptional, but songs of 2,000 to 4,000 or 5,000 lines are not unusual.

In a number of instances in South Slavic literature a previously nonexistent long literary epic has been created by concatenating and expanding short oral-traditional published songs. For example, in the nineteenth century Vuk Stefanović Karadžić published in his classic collection of oral-traditional epic songs in Serbo-Croatian nine or ten short songs, more balladic in nature than epic, connected with the Battle of Kosovo in 1389 in which a Christian coalition under Prince Lazar was defeated by Turkish forces under Sultan Murat. Not one of those songs, however, related the central event of the battle, namely, the killing of Sultan Murat by the Serb Miloš Obilić. In 1974, when Živomir Mladenović and Vladan Nedić edited Karadžić's hitherto unpublished manuscripts, there came to light a version of the Battle of Kosovo with more than 2,434 lines, with a complete account of the battle, including the killing of Murat by Miloš.[10]

Karadžić's famous nineteenth-century Kosovo texts were not, as a matter of fact, the first recorded songs about the battle. Among our oldest manuscript collections from the eighteenth century there is a Kosovo song that also tells of the death of Murat at Miloš's hands. This *bugarštica* is thought by some scholars to be a written literary text rather than an oral-traditional epic.[11] However, it is not of epic length, having only 253 lines. There are also Kosovo texts in the unpublished collections made by Vuk Vrčević in the middle of the nineteenth century, some of

[9] Hörmann, 1933; Marjanović, 1898–99.
[10] For the classical texts see Karadžić, 1958, nos. 44–52. For the long text see Mladenović and Nedić, 1974.
[11] See Bogišić, 1878, nos. 1 and 2, pages 3–10, and Miletich, 1990.

which seem to be of the same kind, although they, too, are not very long.[12]

It is noteworthy, however, that *long, written* epics of the Battle of Kosovo in 1389 were composed during the nineteenth century, and later, using the shorter songs from published or unpublished collections from traditional singers, including the Vuk Karadžić collection of oral tradition epic songs, although Karadžić himself made no such longer songs from his materials. In 1927 one of these, by Sr[eten] J. Stojković, appeared in a sixth edition.[13] Unlike Lönnrot, Stojković did not himself collect any songs. He simply assembled and arranged songs already collected, composing some transitional passages himself—as did Lönnrot. Like Lönnrot, he produced an epic, which he called "national," but which was his own creation, not an oral-traditional epic.

It is clear from these efforts to produce long epic songs, that one of the most important factors in the minds of those who created them was length; an epic poem was though to be long by definition. Had Lönnrot not had such epics as the Homeric poems in his mind, he would not have striven for a long song (see Appendix 1 at the end of this chapter). Like others before and after him, he thought of an epic as a long narrative poem recounting in a high style the deeds of heroes of the past. This concept of epic was derived from a consideration of the Homeric poems and of Vergil's *Aeneid*.

The length of the Homeric poems, however, may well be due to the role of writing in their creation at the moment, or during the hours and days when Homer dictated them to a scribe.[14] It is very likely, I believe, that Homer never sang the songs of the return of Odysseus from Troy or of the wrath of Achilles at the great length in which they appear in our *Iliad* and *Odyssey*. Like the *Kalevala* they were special poems in their composition. But the manner of composition of the Homeric poems was far different from that of the *Kalevala*. Homer was a bona fide

---

[12] Srpska akademija nauka, Belgrade, Vuk Vrčević Ms. Collection no. 62, vol. 1, no. 21; vol. 2, no. 14; vol. 3, nos. 1–3. For a study of these texts see Pešić, 1967. It is noteworthy that Vrčević's texts have affinities with an Albanian version collected by Elezović earlier in the 1900s. See Elezović, 1923, 54–67. See also Parry Text no. 650 (Milman Parry Collection, Widener Library, Harvard University, Cambridge, Mass.), a Serbo-Croatian version collected by Milman Parry in 1934 from Salih Ugljanin, a Yugoslav Albanian, in Novi Pazar. For more on these Kosovo texts and others see Lord, 1984.

[13] Stojković, 1927.

[14] See Lord, A., 1953, Chapter 2 in this volume.

traditional singer who had sung many songs many times in a tradition of singers like himself and songs like his. He expanded two of the songs in his normal repertory, when he dictated them. He did not stitch songs together to make his "monumental" songs, but he composed them in the manner of a living tradition such as those of the Slavs, which on occasion "mix" songs in order to create other, often carefully unified, songs. This is a different process, and one that has not yet been adequately described, from that of Lönnrot in compiling the *Kalevala*. The Homeric poems, on the contrary, were composed, I believe, in dictation in the same way in which Avdo Međedović's *The Wedding of Smailagić Meho* was composed in dictation.

In composing the *Kalevala* Lönnrot gained length in various ways. One of the most striking was the inclusion of ritual songs, for example, incantations and wedding cycle songs. This type of expansion is absent in the South Slavic and in the Homeric songs. It is true that in describing the mourning of Achilles for Patroclus Homer tells how his mother Thetis and the Nereids came out of the sea to comfort him, and Thetis led in singing a threnody for Patroclus, the words of which Homer realistically gives us, in the manner of fullness of narration and description typical of Homeric epic. Homer includes other ritual laments in the *Iliad*.[15] They are not generic laments such as the generic wedding ritual songs in the *Kalevala*, which are independent songs.

Although there are scenes in some of the South Slavic heroic songs which could serve as background for the singing of ritual or lyric songs, the songs themselves that might accompany such rituals are not actually inserted into the epic, as are those set into the *Kalevala* by Lönnrot. For example, some epic songs begin with a group of youths and maidens going to harvest grain in a field near the border with the enemy's country.[16] There are many traditional harvest songs, and it would have been quite appropriate to insert them into the epics, but they were not incorporated, either entire or partially, into the epic songs. Similarly, in South Slavic epic song there are many heroic tales of bride capture that end with an elaborate wedding, but one does not find any wedding ritual songs included.[17]

---

[15] E.g., in addition to the laments of Achilles and of his mother Thetis and the Nereids for Patroclus in *Iliad* 18.22–64, see especially Achilles's lament for Patroclus in 23.13–23 and the laments of Andromache and Hecuba for Hector in 24.723–760. For more on the ritual lament in ancient and modern Greek literature, oral and written, see Alexiou, 1974.

[16] See "The Ragged Border Warrior Wins the Horses," in Parry, 1954, no. 17.

[17] An excellent example of a song telling of the attaining of a bride by the hero,

In the *Kalevala* Lönnrot on occasion inserted separate stories, such as the tragic one of Kullervo, thereby interrupting the flow of another narrative. Even though the events of Kullervo's life are intertwined with that of Ilmarinen, since he eventually murders Ilmarinen's wife, the prophecy of a heroic life for the child Kullervo is inconsistent with the boy's actual future. The unusual results from the tasks that he performs so badly are, in other contexts, indicative of a glorious life; the joinings are not felicitous. In the *Odyssey* Homer tells, through the Phaeacian bard, the story of Ares and Aphrodite. Like the laments of which I spoke earlier, that tale is the result of Homer's desire to tell the story fully. It is not an interruption but a lingering over the details of a scene. On the other hand, Homer interrupts the forward movement of the Telemachy, which is sometimes thought of as a kind of preface to the whole poem, to recount the story of Odysseus, whose adventures in turn are held up at one point for him to recapitulate everything that happened to him up to the time of the telling. But these strands of narrative are related and the juxtaposition of the several portions is the product of a particular technique of narration. The Kullervo poems, on the other hand, are not intimately related to the other narratives in the *Kalevala*. The many deceptive stories in the *Odyssey* are important, integral elements in the main narrative of Odysseus's return. Such stories are found in abundance in South Slavic return songs as well. But they are a different matter from an inserted ritual, lyric, or narrative songs such as those which are so common in the *Kalevala*.

The short Finnish songs, even the narrative ones, are more comparable to the South Slavic "women's songs" than to the South Slavic epics. This is especially true of the Finnish lyric and ritual songs, such as the charms and songs used in the ceremonial acts and speeches attendant upon weddings. For example, South Slavic women's songs have a rich cycle of ritual songs associated with weddings, including the lament of the bride on leaving her home, instructions for the bride from her mother, and so forth. These separately are like the corresponding Finnish songs. They exist independently, but they are not included in epic texts. Here is an example from the South Slavic wedding cycle.[18]

Sunce mi je na zahodu,	The sun is setting,
Hoće da zađe,	It will set,

---

combined with an initiatory journey and a tale of succession, is Avdo Međedović's, "The Wedding of Smailagić Meho," Međedović, 1974a.

[18] Milojević, 1870, vol. 2, no. 171, from Stana Stojanović of Prizren.

Hoće da zađe,	It will set,
I devojka na pohodu,	The maiden is leaving,
Hoće da pođe,	She will leave,
Hoće da pođe.	She will leave.
Žali oca na pohodu,	She is sorry for her father as she leaves,
Oće da pođe,	She will leave,
Oće da pođe.	She will leave.
Žali majku na pohodu,	She is sorry for her mother as she leaves,
Oće da pođe,	She will leave,
Oće da pođe.	She will leave.
Žali seju na pohodu,	She is sorry for her sister as she leaves,
Oće da pođe.	She will leave,
Oće da pođe.	She will leave.
Žali brata na pohodu,	She is sorry for her brother as she leaves,
Neće da pođe,	She won't leave.
Neće da pođe.	She won't leave.
Za svekrvu upituje,	She asks about her mother-in-law,
Hoće da pođe,	She will leave,
Hoće da pođe.	She will leave.

Variants of this song add a number of other members of the family, whom the bride is sorry to have to leave. Here is another example.[19]

Odvoji se devojka od tatka,	The maiden is separated from her father,
Odvoji se devojka od majke,	The maiden is separated from her mother,
Odvoji se devojka od braće,	The maiden is separated from her brothers,
Odvoji se devojka od sestri,	The maiden is separated from her sisters,
Odvoji se devojka od roda,	The maiden is separated from her family,
Svoga roda i rodbine svoje.	Her family and her kin.

[19] Ibid., no. 173, from Nikola Andrejević, priest, in Sretačka-sirinačka, a *župa* (a fertile, protected valley) on Mount Šar; he wrote it down from his brother's wife.

Ona kreće tekne u tudjine.	She leaves for someone else's home.
Tudjeg tatka tatkom zove,	She calls father someone else's father,
On je ćerkom ne nazivlje.	He does not call her daughter.
Tudju majku majkom zove,	She calls mother someone else's mother,
Ona je ćerkom ne nazivlje.	She does not call her daughter.
Tudjeg brata bracom zove,	She calls brother someone else's brother,
On je sejom ne nazivlje.	He does not call her sister.
Tudju ćerku sejom zove,	She calls sister someone else's daughter,
Ona je sejom ne nazivlje.	She does not call her sister.
Tudjeg roda rodom zove,	She calls family someone else's family,
Tudjeg roda i rodbina,	Someone else's family and kin,
Ona je rodom ne nazivlje.	They do not call her family.

The ritual songs in the *Kalevala* are long, having been expanded by Lönnrot, so I have chosen an example from the *Proto-Kalevala*.[20]

The poor girl sighed deeply,   sighed deeply, gasped;
sorrow weighed on her heart,   tears came to her eyes,
she uttered a word, spoke thus: "Now I am really setting out from here,
from this lovely home,   from the house acquired by my father,
from my mother's dancing ground.   I thank you, father,
for my former life,   for the lunches of days gone by,
for the best snacks.   I thank you, mother,
for rocking me when young,   for always washing my head,
for suckling me earlier,   for your sweet milk.
I thank the whole family,   all the companions I grew up with. . . ."

Lönnrot also added to the length of his new poem by expansion of episodes and songs from within, a method used by both Homer and the

[20] Lönnrot, 1963, lines 540–549 of Poem 8.

South Slavic singers. This element is so clear in all three traditions that it seems superfluous to illustrate it.

In sum, both the *Kalevala* and the South Slavic epic songs, different as they are from one another, have something to teach us about the Homeric poems. Of the two, the Slavic tradition is closer in *type* to the Homeric poems than is the Finnish *Kalevala*. In both the Slavic and the Homeric traditions we find independent, integral songs of some length. If there were separate songs telling the story of Telemachus, or of the wanderings of Odysseus, apart from the Homeric *Odyssey*—and I believe there were—they were integrated into the long Homeric poem rather than concatenated in *Kalevala* style.

Part II

I am concerned here with the method of composition of the shorter songs of the *Kalevala*. Fortunately, the shorter songs have published variants, and we have also the forms of them that occur in Lönnrot's own three versions of the *Kalevala*, namely, the *Proto-Kalevala*, the *Old Kalevala*, and the *[New] Kalevala*.[21] The songs from which the *Kalevala* was made were shorter than the South Slavic epic songs or the Homeric. They did not attain great length, by which I mean several thousands of lines. This has been true of traditional songs in some parts of the South Slavic terrain, for example in Bulgaria and in general in the Christian songs among the Serbs. In comparing the three traditions, one must keep in mind that one is not properly comparing the whole *Kalevala* with the *Iliad* or *Odyssey*, but the Finnish songs that were used in the *Kalevala* with the Homeric poems and with individual songs among the South Slavs. Although we do not have variants from ancient Greece of the Homeric songs, we have variants from South Slavic and from Finnish. The variants tell us how the traditions worked.

In his Preface to the *New Kalevala* Lönnrot gave his version of the way in which songs were transmitted.

> As for the authenticity of the songs, the matter runs about as follows: At a feast or some other social gathering someone hears a new song and tries to remember it. Then on another occasion when this person himself is now

[21] All three were translated into English by Francis Peabody Magoun, Jr.. See Lönnrot, 1963 and 1969.

singing it before a new audience, he remembers quite exactly the material proper rather than its narrative word for word in every detail. Those passages which he does not remember in just the original words he tells in his own, in places perhaps better even than they were before. And if some rather insignificant incident among them is left out, another can take its place out of the singer's own head. In the same way, then, second and third persons who hear it proceed to sing it and the song is changed, changed rather in individual words and details than in the material itself.

This is a description by someone who knew the tradition very well and it is a very perspicacious explanation. I believe that by the "someone" he speaks of who hears a new song he means a singer, that is, someone within the singing tradition itself. Otherwise the singer would not be able to compose "new" lines and passages. Lönnrot continues in a remarkable way:

Parallel to this kind of versified story there runs, however, another which keeps closer to the old words and their linking together, namely, a child's learning from its parents from generation to generation. But at the same time that this prevents the other migratory sister-song from deviating too far, it must itself at times follow the other lest it be left far behind.[22]

Lönnrot recognized two kinds of transmittal, one closer to the "original" (my quotation marks) and one more removed. The first recipient, it would seem, tried to *memorize*, that is to get by rote every word through mimicking, as children learn from parents. The other recipient, already, I assume, a competent singer, *remembered*, rather than consciously memorized, the "material," including, presumably, some of the words, naturally enough, but in reality he retold the story in his own way. It is extremely important to realize the distinction between *memorizing*, with its conscious attempt to reproduce every word of an "original," which must be fixed for that process to be meaningful, and *remembering*, the basic, normal process of recall, which is more potent, I believe, than it is generally credited with being. It is through learning the art of verse making and through remembering given, discrete, units of composition, rather than through word-for-word memorization, that the South Slavic songs were both composed and transmitted. I believe that it was

[22] Quoted from Lönnrot, 1963, Appendix I, D, III, *Preface (1849) to the (New) Kalevala*, 376.

in this way that the epic songs in ancient Greek tradition were transmitted from one generation to another.

One of the methods of composition of the *Kalevala* songs which aids in transmission is the repetition of a memorable pattern. An excellent example of what I have in mind is found in Songs 15, 16, and 17 in *Finnish Folk Poetry, Epic.*[23] The songs do not tell exactly the same story, but each has at its beginning a scene in which a girl, bleaching clothes, spies a boat approaching, and asks the boatman where he is going and why. Two or more lying answers are given and finally the truth is told.

Song 15, "The Sampo IV," begins with a stanza devoted to the departure of Väinäimöinen for Pohjola to woo the maid. The second stanza is on the left in the following quotation. The opening stanza of Song 16, "The Courtship I," is on the right:

The girl Anni, matchless maid	Annikki the island maid
	smith Ilmorini's sister
was washing her little things	went off to do her washing
bleaching what she'd rinsed	on the shore of the blue sea
at the end of the long quay	at the end of Laisa Quay
when she saw a shoal of fish.	

Finally, for comparison, on the right in the following quotation we have the opening stanza of Song 17, "The Courtship II," still keeping the second stanza of Song 15 on the left.

The girl Anni, matchless maid	The girl of night, maid of dusk
was washing her little things	was rinsing clothes she had washed
bleaching what she'd rinsed	what she had bleached was bleaching
at the end of the long quay	at the end of the long quay
	a bright-carved bat in her hand
when she saw a shoal of fish.	

The singers of these three songs are not the same.[24] Without another

[23] *Finnish Folk Poetry, Epic,* 1977.
[24] Ibid. Songs 15 and 16 are from A. A. Borenius's collection of 1872 and were written down in Archangel Karelia. Song 17 is from the collection of D. E. D. Europaeus of 1845, written down in North Karelia.

text from the same singers one cannot tell whether they held them in a fixed form in their own mind. But one can say that even the lines that are similar in meaning could not come from a fixed "original" text. The line "at the end of the long quay" is a fixed traditional line, a whole-line formula. In Song 16 it seems to be adapted to its immediate context through substitution of the name of the quay for the epithet, but there the English translation leads us astray. In Finnish the lines are different:

> Song 15 pitam portahan nenassa.
> Song 16 Laisan laiturin nenalla.
> Song 17 pitkan portahan nenassa.

Let us pursue the textual comparison of the three songs. Song 15 continues on the left and Song 16 on the right.

	She spied a black speck on the sea
	something bluish on the waves
	herself put this into words:
	"If you are my father's boat
	turn homeward, turn to your house
	away from other havens!
	Or else if my brother's craft
	away from other havens!
	Or yet Väinämöini's boat
	bring yourself here for a talk!
"If you are a shoal of fish	
then away with you, swim off!	
If you are a flock of birds	If a darling flock of ducks
Then begone with you, fly off!	spread out into flight!
If you are a water-rock	Or again a water-stone
then roll off in the water!	draw the water over you!"
If you're old Väinämöine	
bring yourself here for a talk	
come here for a word!"	
The old Väinämöine came	It was Väinämöini's boat
took himself there for a talk	took itself there for a talk.
went there for a word.	

The foregoing passage does not have an equivalent in Song 17, which continues simply with:

> A red boat went by:
> one side of the boat was red.

There follows immediately the conversation in which the questions and answers concern the destination of the boat and/or its occupant, which we shall consider shortly.

Typical of versions of the same theme by different singers, our texts of the girl's words exhibit variant readings where the subjects are the same. One of the items concerns a flock of birds, another, a water-rock. Here, in Finnish, are the four lines involved; the first two tell of the birds, the last two of the water-rock. Song 15 is on the left, Song 16 is on the right:

Jos lienet lintuine <u>karja</u>	Olit armas alli<u>karja</u>
niin sie <u>lendoho leviete!</u>	sinä <u>lentohon levie</u>
Jos lienet <u>vezikivoine</u>	Elikkä <u>vesikivoni</u>
niin sie <u>vezin</u> vierekkänä!	<u>vesi</u> peälläsi vetähys!"

If you are a flock of birds	If a darling flock of ducks
Then begone with you, fly off!	spread out into flight!
If you are a water-rock	Or again a water-stone
then roll off in the water!	draw the water over you!"

I have underlined the words that are alike in both versions, except for morphological differences. The singers were certainly not going back to the same memorized "original"; the similarities come from the traditional subject matter. Memorization is not needed; one need only remember "flocks," "fly off!" "water-stone," "water." The alliteration of "lendoho leviete!" and "vezikivoine," "vezin vierekkänä!" helps in the remembering as well.

The same is true of the final words of the girl's speech in Song 15 and their corresponding lines in Song 16. Here they are in Finnish:

Jos lienet vanha <u>Väinämöine</u>	Eli pursi <u>Vaïnaïmöisen</u>
<u>pakinoilla painustoate</u>	sie <u>painu pakinoilla!</u>
sanomilla soahustoate!"	

If you're old Väinämöine	Or yet Vänämöini's boat
bring yourself here for a talk,	bring yourself here for a talk!
come here for a word!"	

These lines are, of course, repeated in the description of the action after the girl's words:

Tuli vanha Vainaimöine
pakinoilla painustihi
sanomilla soahustihi.

Se oli pursi Väinäimöisen
se om painu pakinoilla.

The old Väinämöine came
took himself there for a talk
went there for a word.

It was Väinämöini's boat
took itself there for a talk.

In short, the elements that remain textually alike in all versions of a theme, that is, a repeated passage, are the essential ideas as expressed in the traditional word combinations, parts of lines, lines, or groups of lines, especially couplets, that singers have used for generations. These are adapted to the context of the particular song being sung. The similarities are thus the natural ones stemming from the narration of the subject of the passage in traditional garb; they are not the result of memorization of a fixed text, a process which could not have produced the patterns of repetition outlined here.

What we have seen in these examples from the *Kalevala* songs in Finnish is demonstrably true as well of both South Slavic and Homeric oral-traditional narrative song. A single illustration from each will have to suffice, but they can easily be multiplied. First, an example from a South Slavic "return song" at the moment when the hero, who has been long in prison in an enemy city, asks a recently captured prisoner for news of home.[25] Here are two versions of the same passage from the same singer, the one on the left collected November 24, and the one on the right November 20, 1934.

"Sedi lj' moja kula na ćenaru?
Je li' se moja kula podurvala,
Alj' se moja kula harap učinela?
Je lj' mi živa ostarela majka?
Je lj' mi živa svijet mijenila?

A sedi lj' mi sestra neudata,
Sestra Fata u ođaku mome?
Čeka lj' brata Đulić bajraktara?

"Sedi lj' moja na ćenaru kula?
Da se nije kula oburvala,
Alj' je kula jošte na nogama?
Je lj' mi živa u ođaku majka,
Alj' je majka svijet mijenila?
A sedi lj' joj Huso kahveđija?
Čini lj' staroj hizmet do
    odjaka?
A sedi lj' mi sestra neudata,
Sestra Fata Đulić bajraktara?

[25] Parry, M., 1953, no. 4, lines 50–63, and no. 5, lines 33–43, 65–70.

A sedi lj' mi vijernica ljuba?
Da se nije ljuba isprosila?"

A sedi lj' mi dorat u podrumu?
Držu lj' konja dobro u podrumu?
Dalj' mi Huso sedi kahveđija?
Čini lj' staroj hizmet u odaji?"

"Is my house standing on the
    border?
Has my house fallen in,
Or has it been destroyed?
Is my old mother alive?

Is she alive, or has she changed
    worlds?

Is my sister unmarried,
My sister Fata by the hearth?

Does she await her brother Đulić the
    standard-bearer?

Is my chestnut horse in the stable?
Do they care well for the horse in
    the stable?
Is Huso the steward there?
Does he serve the old woman in her
    chamber?"

"Is my house standing on the
    border?
My house has not fallen in?
Is the house still standing?
Is my mother alive by the
    hearth?
Has my mother changed
    worlds?
Is Huso the steward there?
Does he serve the old woman
    by the hearth?
Is my sister unmarried,
Fata, sister of Đulić the
    standard-bearer?

Is my true-love there?
My true-love has not been
    betrothed?"

After the answers to these questions have been given, the hero
continues:

"Sedi lj' moja vijernica ljuba?
Da se ljuba nije isprosila?"

"A sedi lj' mi dorat u
    podrumu,

Sedi lj' dorat u toplom
  podrumu?
Hranu lj' dora konja mojega,
A goru lj' mu četiri svijeće;
Sve mu goru danjem i po
  noći,
Ka' sto ga je Đulić naučijo?

Is my true-love there?
My true-love has not been
  betrothed?"

Is my chestnut horse in the
  stable?
Is the chestnut horse in the
  warm stable?
Are they feeding my chestnut
  horse?
Are the four candles burning
  for him?
Burning day and night,
As Đulić taught him to
  expect?"

There are at least two things that we can learn from a study of those two passages. First, I believe that it is clear that the singer had not memorized a fixed original. Indeed, there never was a fixed original. Yet the text may seem to be amazingly close, so close that in the minds of some the closeness can be explained only by the existence of a fixed original that has been memorized. That leads to the second fact, which we can learn from studying these passages and others like them. They consist of easily remembered, more or less stable, units of two or three lines. Those lines may have one or more lines added to them in elaboration, as the third line in both passages, or the couplet in the passage on the left asking about Djulić's sister. In the question about the chestnut horse in the passage on the right the elaboration is greater and includes a group of three lines at the very end, which themselves form a unit of composition used elsewhere. I should like to suggest that these units of composition are the ones that are more overtly in the mind of the singer than are the individual formulas that make them up, important though they be. It is these units, too, from which "themes" are constructed, as the foregoing passages illustrate.

Let me turn, finally, to an example from the Homeric poems. In recounting the speeches in the assemblies of men or of gods in the *Iliad* Homer has several ways of noting the reactions of the assembly to a speech that has just been made. In three cases he reports that the men shouted, and in several instances the words of the speaker were met with silence. After he has indicated the reaction, Homer has a line leading to another speech. Two of the three shouting passages begin with the same couplet, and vary only in the third line, which introduces the next speaker. Here is the couplet:

Ὣς ἔφαθ', οἱ δ' ἄρα πάντες ἐπίαχον υἷες Ἀχαιῶν,
μῦθον ἀγασσάμενοι Διομήδεος ἱπποδάμοιο.

So he spoke, and all the sons of the Achaians shouted acclaim,
<wondering at> the word of Diomedes, breaker of horses.[26]

The third shouting passage differs from this couplet in its first and second lines:

Ὣς ἔφατ', Ἀργεῖοι δὲ μέγ' ἴαχον, ἀμφὶ δὲ νῆες
σμερδαλέον κονάβησαν ἀϋσάντων ὑπ' Ἀχαιῶν,

So he spoke, and the Argives shouted aloud, and about them
the ships echoed terribly to the roaring Achaians.[27]

The third and fourth lines of the preceding passage are:

μῦθον ἐπαινήσαντες Ὀδυσσῆος θείοιο.
τοῖσι δὲ καὶ μετέειπε Γερήνιος ἱππότα Νέστωρ·

as they cried out applause to the word of god-like Odysseus.
Now among them spoke the Gerenian horseman, Nestor:[28]

[26] *Iliad* 7.403–404. I follow Lattimore's translation except for the words between angular brackets.
[27] *Iliad* 2.333–334.
[28] *Iliad* 2.335–336.

Note that these two lines are variants of the second and third lines of the other two passages:

μῦθον ἀγασσάμενοι Διομήδεος ἱπποδάμοιο.
καὶ τότ' ἄρ' Ἰδαῖον προσέφη κρείων Ἀγαμέμνων.
τοῖσι δ'ἀνιστάμενος μετεφώνεεν ἱππότα Νέστωρ·

<wondering at> the word of Diomedes, breaker of horses.
and now powerful Agamemnon spoke to Idaios:
and now Nestor the horseman stood forth among them and spoke to them:[29]

When the reaction to a speech is silence, the passages (there are five of them) bridging that speech to the next begin with the line:

Ὣς ἔφαθ', οἱ δ'ἄρα πάντες ἀκὴν ἐγένοντο σιωπῇ,

So he spoke, and all of them stayed stricken to silence.[30]

Four of the passages end with a line introducing another speech by the same speaker. In three of them the speaker is Diomedes, and the line is the same:

ὀψὲ δὲ δὴ μετέειπε βοὴν ἀγαθὸς Διομήδης·

but now at long last Diomedes of the great war cry addressed them:[31]

In the fourth the speaker is Athena, and the line is varied to accommodate her name:

ὀψὲ δὲ δὴ μετέειπε θεὰ γλαυκῶπις Ἀθήνη·

But now at long last the goddess grey-eyed Athene answered him:[32]

In the fifth case, although the next speaker is Diomedes, he is not

[29] *Iliad* 7.404–405, and 9.51–52. I follow Lattimore's translation except for the words between angular brackets.
[30] *Iliad* 8.28; 7.398; 9.29; 9.693; and 10.218.
[31] *Iliad* 7.399; 9.31; 9.696.
[32] *Iliad* 8.30.

resuming after the preceding speech, and the line is slightly different. It is like *Iliad* 2.336 in the shouting passages, except for the change of speakers:

τοῖσι δὲ καὶ μετέειπε βοὴν ἀγαθὸς Διομήδης·

but now Diomedes of the great war cry spoke forth among them:[33]

In two cases there are only two lines in the passage, and they have already been discussed. In the remaining three cases there are one or two lines of varying content between the beginning and the ending lines. It is to be noted, however, that the intervening lines have relatives in the other passages, both those with shouting and those with silence. Here, in their entirety, are the three cases in question:

Ὣς ἔφαθ', οἱ δ'ἄρα πάντες ἀκὴν ἐγένοντο σιωπῇ,
μῦθον ἀγασσάμενοι μάλα γὰρ κρατερῶς ἀγόρευσεν.
ὀψὲ δὲ δὴ μετέειπε θεὰ γλαυκῶπις Ἀθήνη·

So he spoke, and all of them stayed stricken to silence,
<wondering> at his word, for indeed he had spoken to them very
        strongly.
But now at long last the goddess grey-eyed Athene answered him:

Ὣς ἔφαθ', οἱ δ'ἄρα πάντες ἀκὴν ἐγένοντο σιωπῇ,
δὴν δ' ἄνεῳ ἦσαν τετιηότες υἷες Ἀχαιῶν·
ὀψὲ δὲ δὴ μετέειπε βοὴν ἀγαθὸς Διομήδης·

So he spoke, and all of them stayed stricken to silence.
For some time the sons of the Achaians said nothing, in sorrow;
but at long last Diomedes of the great war cry addressed them:

Ὣς ἔφαθ', οἱ δ'ἄρα πάντες ἀκὴν ἐγένοντο σιωπῇ,
μῦθον ἀγασσάμενοι· μάλα γὰρ κρατερῶς ἀγόρευσε.
δὴν δ' ἄνεῳ ἦσαν τετιηότες υἷες Ἀχαιῶν·
ὀψὲ δὲ δὴ μετέειπε βοὴν ἀγαθὸς Διομήδης·

So he spoke, and all of them stayed stricken to silence
<Wondering> at his words. He had spoken to them very strongly.
For a long time the sons of the Achaians said nothing, in sorrow,

[33] *Iliad* 10.219.

but at long last Diomedes of the great war cry spoke to them:[34]

The study of these passages indicates clearly that Homer, like the Finnish and South Slavic traditional poets in the passages from them analyzed earlier, had in his mind a more or less stable unit of composition, with some lines very stable but others flexible enough to fit the contexts in which his narrative expressed itself.

As I have already pointed out the *Kalevala* is unique, although the songs that went into its making were not. They were, indeed, like the South Slavic and the Homeric epics in that they had many variants, many other poems, or songs, around them. They were not isolated as is the *Kalevala* itself, a lone monument, without variants.

Yet, having said all that, the *Kalevala* songs are very likely far closer to tradition than those of many edited and published oral-traditional epic texts. The editing process itself, except when it limits itself to correcting such things as spelling or grammatical mistakes, argues the existence of two poetics at odds with one another. When one of the finest of the Croatian collectors of oral-traditional epics at the end of the last century edited his carefully written-down texts for publication he changed them. He standardized the normal variations of metrics, and in many cases he eliminated the regular repetitions which are so much a part of the oral-traditional style but which grated against Marjanović's literary sensibilities, in spite of his profound acquaintance with the oral-traditional epic style. We can see from his edited manuscripts, copies of which are in the Parry Collection at Harvard, exactly what he disapproved of. Sometimes he omitted whole passages or wrote new ones to be inserted into the text. The editor and the singer had different ideas of what constituted acceptable poetics. I have not seen any better proof of the existence of two poetics, one for oral-traditional poetry and the other for written literary poetry.

Part III

There are two main patterns of story in the *Kalevala*. One is that of gaining a bride, the other is the stealing of the Sampo (a magic mill

---

[34] *Iliad* 8.28–30; 9.29–31; and 9.693–696. I follow Lattimore's translation except for the words between pointed brackets.

grinding grain). Clearly the two patterns have much in common. The Trojan legend is concerned with the regaining of a bride, although that is only part of the background of the Homeric poems, not their main focus of action, which is on Achilles in the *Iliad* and on Odysseus in the *Odyssey*. The *Odyssey* is a "return song," to which is joined a story of an initiatory hero setting out on a journey to find his father, and a series of incidents in a tale of wanderings. Whereas there is an abundance of "return" stories in the South Slavic tradition, as well as many tales of initiatory heroes setting out to find their missing fathers or uncles, there are no "wanderings," insofar as I can recall, in South Slavic epic.

Comparetti has analyzed and described the composition of the *Kalevala* in detail.[35] In what follows I shall examine some of the patterns of narrative in that poem to see whether they agree with the traditional patterns in the Homeric poems and in the South Slavic epics with which I am acquainted. I shall first consider the "wedding" sequences. In spite of the differences in the traditions involved, one might expect that some patterning, different though it might be from the Homeric or South Slavic songs, would emerge in repeated traditional sequences in the *Kalevala*. I will thus be treating Lönnrot's epic poem, for the sake of the experiment, as if it were itself an oral-traditional epic.

Väinämöinen is twice offered a bride. In the first case, that of Joukahainen's sister, the pattern is as follows: (1) a bride is offered to the hero by someone else (Joukahainen) under duress; (2) the bride refuses to marry the hero (because he is too old); (3) the bride kills herself (by drowning); (4) Väinämöinen returns without a bride.

In the second case, when the eagle carries Väinänmöinen to North Farm, the pattern is in part repeated: (1) a bride is offered to the hero by someone else (the mistress of North Farm) for a price (forging the Sampo); (2) the offered bride refuses to marry the hero by setting three impossible tasks, two of which Väinämöinen accomplishes, although he fails in the third, building and launching a boat. The third element in the pattern (the bride kills herself) is missing in this instance; (4) Väinämöinen returns without a bride, although he still has the task set by the mistress of North Farm, yet to be fulfilled, namely, to forge a Sampo. The patterns of gaining a bride in the traditions of ancient Greece and of the South Slavs do not fit Väinämöinen's marital adventures, at least not up to this point, although the element of setting tests or a series of tasks

[35] Comparetti, 1898, chap. 3.

for the bridegroom is familiar enough. The best-known instance in South Slavic is found in the "Wedding of Sibinjanin Janko," in which Janko is assisted by his nephew Sekul, in disguise, in performing the various feats required, including shooting an arrow through an apple placed on a spear, jumping over nine horses, and recognizing his bride (whom he has never seen before) among nine maidens.[36] One is reminded of the wooing of Brunhild by Gunter in the *Nibelungenlied*, in which the bridegroom is aided by Siegfried in his "Tarnkappe."

We find the wooing pattern again in the exploits of Ilmarinen: (1) a bride is offered to him by the mistress of North Farm (for forging the Sampo—in Väinämöinen's place); (2) the bride demurred; (3) again the third element is missing, since the maid of North Farm does not kill herself; but (4) Ilmarinen goes home empty-handed.

There is indeed a repeated pattern here, which we might call that of "the jilted bridegroom," an unheroic sequence, the hero being frustrated. Either the girls are unwilling, or the hero cannot meet the requirements set by the girl! While I do not know this pattern in South Slavic epic, it is reminiscent, as is the setting of impossible tasks, of English ballads such as "The Elfin Knight," in which the suitor is an otherworldly figure who seeks to lure the girl into the world of magic and death. By setting him impossible tasks, she is able to save herself.[37] There may be some ambiguity in the pattern in the *Kalevala* caused by this suggestion, because both Väinämöinen and Ilmarinen are certainly associated with the world of shamanism.

The impasse between Väinämöinen and Ilmarinen is solved by one more occurrence of "the jilted bridegroom" pattern for Väinämöinen, and a true wedding sequence for Ilmarinen, who finally wins the maid of North Farm, after performing dangerous tasks set by the mistress of North Farm. The element of testing the bridegroom occurred before, of course, with Väinämöinen, who failed the test!

The "successful bridegroom" pattern, if we may call it that for the moment, is (1) someone offers the hero a bride; (2) a series of tests is imposed on the hero, which he succeeds in performing—sometimes with outside help; (3) the hero wins the bride.

Interestingly enough, in his wooing of Kylliki, Lemminkainen is also

[36]Kačić-Miošić, 1967, 179–180. See also George Kostich's doctoral dissertation at Harvard, "Serbo-Croatian Epic 'Ženidbe': An Investigation of the Multiformity of the Trials and Defenders of the Bridegroom," 1977.

[37]Child, 1965, vol. 1, no. 2, p. 6.

a "successful bridegroom," but in his case no tests are imposed on him. That element is replaced by a straightforward "abduction of the bride."

Lönnrot accomplishes the transition to the adventures of Lemminkainen in the direct way in which the South Slavic singers make the same kind of transition, that is, by saying simply: "It is time to speak of Ahti, to go on about the rascal."[38]

> Now on a certain day   on a certain evening,
> the maidens were sporting,   the fair ones dancing
> secretly on the land side of the island,   on a lovely heath,
> Kylliki supreme over the others,   most famous flower of the Island.
> The ruddy-cheeked rascal came along,   reckless Lemminkainen drove
> his own stallion,   his choice colt
> to the middle of the playing field   of the fair one's dance.
> He snatched Kylliki into the sleigh,   dragged the maiden into his sled,
> put her on his fur rug,   tied her to the slatted bottom of his sleigh.
> He struck the horse with the whip,   cracked the lash, then started
>   sliding along.

In South Slavic epic it is not uncommon to find the hero—or sometimes the villain—riding up to a group of maidens dancing the *kolo*, with the heroine at the head of the dance, and taking her onto his horse, tying her three times to him with his long sash, and galloping home. If this pattern were being followed in the *Kalevala*, one would expect pursuit to complete the pattern, or at least a later rescue.

Lemminkainen's journey to North Farm for a bride follows the pattern of the "unsuccessful"—but not "jilted"—bridegroom, but there are some differences in the pattern from what we have seen so far. (1) The hero *seeks a bride* (he is not offered one by someone else); (2) he is asked to accomplish three tasks, two of which he does successfully; (3) in doing the third task (shooting the swan of Tuonela) he is killed (by Märkähattu, Soppy Hat), but brought back to life—and to home—by his mother. This wedding trip of Lemminkainen is like that of Väinämöinen, in which he is unsuccessful in accomplishing the third of the tasks set him (the building and launching of a boat), but the tests for Lemminkainen were imposed not by the maid of North Farm, but by her mother. Setting tests of the bridegroom, as has already been re-

---

[38] In his version of the Song of Bagdad, Salih Ugljanin, having told of the gathering of the Bosnian armies, changes the subject with "Now let me tell you about Fatima" (Parry, M., 1953, no. 1, line 659).

marked, is common, and has its place in ritual as well, but it is not common for the hero to be unsuccessful in overcoming all obstacles. Ritually this would not be proper.

These, then, are the "wedding songs" in the *Kalevala*. They agree in part with traditional patterns elsewhere, but disagree in some striking ways. The main difference is in the element of frustration of the bridegroom, which gives to some of the hero-bridegrooms in the *Kalevala* a note of pathos, a feature that is missing in the South Slavic epics.

There are no "wanderings" in South Slavic epic, but there are parallels to some of the single incidents in the wanderings of Odysseus, such as encounters with man-eating monsters. The adventures of Lemminkainen in the *Kalevala* come close to forming a series of "wanderings," when the hero sets out to hide on the island where his father had once hidden. In the *Proto-Kalevala* and in the *Old Kalevala* he returns home directly from the island, but in the *New Kalevala* he is shipwrecked and swims to another island, where the lady of the island provides him with a boat, with which he reaches home. There is something Odyssean about the sequence: (1) island of women, (2) acquiring a boat (by building it), (3) shipwreck, and (4) arriving at an island where a woman provides a boat to take the hero home.[39]

> Then reckless Lemminkainen   proceeds on the blue sea.
> He proceeded one day, proceeded a second.   On the third day, indeed,
> a wind got to blowing,   the horizon to rumbling,
> a great northwest wind,   a strong northeast wind blew.
> It caught one plank, caught a second,   it capsized the whole boat.
> Then reckless Lemminkainen   fell straight into the water,
> began to row with his fingers,   to paddle with his feet.
> After he had swum a night and a day,   after he had paddled along quite
>   a distance,
> he saw a little cloud,   a cloud patch in the northwest.
> That indeed changed into land,   became a headland.
> He went onto the headland into a house,   found the mistress baking,
> the daughters shaping loaves. . . .
> The gracious mistress   went out to the storehouse,
> sliced some butter in the storehouse,   a sliver of pork;
> she puts it to roast   for the hungry man to eat,
> brings beer in a stoup   for the man who has been swimming to drink.

[39] Lönnrot, 1963, Poem 29, lines 403–426, 442–453.

Then she gave him a new vessel,   a really well-equipped boat,
for the man to go to other lands,   to proceed home.

One thinks, of course, of Circe and Calypso, and even of the Phaeacians. In fact, since the final incident is not in the earlier versions of the
Kalevala, I wonder if Lönnrot, in inserting it in the *New Kalevala*, was
influenced by Homer's *Odyssey*.

In addition to the narrative patterns mentioned so far, there are journeys to the world of the dead in both the *Kalevala* and the *Odyssey*,
different though they be. Väinämöinen seeks special, magical knowledge, the words of a charm, in several places, among which is Tuonela,
the Land of the Dead. There he is almost ensnared, but he is unsuccessful there in his quest for charms. Not until he encounters Antero
Vipunen and penetrates to his interior, is he able to obtain the words he
needs. The correspondence between this episode and Odysseus's con-
sultation with Teiresias has been noted by Martti Haavio.[40]
    There are actually two episodes in the *Odyssey* in which someone
seeks, and obtains, information. They are multiforms of one another. In
the first, Menelaus inquired of the Old Man of the Sea how he could
leave Egypt and continue on his journey home. The scene is not in the
Land of the Dead, to be sure, but it is in the magic land of Egypt. In the
second episode, just referred to, Odysseus questioned Teiresias, who
was really in the Land of the Dead, about many things, and he learned
much even without asking, including his own fated death. As a matter
of fact, Väinämöinen's journey to Tuonela has little in common with
Odysseus's journey to the Land of the Dead; it is more nearly akin to the
episodes in which Odysseus is almost killed, or detained forever in the
other world, from which, however, he manages to escape.
    The world of the dead, as such, like the "wanderings," is missing in
the South Slavic tradition, but there are journeys into "other worlds" in
the Balkan Slavic epics. In the other world, heroes seek, and usually
gain, brides, horses, and artifacts; and from the other world they rescue
people who are being held there against their will. Such a world is
usually the world of the enemy—appropriately enough, because it is
truly a land of death. One must pass barriers and guardians, which are
sometimes monstrous, before one can enter it, and at the barriers, or in
the foreign land itself, the hero has sometimes to hide his identity

[40]Haavio, 1952, 134.

through disguise. He is asked to identify himself, and his answers are often deceptive at first, and tests are made prior to his recognition by a friend in the enemy land. Such questions are reminiscent of those put to Väinämöinen at the approaches to Tuonela.

The fundamental difference between the Finnish tradition and those of the Slavic Balkans and of ancient Greece is the prevalence and force of shamanism in the *Kalevala* and in the songs and their variants that went into its making. Heroism by magic spells rather than by swords and spears gives the *Kalevala* a very special atmosphere, and it is exciting to enter into that strange world.

It is useful and necessary to be aware of the similarities among traditions, to understand that traditions are not watertight compartments. But it is also important to comprehend the peculiar features of each tradition and to have as firm and sympathetic a grasp as possible of the details and meanings of the traditions in which one works. The haunting, tragic beauty of the *Kalevala* cannot be easily matched anywhere else. Lönnrot expressed in it, however, the same sense of human personal loss that one finds in the *Iliad*. The *Kalevala* also shares with it the ultimate sense of reconciliation with the reality that is symbolized by the fact that only portions of the Sampo can ever be possessed by any one people, ironical though it be that they were clever enough to create it.

Appendixes

The following two passages are taken from *The Traditional Poetry of the Finns*, by Domenico Comparetti, translated by Isabella M. Anderton (New York: Longmans Green, 1898). Appendix 1 is found on page 157, and Appendix 2 on page 9, note 1, of that work. In Appendix 1 the author being quoted is Elias Lönnrot himself from *Helsingfors Litteraturbladet*, 1849, page 16.

Appendix 1

"The order in which the singers chant their runes should certainly not be entirely overlooked. At the same time I have not thought well to attach too much importance to it, as it is a matter in which they differ much from each other. This very difference in the ordering of the runes confirmed me in the idea I had already conceived: that all runes of this kind could be combined among themselves. For I had observed that the disposition adopted by one singer was not the same as that adopted by another; so that, after a great copying of runes recited by various singers, I found very few that had not been sung, by one or another, in various connections. I could not consider one singer's ordering of the runes as more original than that of another; but explained each case by the natural desire of man to bring order into his knowledge, a desire which produces differences according to the different conception of the individual singers. As a consequence, since none of the singers could compare with me in the mass of runes I had collected, I thought that I had the same right which I was convinced most singers assumed: the right, that is, of ordering the runes according as they best fitted into each other."

Appendix 2

"We may refer here to what Lönnrot wrote in this connection after the new edition of the *Kalevala* in *Helsingfors Litteraturbladet*, 1849, n. 1, p. 20: 'No discussion as to the mode of origin of the Homeric poems could ever have arisen had those who have written on this subject had the experience which I have acquired through the Finnish poems, of the influence of tradition on poetry. They would all have agreed that some poet first briefly sang contemporary events, and that tradition then expanded the songs and produced variants of them. He who afterwards collected these variants did much the same as I have done in ordering and weaving together those of the songs of the *Kalevala*; only I beg that no one take these words amiss, as though I wished to place my abilities or the subject I have treated on a par with that other collector and his work. The various dialectic forms which occur so often in the Homeric poems render impossible the belief that the latter were the work of one man or were handed down by tradition without many variants. He who orders and puts together these pieces of a cycle of songs must sometimes insert a connecting line, and I doubt not that such lines can be found, if we look for them, in the Homeric poems. I also have had to introduce some of them into the runes of the *Kalevala*; but it seemed to me, and to others also, that it would have been mere pedantry to draw attention to them, especially as they have nothing to do with the poem itself, and consist generally in such phrases as "He expressed himself in words and spoke thus" (*Sanon virkkoi, noin nimesi*), or, "Then he spoke and said" (*Siita tuon sanokisi virkki*).

CHAPTER 7

Beowulf and Odysseus

Oral tradition leaves its mark not only in the formulaic style of verse making and in the presence of repeated themes but also in the persistence of certain basic narrative patterns, in spite of sea-changes and reinterpretations. There seems to be evidence that one of the patterns found in the story of Odysseus also underlies a section of the first half of *Beowulf.*

Friedrich Panzer's study of the relationship of the Bearson folktale to the story of Beowulf focuses on the struggles of the hero with two monsters, the second of which is in the "other world."[1] There are surely many similarities both in essence and in detail between the folktale and this part of the Old English epic. Rhys Carpenter has reviewed the adventures of Odysseus as told by the hero, concentrating especially on the incident of the Cyclops, and has found a parallel between them (or it) and the folktale of the Bearson.[2] According to the work of these two eminent scholars, Beowulf and Odysseus have much in common. They share at least one traditional story pattern.

It is frequently pointed out that the taunting of Beowulf by Unferth is reminiscent of the challenge and insult to Odysseus by Euryalus at the court of Alcinous on Phaeacia.[3] In this case the parallel is between

Reprinted by permission of New York University Press from *Franciplegius: Medieval and Linguistic Studies in Honor of Francis Peabody Magoun, Jr.*, edited by Jess B. Bessinger, Jr., and Robert P. Creed. Copyright © 1965 by New York University.

[1] Panzer, 1910.
[2] Carpenter, 1946, 136–152, and 184–193.
[3] *Beowulf*, 1968, 149–150.

themes, incidents in a story, namely, calumny of a stranger at a feast, whereas in the previous instance the parallel was between narrative conglomerates.

So far as I am aware, no attempt has been made to compare the events leading up to the Unferth episode with those leading up to the taunt of Euryalus in the *Odyssey* to see if the parallelism goes beyond the single theme to include a larger complex.

In the Old English poem we have the following sequence: (A) Beowulf has a ship built, (B) crosses a body of water, (C) is met by the coast guard on the opposite shore, and (D) after identification, is led to Heorot, (E) where he is graciously received and entertained, except that (F) during the entertainment he is, without provocation, insulted by Unferth, but (G) after he has proven himself by the long story of his adventures with Breca, (H) the entertainment continues and is ended (I) when all go to bed.

In the *Odyssey* the pattern is as follows (A) Odysseus builds a raft on the island of Ogygia, where he is being detained by Calypso, (B) crosses a body of water, on which he loses his ship but is provided a substitute for one by Ino, (C) encounters Nausicaa and her maidens on the shore, and (D) is directed to the palace of Alcinous, (E) where he is graciously received and entertained, except that (F) during the games he is, without provocation, insulted by Euryalus, but (G) after he has proven himself, (H) the entertainment continues, including his identification and story of his adventures, and is ended (I) by all going to bed. It is clear that the two narratives share some elements. It will be worthwhile to examine some of the subdivisions in more detail.

A. Both Beowulf and Odysseus are depicted as having neither means of transportation nor companions at the beginning of this section. They both acquire a new ship by building it or having it built. Beowulf at this same time acquires companions. These companions are, however, not a necessary element in the section of story that we are considering. Only later, when one of them is destroyed by Grendel before the attack on Beowulf himself, do the companions enter the essential plot. At the moment of which we are speaking, namely the sequence of events from the departure of Beowulf from home to the end of the banquet, the companions are not necessary. In the *Odyssey*, although the companions have all been lost at the moment we are studying, they are, of course, a significant element in Odysseus's complete story.

B. Beowulf's sea voyage is uneventful. As indicated earlier, Odysseus suffers shipwreck, then loses his raft, and acquires Ino's wimple to assist him. Loss of comrades and/or ship seems to be part of a larger pattern. Beowulf also loses a comrade to Grendel. As a matter of fact, the "shipwreck" (the loss of the raft) in the *Odyssey* pattern under consideration could be thought of as a duplication of the great shipwreck in which the remnant of his companions was finally lost, just before his arrival at Ogygia. Thus the sea voyage between Ogygia and Phaeacia with its method of landing, that is by swimming to shore with or without a wimple, is in reality a duplication of the journey from the Isle of the Sun, Thrinacia, to Ogygia. Duplications are characteristic of Homer's poems, especially the *Odyssey*. But, granted all that, Beowulf's sea voyage from the land of the Geats to Denmark is not at all like that of Odysseus from Ogygia to Phaeacia.

C. In both *Beowulf* and the *Odyssey* the traveler is met by someone. The coast guard fits well the stark Germanic heroic scene; Nausicaa and her maidens on the shore of Phaeacia are meaningful in their setting also. Indeed, the comparative absence of women in *Beowulf* contrasts strikingly with their important role in the *Odyssey*. Actually, most of Odysseus' landfalls involve female figures; the land of the Cyclops is one of the few exceptions. What distinguishes the arrival of Beowulf in Denmark is the coast guard's questioning of him as to who he is.

D. Identification of the hero is present at this point in the northern song, but not in Homer. This element is in reality found in the *Odyssey*, but it is delayed until after the gracious reception of the stranger. It occurs at a different point in the story. In both poems, however, the person who meets the hero conducts him to the abode of the leader, although Nausicaa, for reasons of propriety, does not personally take Odysseus all the way into town, but gives him directions.

E. The correspondences in the theme of entertainment are transparent and do not need to be commented on further here.

The themes of insult and reply are the most distinctive in our sequence in both poems, because they mar the joy and peace of the banquet and entertainment. There is an interesting sequel to the relationship between Beowulf and Unferth and between Odysseus and Euryalus that is found later in each poem. Unferth gives to Beowulf his sword to use in fighting Grendel's mother in the mere, in spite of the fact that Beowulf has a sword of his own. This incident is outside of our sequence in *Beowulf*, but it has a parallel within the sequence in the *Odyssey*. During the entertainment that continues after the insult to Odysseus, Euryalus approaches and gives to our hero a beautiful sword and an apology.

Another element associated with the theme of Unferth's taunt is the flashback related by Beowulf in answer to Unferth's insult, the relating of a past adventure. It is in the continuation of the entertainment at the court of Alcinous that Odysseus relates his wanderings at such great length. In other words, the telling of a story from the past is a constant, and hence significant, element in our sequence. It has reached the ultimate in expansion in the *Odyssey*.

There are, therefore, some parallel elements in the sequence in *Beowulf* leading up to and surrounding the Unferth incident and the sequence in the *Odyssey* leading up to and surrounding the taunting of the hero by Euryalus. What follows in *Beowulf*, namely the fight with Grendel, has a parallel in the *Odyssey*, as Carpenter has pointed out, in the blinding of the Cyclops, but it does not occur at the same point in the story.[4] The subsequent events in the *Odyssey* are the equiping of Odysseus for his return to Ithaca after he has recounted all his adventures.

The same pattern of equipping, sailing over the sea, landing, being met by someone, being entertained and reviled, is repeated in Odysseus's return to Ithaca. The sequence is even closer to that in *Beowulf* than that from Ogygia to Phaeacia. The Phaeacians provide Odysseus with a special ship and a mysterious crew for his voyage to Ithaca. Like the journey of Beowulf, that of Odysseus in this case is uneventful, but far more wondrous. As for a possible vestige of the loss of both ship and companions, it should be noted that the ship of the Phaeacians was turned to stone on its return, but of its crew nothing was said.

We have seen that it is typical of the *Odyssey* that the hero is met on the shore by a female figure. In this case it is Athena. Straightway in the exchange between Odysseus and Athena the question of identity arises, in one of the most delightfully playful scenes in the *Odyssey*.

From here to the end of the poem the sequence is not always clear because of the tendency of the *Odyssey* to duplication and ornamentation, but what does stand out is that the poem contains the distinctive

[4]For a discussion of the pattern to which the monster fights belong see Lord, A., 1980, Chapter 8 in this volume.

elements of entertainment, vilification, acquiring of weapons (cf. Un-ferth), the long flashback (Odysseus to his wife), and finally bed. The elements are all there.

Identification of the hero is repeated a number of times, but it is still identification. Vilification also takes several forms. But in this final instance of the sequence in the *Odyssey* the hero meets and slays those who unlawfully possess his house, namely the suitors of Penelope. The events in Phaeacia have been a foreshadowing of events that are to happen in Ithaca up to the end of the banqueting, when the story takes the same turn as in *Beowulf.* In the *Odyssey* the sequence of the narrative goes from release from detention (Calypso on Ogygia, Queen Arete on Phaeacia; an element common to these two examples in the *Odyssey*, but missing in *Beowulf*) to the end of feasting, in which the hero is taunted, and all retire for the night. The parallel in *Beowulf* then, is to the home-coming of Odysseus and the slaying of the suitors, the disturbers of the peace, and the bringing of order to Odysseus's halls.

We might carry the comparison still further. The slaying of the suit-ors begins a feud with their families, and the relatives set out to take revenge upon Odysseus and Telemachus, who have gone off to Laertes' farm. Can this be parallel to the desire for revenge on the part of Grendel's dam? In the *Odyssey* the theme is abortive, because Athena, the dea ex machina stops the feud. Yet, it should be noted that the story persists in describing a descent to the lower world (the so-called Second Nekyia) at this point in the sequence where in *Beowulf* the hero goes down into the mere.

At the other end of the story, at its beginning, there are correspon-dences that are, at least, suggestive. In both *Beowulf* and the *Odyssey* considerable point is made of the fact that a "time of troubles" has lasted for twelve (*Beowulf*) or twenty (*Odyssey*) years. During this period a monster has killed the inhabitants, or suitors have devoured the sub-stance, of a kingdom. The return of Odysseus and the arrival of Beowulf have the same salutary effect. Evildoers are punished and order is restored.

Does this mean that the story of the first part of *Beowulf* is a "return story"? Not necessarily, but it does mean that the narrative frame of part of the return story is similar to, if not identical with, the sequence of events in another kind of adventure tale.

There is still one more example in the *Odyssey* of the pattern "ship

journey—taunting at banquet or games—bed." This section of narrative, it would seem, is distinctive or separate enough to have an existence of its own.

In the early books of the *Odyssey*, Telemachus, who even before this
has had his share of vilification and taunting, at last is able, with the help
of Athena, to equip a ship and to cross the sea to Pylos, where he is
entertained by Nestor. In the course of the conversation with Nestor,
there is very probably the vestige of a taunt. Nestor has expressed the
pious hope that Athena may show the same care for Telemachus that she
did for Odysseus. Telemachus, ever the defeatist, says that this is too
much to be hoped for. He dare not expect such happiness. Athena, in
disguise as Mentor, rounds on him with

> Telemachus, . . . What a thing to say! However far a man may have
> strayed, a friendly god could bring him safely home, and that with ease.
> And for myself, I would rather live through untold hardships to get
> home in the end and see that happy day, than come back and die at my
> own hearth, as Agamemnon died by the treachery of Aegisthus and his
> wife.[5]

Certainly this is not a strong taunt, but this upbraiding does take place
at the proper point in the frame, and it should be remembered that
taunting has been a characteristic of the story of Telemachus up to this
point, taunting both at banquet and at assembly. When the exact sequence is not kept in oral-traditional narrative, often the elements may
all occur in the story but in different order. After the banqueting and
entertainment, during which Nestor tells a long story (like Odysseus's
tale of his wanderings), all go off to bed.

This example of the pattern occurs not as "return" but on the outward
journey, as the young hero goes forth on his first adventure. In the
Odyssey the story of Telemachus is abortive in that he does not find his
father, unless one sees in Theoclymenus a vestige of Odysseus. *Beowulf*
shows the heroic conclusion with its slaying of monsters.[6]

I am reminded of the story of the rescue of the maiden in some
Yugoslav oral-traditional epics. The hero finds himself in disguise in the
city of the enemy whither he has gone, after varying degrees of vilification, in order to rescue a girl whom he has already accepted as his

[5] *Odyssey* 3.229–238, translated by E. V. Rieu, 1946.
[6] For more on Telemachus see Bynum, 1968.

betrothed.[7] His journey, which is overland, has been uneventful, and on arrival in the enemy city he betakes himself to a tavern, where he is cared for by the tavernkeeper, a woman. She thinks that she recognizes the hero. In the course of recognition she recounts a long history of their previous encounter many years before. Then she leads him to his betrothed and advises how the escape may be managed. After the slaughter of those who hinder the girl's marriage, including a suitor, the wedding takes place.

The examples of the narrative sequence we have been investigating seem to indicate that this sequence is useful and has meaning both on the return of the hero to his home to set everything in order and to remarry his wife and on the outward journey of the young hero to win a wife. The identity of the hero on the boundaries between the "other" world and the real one is the pivot of the sequence. Vilification appears to have a function in the pattern. That it is a necessary element is demonstrated by its constant appearance.

The *Odyssey* of Homer had no direct influence on *Beowulf;* the Old English poet did not borrow from Homer. But they both belonged, as the present-day Yugoslav singer of tales does also, to the same oral epic narrative tradition. The story patterns in such a tradition are very old, amazingly stable, surprisingly alive, whether we observe them in the eighth century B.C., the eighth century A.D., (if we accept an early date for *Beowulf*), or in our own time.[8]

[7] See Parry, M., 1954 and 1953, no. 24.

[8] For another aspect of comparison of elements in *Beowulf* with elements in the Homeric poems see Creed, 1962, 44–52.

CHAPTER 8

Interlocking Mythic
Patterns in *Beowulf*

There are two discrete narrative patterns that are found fairly widely disseminated in epic or story tradition, the possible presence of which I should like to explore in *Beowulf*. The first of these involves three stages. (1) A powerful figure is not present or, for various reasons, is powerless in a situation of danger to his people. (2) During the period of his absence, or of his inability or unwillingness to act effectively, things go very badly for those around him, and many of his friends are killed. Finally, (3) the powerful figure returns or his power is restored, whereupon he puts things to right again. The first element in the pattern is sometimes preceded by a quarrel, which motivates either the absence of the powerful figure or his loss of power.

Readers of the *Iliad* will recognize, of course, that this is the often remarked pattern of the main part of the poem with (1) the withdrawal of Achilles from battle because of his quarrel with Agamemnon, (2) the ensuing difficulties of the Achaeans and the death of Patroclus, which motivates (3) the return of Achilles to the battle and the victory of the Achaeans that follows.[1] Its other classical example is in the *Odyssey*, where (1) Odysseus's absence causes (2) the nefarious activities of Penelope's suitors, which are halted by (3) the return of Odysseus. There

The original form of this paper was delivered at an Old English Colloquium at the University of California, Berkeley, in May 1978 and published in *Old English Literature in Context: Ten Essays,* edited by John D. Niles (London: D. S. Brewer, 1980).

[1] See Lord, A., 1960, chap. 9, "The *Iliad*," 186–97, and Nagler, 1974, chap. 5, "The 'Eternal Return' in the Plot Structure of the *Iliad*," 131–136. For further references see Foley, 1980, n. 6.

are numerous examples of the pattern in oral-traditional Slavic epic, both Russian and South Slavic.[2] Its existence in English is attested by the story of King Horn, known especially in the romance of that name and in the ballad of "Hind Horn."[3] Horn returns in disguise after long absence and many adventures to find his beloved about to be married to another. He tells a deceptive story about his own death, recognition occurs, and Horn kills the king who was her suitor and all others in the castle except old friends. This is only part of the story, which is rich in duplications.

For the first element (1), we find in *Beowulf* that Hrothgar is powerless against Grendel. The resulting difficulties (2) over a long time— twelve years—are clear, and need not be elaborated. With the advent of Beowulf (3), Hrothgar's surrogate, the difficulties begin to be overcome, although they cost Beowulf the death of his companion Hondscio. Beowulf maims and drives away the monster Grendel, and the ancient joy and peace return to Heorot.

One is tempted to view the absence of Beowulf himself at the beginning of the poem as the proper first element of the pattern. It may be so vestigially. If that is true, then the lack of a leader is indicated in two ways in *Beowulf,* namely by Beowulf's absence and Hrothgar's impotence.

This pattern, or the continuance of its central period of difficulty, is repeated with the coming of Grendel's dam, whose elimination of Æschere duplicates and deepens the pattern, because Æschere is emphatically identified as Hrothgar's favorite counselor (see lines 1708–1709, 1323b–1329). Hondscio's relationship to Beowulf is "unmarked," and in the early part of the poem he is not even named. In contrast, Æschere is mentioned by name and "marked" in his appearance in this episode. I have sometimes wondered whether the telling of the Grendel episode in Beowulf's recapitulation of the event (lines 2000–2100) actually represents the incident in its form before it was combined with that of Grendel's dam. In that case, Hondscio's name would have occurred in the early part of the poem. At any rate, Hondscio and/or Æschere are

---

[2] For selected examples in Serbo-Croatian see Lord, A., 1960, Appendix III, "Return Songs," 242–259. For the Russian *bylina* of "Dobrynja and Alyosha" see Rybnikov, 1909, vol. 1, nos. 26, 41; vol. 2, nos. 129, 160, 178, 193; also Hilferding, 1950, vol. 1, nos. 5, 23, 26, 33, 38, 43, 49, 65; vol. 2, nos. 100, 145, 168, 187. For a German translation and discussion of Hilferding, no. 5, verses 734–1093, see Trautmann, 1935, no. 26, 280–291.

[3] For the Middle English "King Horn" see Hall, 1901, and for the English ballad see Child, 1965, vol. 1, no. 17, 187–208.

killed, and after the death of the second, Beowulf again appears to remove the difficulties and once again restore peace and joy to Heorot.

The pattern does, then, seem to occur in *Beowulf*, and it is possible that the deaths of Hondscio and Æschere can be interpreted as vestiges of the death of the substitute. They correspond to Patroclus in the *Iliad* or Enkidu, Gilgamesh's companion, in the *Epic of Gilgamesh*. This interpretation would remove what to me has been a puzzling difficulty in the Grendel episode, namely the death of Hondscio while Beowulf looks on. The death of Æschere causes no such difficulty because Beowulf was not in Heorot at the time of the second attack.

One should also remark that the pattern of absence, devastation, and return often, and indeed, originally or ideally, includes elements of disguise, deceptive story, mocking or testing, and recognition, as in the seasonal pattern in the Homeric Hymn to Demeter.[4] All these elements are associated with the hero's return and with the establishment of his identity. They are all to be found in the classic example of the pattern in Homer's *Odyssey*. They are present in more modern oral epic traditions, for example, in the Turkic epics and in Slavic return poems, both Russian and South Slavic, to mention only two out of the numerous contemporary cultures still preserving their traditional narratives with all their traditional elements observed. The challenge of Unferth, beginning "Are you that Beowulf who?" (lines 506–528), fits into this pattern as an element of mocking or testing.[5] Whether or not this episode is an example of a traditional Germanic flyting, as Carol Clover argues, a challenge of the hero suits the pattern and is appropriate where it is in *Beowulf*.[6] In other words, the flyting might be used in the Germanic version of the pattern where the mocking or testing appears in the basic Indo-European tradition, to which Slavic and ancient Greek belong. Be that as it may, mocking in the context of determining identity, feigned or otherwise, is a part of the complex of the return pattern, and I would like to suggest that it may occur here in that complex in *Beowulf*.

Let me turn now to an investigation of the second pattern that was mentioned at the beginning. Stories with this pattern tell of the encounter of the hero and a companion, or companions, with first a male monster, which he overcomes, and then a female monster, or a divine temptress who wants to keep him in the "other" world. His escape from

---

[4] For further discussion of these elements in the Hymn, see Lord, M., 1967.
[5] See Lord, A., 1965, "Beowulf and Odysseus," Chapter 7 in this volume.
[6] Clover, 1980.

the one and his rejection of the offers of the other involve breaking a taboo and/or insulting a deity, and as a result one or more of his companions is killed. The hero, then, with a question in his mind concerning his own mortality or immortality, goes on a journey in which he learns the answer to that question.

The Homeric example of this is in the wanderings of Odysseus. The hero blinds the Cyclops Polyphemus, thus offending Poseidon, and with Hermes's help he defies the powers of Circe, who wishes to detain him in the "other" world. In the Polyphemus episode Odysseus loses some unnamed companions, but in the second incident, that with Circe, he loses a named and otherwise "marked" (the youngest) companion, Elpenor. After this, Odysseus goes to the Land of the Dead and there learns when death will come to him.

This second pattern, then, also contains a death at a climactic point. In it a hero, often a unusual birth, with a companion or companions, encounters a monster of cannibal propensities who kills one or more of the hero's companions, but he overcomes the monster by seriously maiming him. That episode constitutes the first element in the pattern. We have seen it in the encounter of Odysseus and his companions with Polyphemus (and it is duplicated in the episode with the Laestrygonians) but it fits the Humbaba episode in *Gilgamesh* also, so far as we can tell, although some details are not clear. In that episode the hero of the epic, Gilgamesh, who is part god and part man, and his mortal companion, Enkidu, penetrate into the apparently sacred Cedar Forest where they overcome and kill the monster Humbaba. These elements correspond to the Grendel episode in *Beowulf*, of course.

Following the episode with a male monster, the hero comes into conflict with a female figure who wishes to keep him with her in her world but whom he thwarts. His companion or companions are also involved in this episode, but they are not immediately or literally killed in it. I have in mind the incident of Odysseus and Circe in the *Odyssey* and of Gilgamesh and Ishtar in the *Gilgamesh* epic. In the latter, Gilgamesh, returning in glory from his conquest of Humbaba, is seen by the goddess Ishtar. She falls in love with him and wants him to be her lover. He refuses and she calls on her father to send the Bull of Heaven against the two heroes. They slay the Bull, and Enkidu throws a haunch of the animal at the goddess, who is furious. Finally the gods in assembly decree that one of the two must die, and the choice falls on the mortal Enkidu. The episode with Grendel's dam in *Beowulf* fits in the sequence in this pattern, but there are clearly points of divergence, particularly in that Grendel's dam is killed, whereas Ishtar and Circe are only frustrated.

The third element in this pattern is the climactic one to which the first two have been leading. It is the death of one of the hero's companions, a death that is caused by the actions of the hero and his companions in elements one and two. It is clearest in *Gilgamesh* where Enkidu's death is caused by the breaking of taboos or the insulting of the gods by the two protagonists in killing Humbaba and thwarting Ishtar. This third element is vestigial in the *Odyssey* in the death of Elpenor, which occurs at the proper position in the story to fit into the pattern. It is preceded by the episodes of Polyphemus and Circe; it is followed by a journey during which the hero's ultimate destiny, death, is discovered.

The element of death is certainly not clear *at this point* in *Beowulf.* One may see it vestigially in the deaths of Hondscio and Æschere, but these do not occur in the expected place. That answer may be correct, yet in the Scandinavian analogues usually cited for these episodes (for example, the incident of the she-troll and the giant at Sandhaugar in the *Grettis saga*) the same positioning of a death before each of the fights is to be found.[7] The stories in those analogues are complete in themselves and do not go on to a sequel, as in *Beowulf* and in my two main sources for the pattern, the *Odyssey* and the *Gilgamesh* epic.

Whether we accept Hondscio and Æschere as possible vestiges that have been misplaced or simply as pointing forward to a death not present, or whether we simply note the absence in *Beowulf* of this crucial element, this absence (or vestige) must somehow be explained. To do so is not difficult, as a matter of fact, and the explanation leads us, I believe, to a clearer indication not only of the presence but, more significantly, of the importance of this pattern in that poem.

There is an essential difference between the adversaries in the ancient examples and those in the Germanic ones in *Beowulf* and in the sagas. In the former the adversaries are "sacred," and therefore the opposition to them by the hero is tantamount to sacrilege. Although the details are not clear, it is apparent that when Gilgamesh and Enkidu slay Humbaba in the Cedar Forest they have incurred some degree of guilt. This guilt is, of course, crystal clear in the incident with Ishtar and the Bull of Heaven. Death for one of the two heroes must follow, and the gods choose

---

[7] See Klaeber's account of analogues, especially in *Grettissaga*, in *Beowulf,* 1950, xiv–xxiii; also *Beowulf and Its Analogues,* especially 302–316.

Enkidu, the mortal companion of the partly divine Gilgamesh, as the one who must die. The death of the companion is motivated by the guilt of the pair. In the case of the *Odyssey,* the fact that Odysseus had offended the god Poseidon by blinding his son, however justified the hero's actions might be, is made abundantly clear in the song. That Odysseus in the episode with Circe has thwarted her wishes to turn him into a swine and to keep him with her forever is also apparent. But the death of Elpenor is no longer evident as the result of Odysseus's deeds, partly, of course, because his punishment for the maiming of Polyphemus was already realized in his eventual wanderings and shipwreck. The pattern is weakened but it is still there, for Odysseus goes to the Land of the Dead and there learns, among other things, that death will at some time come to him quietly from the sea.

The loss (or perhaps better the absence) in Germanic tradition of the sense of guilt in breaking taboos and insulting the gods, explains the breaking of the pattern in *Beowulf* at this particular place in the poem by the omission of a special death, or at best by its vestigial survival earlier in the poem. The hero not only does not incur any guilt in the Germanic reinterpretation of the pattern, but, quite the opposite, he gains great glory by overcoming the evil chaos caused by Grendel and Grendel's dam.

The pattern may be seen to be resumed, however, in the return journey of Beowulf to his homeland, although this is on another level of reality. We are given not the prophecy of death, as in the *Odyssey*, but its actuality.

We see then in these three cases of the pattern, first, a clear working out of it in *Gilgamesh*, replete with guilt that causes death; second, a form in the *Odyssey* that still holds a strong element of guilt, but death as the result is, while clearly present, only vestigial, since the hero's guilt is punished otherwise; and third, a form in *Beowulf* in which guilt has become virtue and the pattern is broken, leaving either a gap or at best an enigmatic and unclear vestige.

The interlocking of these two patterns from the deep past of the story, modulating from the hopeful eternal return of the cyclical myth of annual renewal, through the death of the substitute, to the eventual acceptance of human mortality, provides a mythic base both for the triumph of Beowulf over the evil generations of Cain and for the inevitable death of the hero in old age, still fighting against destructive forces.

But Beowulf's last deed and his last words held hope within them:

Dyde him of healse   hring gyldenne
þioden þristhydig,   þegne gesealde,
geongum garwigan,   goldfahne helm,
beah ond byrnan,   het hyne brucan well;
"þu eart endelaf   usses cynnes,
Waegmundinga;   ealle wyrd forsweop
mine magas   to metodsceafte,
eorlas on elne;   ic him æfter sceal."
þæt wæs pam gomelan   gingæste word
breostgehygdum,   ær he bæl cure,
hate heaðowylmas;   him of hræðre gewat
sawol secean   soðfæstra dom.[8]

Then the prince, bold of mind, detached
his golden collar and gave it to Wiglaf,
the young spear-warrior, and also his helmet
adorned with gold, his ring and his corslet,
and enjoined him to use them well;
"You are the last survivor of our family,
the Waegmundings; fate has swept
all my kinsmen, those courageous warriors,
to their doom. I must follow them."
   Those were the warrior's last words
before he succumbed to the raging flames
on the pyre; his soul migrated from his breast
to meet the judgement of righteous men.[9]

---

[8] Ibid., lines 2809–2820.
[9] *Beowulf*, 1968, 109.

CHAPTER 9

The Formulaic Structure of Introductions to Direct Discourse in *Beowulf* and *Elene*

This paper is an attempt, after a long silence, to continue work along lines suggested by my distinguished colleague Larry Benson, in an article published in 1966.[1] In it he indicated that a number of the Anglo-Saxon poems that are clearly products of written literature, such as *Phoenix* and *The Metres of Boethius*, which are translations of Latin originals, have approximately as many formulas as *Beowulf* and that the test for orality by formula count is not conclusive for Anglo-Saxon poetry. Shortly after that, Donald K. Fry called for caution together with continued research.[2] Ann Chalmers Watts, after a full and very fair review and further impressive research, came to the same conclusion in *The Lyre and the Harp*.[3] Although there have been some fine articles on *Beowulf* since then, formulas in *Beowulf* have not been the subject of any deep or comprehensive study. Larry Benson concluded his article as follows:

> Indeed, I believe that a recognition that Old English poetry is both formulaic and lettered would lead to an even more exciting and fruitful development in our discipline, for the most significant contribution of the formulaic and thematic studies made thus far has been the demonstration

This paper in its original form was read at the annual International Congress on Medieval Studies at Kalamazoo, Michigan, in May 1982. It has not been published before.

[1] Benson, 1966.
[2] Fry, 1967.
[3] Watts, 1969.

that the Old English poetic language carried with it a richness of reference that allows us to approach these poems with an aesthetic sympathy unknown to critics in the days of [W. J.] Sedgefield. Perhaps more such studies combined with more widespread recognition that the poems we study are indeed poems will bring us closer than ever to an understanding of those distant poets.[4]

It is in that spirit, like Donald K. Fry, who used this same quotation, that I write to take up Benson's challenge to continue to study the formulaic style in *Beowulf* and in other Anglo-Saxon poems.

Formula Clusters

In the Introduction to *The Web of Words* Huppé discusses in rhetorical terms the units of structure, or of construction, of Anglo-Saxon verse.[5] The hemistich and the line are the most obvious, and the repeated phrases and formulas point up this fact very clearly. But the rhetoric, behaving according to the dictates of syntax, meter, and alliteration, often leads beyond the line, to enjambement with the following line. There is nothing peculiarly Anglo-Saxon, of course, in the principles of enjambement. Although it is not very common in the *Chanson de Roland*, it can be found there.[6] Line 1289, for example,

> E Engelers li Guascuinz de Burdele

requires a second line,

> Sun cheval brochet, si li laschet la resne. . . .

just as inexorably as the first line of *Beowulf*,

> Hwæt! We Gar-Dena   in geardagum,

requires a second line

> þeodcyninga   þrym gefrunon.[7]

---

[4] Benson, 1966, 340–341.
[5] Huppé, 1970.
[6] Quotations from the *Chanson de Roland* are from *Roland*, 1937.
[7] Quoted from *Beowulf*, 1968.

The essential ideas of the two lines just quoted at the beginning of laisse 100 of the *Chanson de Roland* are, "Engelers spurs on his horse and loosens the reins." Their expression fills only a line and a half. The subject, "Engelers," occupies, even with the conjunction "e," only a half line. A phrase is needed to complete the line and the appositive, "li Guascuinz de Burdele," performs that function. Still the subject needs a predicate, and so the first two lines have to be taken together. Similarly, the essential ideas of the first two lines of *Beowulf* are "We have heard of the glory of the Spear-Danes in times past." Their expression, too, fills only a line and a half. An alliterative phrase is needed in the a) verse of the second line; the appositive "þeodcyninga" performs that function.

To units of hemistich and line must be added units of three and four hemistichs, or even more, in succession, and beginning in either an a) or a b) verse. For example, *Beowulf* 662,

Ða him Hroðgar gewat   mid his hæleþa gedryht,

requires a second line to complete it, namely 663

eodur Scyldinga,   ut of healle.

Here also we encounter a larger structural unit of four successive hemistichs, the first two and the last of which express the essential idea, or, more accurately, the essential ideas, of the unit, that is, "Hrothgar departed from the hall with his company of retainers." Alliteration requires the appositive, *eodur Scyldinga*, "prince of the Scyldings."

The cluster of formulas operates as does a single formula. Instead of "a word or group of words" one has "a group of formulas regularly used to express a cluster of essential ideas under given metrical conditions." One has merely expanded the "group of words" to "cluster of formulas" and "essential idea" to "cluster of essential ideas." The "given metrical conditions" have also been extended beyond the hemistich and the line. The *principle* of the formula has been preserved intact. The question naturally arises whether any given cluster is "regularly used." The following clusters from *Beowulf*, covering two couplets, are helpful in answering that question:

258–259   Him se yldesta   ondswarode,
             werodes wisa,   wordhord onleac:

340–341   Him þa ellenrof   andswarode,
           wlanc Wedera leod,   word æfter spræc.

The second of the four hemistichs are identical in each couplet, and the syntactic patterns and paratactic structures are the same in both. Moreover, the essential idea of the four hemistichs is the same, namely, "someone spoke to him." I am inclined to call these couplets "formulaic expressions," the more so since the several elements constituting the couplets are themselves demonstrably formulaic.

A number of scholars have written about formulas of more than one line or about clusters of formulas. David Bynum has worked with this concept for several years. Kenneth Goldman investigated various aspects of that phenomenon in South Slavic epic, and John Miles Foley and Robert Payson Creed among others have dealt with clusters of formulas. The most recent work I know of on the subject is found in two articles by Jean Ritzke-Rutherford in the book on the Middle English alliterative *Morte Arthure* edited by K. H. Göller in 1981.[8]

The clusters of which I am thinking, however, differ from those that Robert Creed calls "gnomes" or that John Foley calls "responsions," as well as from those in Ritzke-Rutherford's work. My clusters of formulas are bound together syntactically and are involved in the process of verse making. I am still deeply concerned with composing traditional poets and the means and processes that the tradition provides them to express their ideas. The elements of various kinds and sizes that are used to adjust ideas to spaces are not to be thought of as "mere fillers." Their meaning and force are as important as their compositional usefulness.

Once I left the emphasis on single formulas and moved to the larger units, or clusters, not only did the style become a living organism, but the formulas in context did also. In what follows I try to look beyond the hemistich and the line, wherever appropriate, to the rhetorical "clausules" or "periods," as Huppé calls them, or to formula clusters, for they, too, are units of composition. I have concentrated on the passages introducing speech, paying special attention to those of more than one line and to those beginning in the b) verse.[9]

---

[8] Ritzke-Rutherford, 1981a and 1981b.

[9] The fullest study of verbs of speaking in older Germanic poetry is the work of Teresa Pàroli (1975). Her Tavola 2 at page 182, giving the frequency of the several *verba dicendi* in Anglo-Saxon poetry, is particularly helpful.

Introductions to Speech

Beowulf

In 1978 Paule Mertens-Fonck studied the structure of passages introducing direct discourse in *Beowulf*, and her tabular checklist of the forty-
five passages involved in introductions to speech is very useful.[10] Her
four categories, especially those dealing with *maþelode*, point out some
of the phenomena that I discuss in this paper, but her criteria for de-
limiting the passages are different from those I have used, since I was
thinking in terms of formulaic structure.

Speech introductions are handled differently by the *Beowulf* poet than
by any other Anglo-Saxon poet whose works we have. The *maþelode*
formula systems so characteristic of *Beowulf* are not used at all in *Christ*,
for example, although they are employed, especially in one prolonged
passage in Cynewulf's *Elene*, almost as often, proportionately, as in
Beowulf. They are found very sparingly in *Genesis*. Yet they belong to
Beowulf par excellence; in fact, they are used twenty-six times in *Beowulf*
compared to nine in *Elene* and four in *Genesis*—twice as many in *Beowulf*
as in the other two combined.

The *Beowulf* poet uses other words to introduce speech as well, as can
be seen from the following list:

maþelode	26 times
spræc	5 times
gecwæð	3 times
gespræc	once
cwæð	once
acwæð	once
acwyð	once
frægn	twice
fricgan	once
sægde	once
abead	once
wordhord onleac	once
andswarode	twice
ondswarode	once

It is not, however, merely that the formula systems on *maþelode* are
used more frequently than any other system in *Beowulf* or than else-

[10] Mertens-Fonck, 1978.

where in Anglo-Saxon poetry. What is more significant is that they are used differently. The poet of *Beowulf* does not hesitate to employ these formulas over and over again, even in long sequences, without striving for variety, although we can see from the list just given that he had alternatives in his repertory, if he chose to use them.

The first seven speeches in *Beowulf*, which lead into and overlap with a "run" of *maþelode*s, follow a duplicated pattern, as seen below, and include two instances of *maþelode*.

coast guard	236	frægn
Beowulf	258–259	ondswarode—wordhord onleac
coast guard	286	maþelode
coast guard	315	cwæð
Wulfgar	332	frægn
Beowulf	340–341	andswarode—word æfter spræc
Wulfgar	348	maþelode

In these cases *maþelode* introduces a statement made by the person who was first asked a question and received an answer. His statement is followed by some action. The new arrivals on the shore, Beowulf and his men, proceed inland according to instructions given in the first statement, and Wulfgar reports their desire for an audience to Hrothgar after the second.

It will be useful to see the list filled out with the complete introductory passages in each case.

234–236	Gewat him þa to waroðe wicge ridan þegn Hroðgares, þrymmum cwehte mægenwudu mundum, meþelwordum frægn: speech 237–257
258–259	Him se yldesta ondswarode, werodes wisa, wordhord onleac: speech 260–285

286–287a	Weard maþelode, ðær on wicge sæt,
	ombeht unforht:
	        speech 287b–300
	        narrative 301–311

314b–315   guðbeorna sum
              wicg gewende,   word æfter cwæð:
                          speech 316–319
                          narrative 320–331a
331b–332   Þa ðær wlonc hæleð
              oretmecgas   æfter æþelum frægn:
                          speech 333–339
340–342a   Him þa ellenrof   andswarode,
              wlonc Wedera leod,   word æfter spræc
              heard under helme:
                          speech 342b–347
348–350a   Wulfgar maþelode   (þæt wæs Wendla leod;
              wæs his modsefa   manegum gecyðed,
              wig ond wisdom):
                          speech 350b–355

In these seven speeches there are no one-line introductions, although there are three of one and a half lines, two of two and a half lines, one of two lines, and one of three lines.

More important than the length of the passages is the way in which that length is gained. The three-line introduction with which the passage opens (lines 234–236) consists of three clauses, only the third of which has a verb of speaking: "the thane of Hrothgar rode his horse to the people, he shook his spear at the host, and asked in a speech." The subject of all three verbs is in the third hemistich, a delayed subject of "gewat. . . ridan" in the preceding line; forming a one-and-a-half-line unit (lines 234–235a). Hrothgar's thane is also the subject of the verb in the fourth hemistich, which is modified by the phrase in the fifth, forming another one-and-a-half-line unit (lines 235–236a), sharing a subject with the preceding. The unit introducing speech, with the verb of speaking in the sixth hemistich of the passage, covers two lines (235–236), including the previous unit. This passage is a superb example of the "weaving style" typical of oral traditional composition.

The two-line introduction that follows (lines 258–259) is a "duplicated" one-liner, a frequent pattern in Anglo-Saxon poetry, of course, with its fondness for parataxis.

Two of the one-and-one-half-line introductions (lines 314b–315 and 331b–332) begin in the b) verse, and the a) verse of the following line is, in one case, in apposition with the subject in the preceding b) verse and, in the other, the direct object of the "asking" verb in the second line.

The other one-and-one-half-line passage (lines 286–287a) begins in the a) verse, and the third hemistich is in apposition with the subject in the first hemistich. In short, it is an extended one-line introduction.

The two two-and-one-half-line introductions that end the sequence (lines 340–342a and 348–350a) are extended two-liners in which the fifth hemistich is an elaboration of the third.

To sum up so far: one of the basic methods of composition is to extend a one-line introduction to one and a half by adding an appositive or to duplicate a one-liner by parataxis; similarly one can extend a two-line passage by a fifth hemistich which is an appositive of the third; the two-line passage itself turns out to be a one-liner that has been duplicated by parataxis, as in lines 340–341, or has been otherwise elaborated, as in lines 348–349. One begins with one line, builds it to one and a half by extension or to two by duplication or some other form of elaboration, and then builds the two-line product to two and a half by extension with an appositive.

We must go further to see whether these patterns are found only in *Beowulf* or are characteristics of all Anglo-Saxon narrative poetry. We suspect that the latter is true.

The last introduction in the preceding sequence also begins a series of eight *maþelode*s between lines 348 and 631, interrupted only once:

348 Wulfgar m.	þæt wæs Wendla leod
360 Wulfgar m.	to his winedrihten:
371 Hroðgar m.	helm Scyldinga
389b–390	[Þa to dura eode
widcuð hæleð,]	word inne abead:[11]
405 Beowulf m.	on him byrne scan
456 Hroðgar m.	helm Scyldinga:
499 Unferð m.	Ecglafes bearn
529 Beowulf m.	bearn Ecgþeowes:
631 Beowulf m.	bearn Ecgþeowes:

The foregoing are *all* the introductions to speech between lines 348 and 654. They cover the arrival of Beowulf at Heorot and his exchanges with Hrothgar and with Unferth.

It will be useful to see the above list filled out with the complete introductory passages in each case.

---

[11] Lines 389–390 reconstructed in *Beowulf,* 1950.

348–50a   Wulfgar maþelode   —ðæt wæs Wendla leod,
               wæs his modsefa   manegum gecyðed,
               wig ond wisdom—:
                       speech 350b–355
                       narrative 356–359
360   Wulfgar maðelode   to his winedrihtne:
                       speech 361–370
371   Hroðgar maþelode,   helm Scyldinga:
                       speech 372–389a
389–390   Deniga leodum,"   Þa to dura eode
               widcuð hæleð,   word inne abead:
                       speech 391–398
                       narrative 399–404
405–406   Beowulf maþlode   (on him byrne scan,
               searonet seowed   smiþes orþancum):
                       speech 407–455
456   Hroðgar maþelode,   helm Scyldinga:
                       speech 457–490
                       narrative 491–498
499–505   Unferð maþelode,   Ecglafes bearn,
               þe æt fotum sæt   frean Scyldinga,
               onband beadurune   (wæs him Beowulfes sið,
               modges merefaran,   micel æfþunca,
               forþon þe he ne uþe,   þæt ænig oðer man
               æfre mærða þon ma   middangeardes
               gehedde under heofenum   þonne he sylfa):
                       speech 506–528
529   Beowulf maþelode,   bearn Ecgþeowes:
                       speech 530–606
                       narrative 607–628a
628b–631   He þæt ful geþeah,
            wælreow wiga   æt Wealhþeon,
            ond þa gyddode   guþe gefysed;
           Beowulf maþelode,   bearn Ecgþeowes:
                     speech 632–638

The one exception to the *maðelode* series (lines 389–390) occurs in a passage in which the text is corrupt! Four of the remaining introductions are one-liners: two refer to Hrothgar as *helm Scyldinga* (lines 371 and 456), one to Beowulf as *bearn Ecgþeowes* (line 529), and one to Wulfgar, in which the phrase *to his winedrihten* completes the line (line 350). Although the remaining four passages have more than one line, they are all basically one-liners that have been extended.

Before another long sequence of *maþelode* begins, there are five speeches, two of which are introduced by *maþelode*. Here are the five introductions:

First Hrothgar and Beowulf salute one another:

652–654   Gegrette þa   guma oþerne,
           Hroðgar Beowulf,   ond him hæl abead,
           winærnes geweald,   ond þæt word acwæð:
                     speech 655–661
                     narrative 662–674

Before going to rest, Beowulf utters a boast:

675–676   Gespræc þa se goda   gylpworda sum,
           Beowulf Geata,   ær he on bed stige:
                     speech 677–687
                     narrative 688–924

There follow then two passages introduced by *maþelode* in the exchange between Hrothgar and Beowulf the day after Beowulf's fight with Grendel. Hrothgar looks upon Grendel's paw and Beowulf responds to his wonder. Their speeches are introduced by:

925–927   Hroðgar maþelode   (he to healle geong,
           stod on stapole,   geseah steapne hrof,
           golde fahne   ond Grendles hond):
                     speech 928–956
957   Beowulf maþelode,   bearn Ecgþeowes:

After the gifts have been given in the great hall and the tale of Finn sung, the queen comes forward and speaks, opening the feasting and further gift giving:

1168b   Spræc ða ides Scyldinga:
                     speech 1169–1187
                     narrative 1188–1214

When Wealhtheow speaks a second time, another lengthy *maþelode* series begins in earnest. There are *nine* instances between lines 1215 and 1999, as can be seen in the list below. Lines 1698 and 1983b–1986 are the

only non-*maþelode* introductions in this sequence of passages. The series
begins at line 1215 with a one-liner.

1215	Wealhðeo m. heo fore þæm werede spræc
	speech 1216–1231, narrative 1232–1320
1321	Hroðgar m. helm Scyldinga
	speech 1322–1382
1383	Beowulf m. bearn Ecgþeowes
	speech 1384–1396, narrative 1397–1472
1473	Beowulf m. bearn Ecgþeowes
	speech 1474–1491, narrative 1492–1650
1651	Beowulf m. bearn Ecgþeowes
	speech 1652–1676, narrative 1677–1686
1687	Hroðgar m., hylt sceawode

ealde lafe,   on ðæm wæs or writen
fyrngewinnes;   syðþan flod ofsloh,
gifen geotende   giganta cyn
frecne geferdon;   þæt wæs fremde þeod
ecean Dryhtne;   him þæs endelean
þurh wæteres wylm   Waldend sealde.
Swa wæs on ðæm scennum   sciran goldes
þurh runstafas   rihte gemearcod,
geseted ond gesæd,   hwam þæt sweord geworht,
irena cyst,   ærest wære,
wreoþenhilt ond wyrmfah.   Ða se wisa spræc
sunu Healfdenes   (swigedon ealle):
speech 1700–1784, narrative 1785–1816

1817	Beowulf m. bearn Ecgþeowes
	speech 1818–1839
1840	Hroðgar m. him on ondsware
	speech 1841–1865, narrative 1866–1983a
1983b–1986	Higelac ongan

sinne geseldan   in sele þam hean
fægre fricgcean,   (hyne fyrwet bræc,
hwylce SæGeata   siðas wæron):
speech 1987–1998

| 1999 | Beowulf m.   bearn Ecgðioes |
| | speech 2000–2151 |

Before the last two introductions Beowulf and his men have returned
home, and in lines 1987–1998 Higelac asked him how he fared in Denmark. Unlike Hrothgar, Higelac has no *maðelode* formula! Line 1999

introduces Beowulf's famous retelling of events at Heorot. As the events at Higelac's hall move on, we move also away from the "Beowulf maðelode   bearn Ecgþeowes" formula to other forms of introduction. The sea of *maþelode*s is disturbed by a non-*maþelode* introduction of six lines leading into a speech within a speech in lines 2047–2056.

> 2041–2046   Þonne cwið æt beore   se ðe beah gesyhð,
> eald æscwiga,   se ðe eall gem(an),
> garcwealm gumena   (him bið grim sefa),
> onginneð geomormod   geong(um) cempan
> þurh hreðra gehygd   higes cunnian,
> wigbealu weccean,   ond þæt word acwyð:

The scene between Higelac and Beowulf concludes with a three-line introduction (lines 2152–2154) to Beowulf's words about the armor that Hrothgar had given him:

> Het ða in beran   eaforheafodsegn,
> heaðosteapne helm   hare byrnan,
> guðsweord geatolic,   gyd æfter wræc:

This is the first and only time that "gyd" is used in any of the introductions to speech in *Beowulf*. In sum, the scene with Higelac contains only four introductions to speech, one of which leads to a speech within a speech. The other two speeches are the opening one by Higelac and the closing one by Beowulf commenting on the gifts of armor that are brought into the hall for him to show to his king.

The two great scenes at Heorot are marked with due ceremony by the repeated trumpeting of *maþelode* announcing the rising to speak of the great characters of the poem. The note sounded by the coast guard and by Wulfgar is prolonged throughout the great scenes. As the action shifts to the land of the Geats the dignity of *maðelode* is reserved for Beowulf in his formal line "Beowulf maðelode,   bearn Ecgþeowes," (line 1999) when he begins his account of his adventures abroad.

The dragon episode begins with the speech of the last survivor, introduced by lines 2244–2246:

> Þær on innan bær   eorlgestreona
> hringa hyrde   hordwyrðne dæl,

> fættan goldes,   fea worda cwæð:
> speech 2247–2266
> narrative 2267–2424

There follows a long speech by Beowulf, which has three parts, each with its own introduction. The first part is introduced by his formal line (line 2425):

> Biowulf maþelade,   bearn Ecgþeowes:
> speech 2426–2509;

the second by lines 2510–2511a:

> Beowulf maðelode,   beotwordum spræc,
> niehstan siðe:
> speech 2511b–2515;

and the third, by an appropriate introduction to further words by Beowulf as he turns to address each one of his men (lines 2516–2518a):

> Gegrette ða   gumena gehwylcne,
> hwate helmberend,   hindeman siðe,
> swæse gesiðas:
> speech 2518b–2537
> narrative 2538–2630.

After that, *maðelode* is taken over, fittingly enough, by Wiglaf, who has three speeches using *maðelode*, the first of which is introduced by lines 2631–2632:

> Wiglaf maðelode,   wordrihta fela
> sægde gesiðum   (him wæs sefa geomor):
> speech 2633–2660

and followed immediately by his words to Beowulf, introduced by lines 2661–2662:

> Wod þa þurh þone wælrec,   wigheafolan bær
> frean on fultum,   fea worda cwæð:
> speech 2663–2668
> narrative 2669–2723.

The wounded Beowulf speaks again and his words are introduced by lines 2724–2728:

> Biowulf maþelode   —he ofer benne spræc,
> wunde wælbleate;   wisse he gearwe
> þæt he dæghwila   gedrogen hæfde,
> eorðan wyn[ne];   ða wæs eall sceacen
> dogorgerimes,   dead ungemete neah—:
> speech 2729–2751
> narrative 2752–2790a

At this point Beowulf gives instructions about his funeral pyre; his words are introduced by lines 2790b–2793:

> he hine eft ongon
> wæteres weorpan,   oðþæt wordes ord
> breosthord þurhbræc.   (þa se bearn gespræc,)
> gomel on giohðe   (gold sceawode):
> speech 2794–2808. (Line 2792b em. C. L. Wrenn.)

After this, Beowulf places his gold collar on Wiglaf's neck (lines 2809–2812a) and, in a hemistich that serves as introduction to Beowulf's very last words, the poet says: (line 2812b)

> het hyne brucan well:
> speech 2813–2816
> narrative 2817–2861

The next speech is by Wiglaf, and for the first time his words are introduced by "his" formal line: (lines 2862–2863)

> Wiglaf maðelode,   Weohstanes sunu,
> sec, sarigferd   (seah on unleofe);
> speech 2864–2891
> narrative 2892–2897a

The messenger's announcement of Beowulf's death to all his men is introduced in lines 2897b–2899:

Lyt swigode
niwra spella   se ðe næs gerad,
ac he soðlice   sægde ofer ealle:
speech 2900–3027
narrative 3028–3075.

Wiglaf speaks again in line 3077, introduced by "his" single formal line 3076:

Wiglaf maðelode,   Wihstanes sunu.
speech 3077–3109

And his final words were introduced immediately after that speech with lines 3110–3114a:

Het ða gebeodan   byre Wihstanes,
hæle hildedior,   hæleða monegum,
boldagendra,   þæt hie bælwudu
feorran feredon,   folcagende,
godum togenes:
speech 3114b–3119
narrative 3120–3182.

It is important to be aware of the place of *maþelode* among the other words introducing speech in *Beowulf* and it is especially significant to observe the two "runs" of eight or nine *maþelode*'s. They, as well as the word itself, differentiate *Beowulf* from the other Anglo-Saxon poems. Within the poem they also appear to distinguish the scenes in Heorot from that in Higelac's hall and to show a continuity with the dragon episode, marking significantly the generational succession from Beowulf to his kinsman Wiglaf.

Elene

Cynewulf's *Elene* has nine instances of *maþelode* and serves as a useful comparison with *Beowulf*.[12] As in the case of *Beowulf*, to obtain a true

---

[12] Quotations from *Elene* are from *ASPR*, 2, 1932.

concept of Cynewulf's handling of speech introductions it is necessary to look at other formulas introducing speech in *Elene* and to see how they sometimes dovetail together with the *maþelode* systems. The list below schematizes by their verbs the speech formulas from line 78 to line 537.

1. Angel to Constantine	78b	wið þingode	
2. Elene to the Hebrews	287b	wordum negan	
3. Elene	332	E. maþelode / ond for eorlum spræc	
a. Moses	338b	word gecwæð	
b. David	344b	word gecwæð	
c. Isaiah	352b	wordum mælde	
4. Elene	385a	wordum genegan	
5. People	396b	ondsweredon	
6. Elene	404	E. maþelode / ond for eorlum spræc	
	405b	ides reordode	
7. Judas	417	an reordode	
a. father	440b	ond þæt word gecwæð	
b. Judas	455b	ageaf ondsware	
c. father	462b	ageaf ondsware	
	463b	fæder reordode	
8. The wisest	537b	wodum mældon	

The first speech in *Elene* is that of the Angel who appears to Constantine in a dream:

76–78   Him se ar hraðe,
        wlitig wuldres boda,   wið þingode
        ond be naman nemde,   (nihthelm toglad):

When Elene herself first speaks to the assembled Hebrews, her speech is introduced by:

286b–287   Ongan þa leoflic wif
            weras Ebrea   wordum negan:
        speech 288–319, narrative 320–331

Elene's second speech is dignified with the *maþelode* formula—its first appearance in the poem—in tandem with *spræc* in line

332:   Elene maþelode   ond for eorlum spræc:
            speech 333a–376b

Within that major speech there are three quotations from the Old Testament, presented in direct discourse. One is by Moses, one by David, and one by Isaiah. The first is introduced by:

337b–338   Be þam Moyses sang,
          ond þæt word gecwæð   weard Israhela:

The second uses the same formula:

342–344   Be þam David cyning,   dryhtleod agol,
          frod fyrnweota,   fæder Salomones,
          ond þæt word gecwæþ,   wigona baldor:

The third speech within a speech, that by Isaiah, is introduced by lines

350–352   Swa hit eft be eow   Essaias,
          witga for weorodum,   wordum mælde:
          deophycggende   þurh dryhtnes gast:

Elene's long speech with its three speeches within it is followed by narrative in lines 364–384a. Her next speech is introduced by:

384b–385   Hio sio cwen ongan
          wordum genegan   (wlat ofer ealle):
                  speech 386–395

The answer follows immediately, introduced by

396   Hie þa anmode   ondsweredon:
              speech 397–403

Elene's next speech is introduced beginning with the now familiar formula:

404–406a   Elene maðelade   ond for eorlum spræc

undearninga,   ides reordode
hlude for herigum:
speech 406b–410, narrative 411–416

Judas's first speech is introduced by

417–419a   Þa þær for eorlum   an reordode,
gidda gearosnotor   (ðam wæs Iudas nama),
wordes cræftig:
speech 419b–535

This long speech contains three other speeches. The first of these has a complicated introduction, which is not helped by a corrupt text.

436–440   swa þa þæt ilce gio   min yldra fæder
sigerof sægde,   (þam wæs Sachius nama),
frod fyrnwiota,   fæder minum,
*   *   *   *
eaferan,
wende hine of worulde   ond þæt word gecwæð:

The second and third speeches within a speech are introduced each by a simple couplet:

454–455   Þa ic fromlice   fædere minum,
ealdum æwitan,   ageaf ondsware:

and

462–463   Ða me yldra min   ageaf ondsware,
frod on fyrhðe   fæder reordode:

Judas's long speech is followed immediately by a couplet introducing a short one spoken by the wisest (*gleawestan*) of the Hebrews:

536–537   Him þa togenes   þa gleawestan
on wera þreate   wordum mældon:
speech 538–546

The next scene opens after three and a half lines of assembling with the proclamation of the heralds:

551a–552b   Hreopon friccan,
                  caseres bodan:

The list of verbs given above shows a somewhat different vocabulary
in *Elene* from what one finds in *Beowulf* in introductions to speech.
Mælian is not found in *Beowulf; reordian* is used only once in *Beowulf* and
not in an introduction to speech; the same is to be said for *þingian; negan*
(*nægan*) or *genegan* is also used once in *Beowulf* in the formula *wordum
nægde* (line 1318), but not introducing a speech.

The second major group of exchanges of speeches in *Elene* begins
with Elene's address to the assembled people:

573   Elene maþelade   ond him yrre oncwæð:

The reply of the people is to indicate Judas as their wise man and
spokesman. There is no introductory formula to the speech, which
extends from line 588b to line 597b. Now that her interlocutor for the
formal exchange has been named, the series begins in earnest as Elene
tries to persuade Judas to tell her where the cross is hidden. It might be
reasonable to expect a series of *maðelode*s at this point, following the
pattern in *Beowulf;* or rather, this expectation would be reasonable if we
knew for certain that Cynewulf was acquainted with the *Beowulf* text,
or—a different matter entirely—with the tradition to which the *Beowulf*
poet belonged. Actually, that expectation is not fully realized; the series
is broken. This fact is the more amazing because in the passage in
question Cynewulf is following the Latin source very closely, and the
Latin speeches are all, without exception, introduced by *dixit*. Cynewulf
varies the verbs of speaking more than either the *Beowulf* poet or the
Latin does. In addition Cynewulf in this passage employs the epithet for
Elene used regularly in the Latin text, *beata*, which becomes *eadige* in
Anglo-Saxon, only *once* (619) in *Elene*. Cynewulf also uses *tireadig* (605)
and *æðele* (662). In short, here too, as in the sequences of verbs introduc-
ing speech, Cynewulf prefers variety.

There is one more passage from *Elene* with a number of *mapelode*s.
The list below presents the introductions to direct discourse from lines
604 to 685, including one example of introduction to indirect discourse
(lines 667–668). The speech formulas are underlined.

604	Elene maþelode	to þam anhagan
605	tireadige cwen:	"þe synt tu gearu,
609	Judas hire ongen þingode	(ne meahte he þa gehðu bebugan,
610	oncyrran rex geniðlan.	He wæs on þære cwene gewealdum):
619	Him þa seo eadige	andwyrde ageaf
620	Elene for eorlum	undearnunga:
627	Judas maðelade	(him wæs geomor sefa,
628	hat æt heortan	ond gehwæðres wa,
629	ge he heofonrices	hyht swa mode
630	ond þis ondwearde	anforlete,
631	rice under roderum,	ge he ða rode tæhte):
642	Elene maðelade	him on andsware:
655	Judas maðelade	(gnornsorge wæg):
662	Him seo æðele cwen	ageaf andsware:
667	Judas hire ongen þingode,	cwæð, þæt he þæt on gehðu gespræce
668	ond tweon swiðost,	wende him trage hnagre.
669	Him oncwæð hraðe	caseres mæg:
682	gasta geocend."	Hire Judas oncwæð
683	stiðhycgende:	"ic þa stowe ne can
684	ne þæs wanges wiht	ne þa wisan cann."
685	Elene maðelode	þurh eorne hyge:

There are several things to comment on here. First, it is clear that the *maþelode* series is broken. Second, there is an example of "ring-composition" in this passage, a type of composition known in both oral and written literary style, but original, it would seem, in the former, as we see it in Homeric composition.[13] Third, one can see in the list some of the varying lengths of the introductory clusters of formulas in *Elene* leading to direct discourse.

We have been able to discern differences between *Beowulf* and *Elene* in the poets' choice of words introducing speech, and in the sequences of such words in passages in which there is sustained dialogue. The next step is to analyze the formulaic structure of the passages introducing direct discourse. Such an investigation can serve as a model for the analysis of other structural groups. Something of the variety of the structures one finds in *Elene*, in comparison with *Beowulf*, is apparent from the list above.

In the group you will see, for example, introductions of one-half line, plus a parenthetical hemistich (line 655), and introductions of two con-

13 See Whitman, 1958, chap. 11, "Geometric Structure of the *Iliad*," especially 252–284.

secutive hemistichs in the b) verse of one line and the a) verse of the following (lines 682b and 683a). Note that *stiðhycgende* (courageous) is an alliterative helper, even as was the parenthetical hemistich in the previous case. The repeated necessity of fitting essential ideas into a given space is found in both *Beowulf* and *Elene*, of course. It is one of the realities of composing, whether orally or in writing, in the alliterative Germanic meters, but the precise ways in which it is accomplished are varied, and may be significant in differentiating one composer from another. This is a fruitful field for research, but I cannot here analyze all the passages in the foregoing group.

Let me make special mention, however, of the longest passage, lines 627–631, five lines. This is in reality a single *maþelode* hemistich plus a parenthetical sentence extending over four and one half lines! In other words, it is structurally like line 655. Finally, lines 667–669 are actually two separate, consecutive cases of introduction to speech. Lines 667–668, which I have included for the sake of the ring-composition involved, are a case of indirect, rather than direct, discourse. The introduction to direct discourse with which it is associated is the single-line formula in 669. Of the ten introductions to direct discourse under consideration, three consist of a single hemistich (609, 627, and 655), four consist of a single line (642, 662, 669, and 685), one consists of two consecutive hemistichs in two separate lines(682–683), one consists of a line and a half (604–605), and only one introduction, that to indirect discourse, is a bona fide two-line passage (667–668).

There are ten more speeches in *Elene*, but only one uses *maþelode*. For the sake of completeness, I list below the verbs used in the introductions to those speeches:

691–698	cleopigan ongan (696)	8 lines
723b–724	word . . . ahof—spræc	1-1/2 lines
806	Iudas *maþelode*	1 line
848b–851	frignan ongan (849)	3-1/2 lines
900–901	ongan þa hleoðrian (900)	2 lines
934–938	oncwæð—word gecwæð	5 lines
1067b–1072	frignan ongan—bæd—	
	word acwæð—reordode	5-1/2 lines
1119b	Hie cwædon þus	1/2 line
1166b	He hire þriste oncwæð	1/2 line
1188b–1190	sang—word gecwæð	2-1/2 lines

Not only is the *maþelode* sequence broken, but variety is evidenced in the words used—although beginning in lines 934–938 some form of *cwæð* is found—and in the syntactic structures. The reader of *Beowulf* is aware that this long passage could not have been by the same poet who wrote of Heorot.

Conclusion

It is appropriate to end our analyses with a summary of the results of the comparison of one-line speech introductions in *Beowulf* and *Elene*. By noting the role of *maþelode* in *Beowulf*, one is able to distinguish that poem from *Elene* by the structure of their one-line speech introductions, using the following criteria:

1. There are fourteen one-line introductions in *Beowulf* and nine in *Elene*. All fourteen from *Beowulf* are *maþelode* formulas in the a) verse; seven of the nine from *Elene* are *maþelode* formulas in the a) verse. In those cases where the subject and the verb of speaking are in the a) verse and the direct discourse begins in the a) verse of the following line, the two most common possibilities for the b) verse of the speech introduction are either an epithet phrase in apposition with the subject, or another verb of speaking in tandem with *maþelode*.

2. Twelve of the fourteen *maþelode* formulas in *Beowulf* are completed in the b) verse with an epithet phrase (*bearn Ecgþeowes, helm Scyldinga,* and so forth); *none* of the *maþelode* formulas in *Elene* is completed by an epithet phrase. This might be taken as an indication that none of the figures in the biblical poem belonged to Anglo-Saxon tradition, as did Beowulf, Hrothgar, Unferth, or Wiglaf. They were not identifiable in Anglo-Saxon by their patronymics.

3. There are three one-line speech introductions in *Elene* that use another verb than *maþelode*. In two cases this verb is found in the b) verse, with the subject in the a) verse, and is some form of answering (line 396, *Hie þa anmode   ondsweredon*; line 662, *Him seo æðele cwen   ageaf ondsware*); in the third case the verb is in the a) verse and the subject in the b) verse (line 669, *Him oncwæð hraðe   caseres mæg*).

One can, therefore, distinguish *Beowulf* from *Elene* by the structure of the one-line introductions to speech, using the criteria just enumerated.

Our ultimate purpose is to determine whether formulaic analysis, or any other type of stylistic analysis, can successfully differentiate between oral-traditional narrative sung verse and "written" narrative verse, or even distinguish among several degrees of transitional, or mixed, or imitative styles. Our first step in that direction has been to see if we could find ways in which *Beowulf*, as a possible member of the oral-traditional or transitional groups, differs from *Elene*, which is clearly a "written" literary composition. We have succeeded in a limited way with a well-defined body of material, but the careful analysis and interpretation of all of that material has not yet been completed. At the beginning of this analysis I set down some thoughts about structures covering more than one line, which may serve to guide further research, including the analysis of sentences beginning in the b) verse.

CHAPTER 10

The Influence of
a Fixed Text

In *The Singer of Tales* I attempted primarily to describe the workings of a *pure* oral tradition of narrative song, one in which written texts had no influence, or were nonexistent.[1] A knowledge of the processes of oral composition and transmission in their pure form was necessary for an understanding of such texts as those of the Homeric poems, which we may safely assume were written down before other texts were recorded, in a precollecting era.

Once texts have been written down and are available to those who sing or tell stories, they can in fixed form have an influence on the tradition. With the Homeric rhapsodes we are studying a somewhat different phenomenon from Homer himself, from the *aoidos* (epic singer, bard). A realization of this difference is especially significant for the medieval period in Europe, where we are surely dealing, to a large extent, perhaps, with texts thus influenced by a preexistent fixed text. The question, therefore, arises: In exactly what ways do the written texts affect the oral tradition? I should like in this paper to address myself briefly to that question and to examine some of the evidence that is furnished by the material in the Milman Parry Collection of Oral Literature.[2] I shall limit myself here almost entirely to textual or verbal influence.

First published in *To Honor Roman Jakobson: Essays on the Occasion of His Seventieth Birthday (11 October 1966)*, Janua Linguarum, Series Maior, 32, vol. 2 (The Hague and Paris: Mouton, 1967), 1199–1206. Reprinted by permission of Mouton de Gruyter.

[1] Lord, A., 1960.

[2] Although, owing to misunderstandings in the small villages in which Parry worked in the early 1930s, the Milman Parry Collection in Widener Library at Harvard Univer-

Among the best songs in the older repertory collected by Vuk Karadžić in the early part of the nineteenth century, those from Tešan Podrugović of Gacko, Hercegovina, are outstanding.[3] In the second volume of Karadžić's collection, the volume that contains the heroic songs of the older period, there are thirteen songs from Podrugović.[4] For all but one of those there is at least one corresponding text in the Parry Collection. I have examined them all and compared each of them with the corresponding Karadžić text to determine what influence, if any, the printed text had on the songs collected approximately one hundred years later.

In this respect, the Parry texts may be divided into three unequal categories. There are some texts (Category A) that seem to be independent of the Karadžić tradition. Category A, provided that we could show that the songs in it are not influenced by other printed collections, could be assumed to be "pure" in their traditional orality. Into Category B, a much larger one than A, we have placed those texts that show a clearly discernible influence of the Karadžić printed text. Category C contains texts that are clearly cases of direct copying or of word-for-word memorization from the songbook. I wish to examine at least one text in each category to see exactly what the differences are between the later and earlier texts, and for this purpose I shall begin with Category C, and with a text from Parry's early days of collecting.

Adam Parry published some of the notes that his father dictated in Dubrovnik as commentary to the first six songs that he collected in 1933. In those notes he included digressions on various subjects that were in his mind as he worked in the field and gained experience in

---

sity contains some texts that were copied from published songbooks, they are a very small proportion of its more than 12,000 texts. Even the songs that were memorized from fixed texts are comparatively few, because, especially in 1934 and 1935, Parry made a point of not collecting from singers who had learned any of their repertory from the published collections. Those that slipped through due to misrepresentation have proved to be of value in research, but their presence in the collection was accidental. Some were given or sent to Parry unsolicited. Even they can be useful.

[3] Vuk Karadžić tells us much about Podrugović in the Introduction to Karadžić, 1958, 4:x–xi. It is worth mentioning that Podrugović did not sing his songs; he recited them. Karadžić notes: "Pesme se, i ženske i junačke, *kazuju*, kao kad čovek čita iz knjige, tako da se poznaje i stih i odmor (caesura). Stari ljudi pesme deci više *kazuju* nego *pevaju*. Sila ljudi i žena ima koje je mlogo lakše namoliti da pesmu *kazuju* nego da *pevaju*" (Songs, both women's and heroic, are *recited*, as when a person reads from a book, so that both the verse and the rest (caesura) are recognizable. Old people *recite* songs to children rather than *sing* them. There are many men and women whom it is much easier to ask to *recite* a song than to *sing* it).

[4] Karadžić, 1958.

understanding the songs and the processes of traditional composition and transmission. In a portion of "Ćor Huso" (the name that he gave to these writings) that Adam Parry published, Milman Parry, wrote (December 3, 1934) some observations on the subject of the influence of a fixed text. Among the comments that still remain unpublished he made the following remarks about the singer Milovan Vojičić of Nevesinje, Hercegovina: "Milovan from his school days, he told me, had read every word of all the *pjesmarice* [song books] on which he could lay his hands. At one time, he said, he had a very large collection of his own which later on in days of poverty he sold for ten dinars a kilo. His repertory of the classical Serbian songs, as far as I could judge by his questioning, was very large, and the *Ženidba Kralja Vukašina* [The Wedding of King Vukašin] (autograph text 29) which I picked at random and asked him to write out for me shows that he had learned those texts with an exactness that varies from the original only in the omission or rearrangement of a few lines and in the reordering or changing of words in the phrase." What follows illustrates in detail the kinds of differences that exist in another experiment with a song sent by Milovan Vojičić to Parry at Kirkland House, Harvard University.

During the winter of 1933–34, Milovan wrote out himself a version of "Nahod Simeun" and mailed it from Nevesinje on February 19, 1934, to Milman Parry at Kirkland House, Harvard University.[5] The Karadžić text, from Podrugović, has 197 lines; Vojičić's is 198 lines in length. The added line is the last, "Simeun se mladan posvetijo," "The young Simeun became a saint." Of the remaining 197 lines, 116 are identical with Podrugović's text, 79 of them are very close, 2 correspond in meaning but have different wording. No lines from Karadžić are omitted in sense.

In the category of lines that are very close to those of the Karadžić text some reflect only slight differences of pronunciation: for example, "uranijo" for "uranio," "namastir" instead of "manastir," "jevanđelje" for "evanđelje," "zavati" for "zafati," "dvanajes'" for "dvanaest," and so on.

Milovan preferred the normal forms "tebi" and "meni" for the dative of the pronouns "ti" (you, sing.) and "ja" (I) to the dialect forms "tebe" and "mene," and he used the form "đogin" rather than "đogat," meaning "white horse."

[5]Ibid., 1958, vol. 2, no. 13; Parry Text no. 120.

In several lines one preposition is used instead of another: for example, "na obalu," "on the shore," rather than Karadžić's "pod obalu"; and "niz bijelo lice," "down his white face," instead of Karadžić's "od bijela lica," "from his white face."

Other cases of change of a single word are (1) change of verbal aspect, as "posjede đogina" for "usjede đogata," "mounted his white horse" (line 131); (2) avoidance of an obsolete form, as "misli" for "mlidijaše," "thought" (line 8), and "čita" for "čati," "reads" (lines 48 and 141); (3) one epithet for another, as "divno odijelo," "wondrous clothes," for Podrugović's "svjetlo odijelo," "bright clothes" (line 69), and "na noge junačke," "to his heroic feet," instead of "na noge lagane," "to his light feet" (line 126); (4) in one instance Vojičić has been influenced in his change by the rhetoric of the line; in prefering "namjera je starca namjerila," "the old man intended" (line 5), to "namjera je starca nanijela," "intention came over the old man." In this latter case, he seems to have liked the combination of cognate verb with cognate noun subject.

Of the changes that effect more than one word the following are typical: (1) in line 53 "šta ti fali," "what is lacking to you," takes the place of "šta je malo," "what is little"; (2) in line 107 Vojičić prefers "zdravlje prifatila," "she accepted his greeting," to "božju pomoć prima," "she received his 'God's help!'" In both cases the alternates are natural replacements.

The most concentrated degree of change (underlined in Vojičić's version in the Parry Collection) is found in lines 23–27:

<table>
<tr><td>Karadžić</td><td>Parry</td></tr>
<tr><td>Kad je bilo od tri godinice,</td><td>Kad <u>mu</u> bilo <u>tri godine dana,</u></td></tr>
<tr><td>kolik' drugo od sedam godina!</td><td>Kolik' drugo od sedam godina!</td></tr>
<tr><td></td><td></td></tr>
<tr><td>A kad bilo od sedam godina,</td><td><u>Kad mu</u> bilo <u>sedam godinice,</u></td></tr>
<tr><td>kolik' drugo od dvanaest ljeta!</td><td><u>Kao</u> drugo od <u>dvanes' godina!</u></td></tr>
<tr><td>Kad je bilo od dvanaest ljeta,</td><td><u>A kad</u> bilo <u>dvanajes' godina,</u></td></tr>
<tr><td>kolik' drugo od dvadest godina!</td><td>Kolik' drugo od <u>dvades'</u> godina!</td></tr>
</table>

When he was three years old,
He was like another of seven!
When he was seven years old,
He was like another of twelve,
When he was twelve years old,
He was like another of twenty!

It is useful to see exactly in what way Vojičić's text varies from that in Karadžić, but, in spite of a few details like those just cited, *the differences are minimal*, and Vojičić's text is very close to that of Podrugović. There are only two lines in the Vojičić text that seem to correspond in general sense with the Karadžić text but to differ from it almost completely in wording. These are lines 37 and 163.

Karadžić	Parry
Preskače im Nahod Simeune,	Preskače im Nahod Simeune,
preskače im, kamenom odmeče.	I pretura kamena s ramena.

In these pairs of lines, Podrugović has repeated the sense of line 36 in the first half of line 37, and in that same line (37) he has also added a new thought. Thus, "Nahod Simeun jumped farther than the rest, / He jumped farther, and hurled the stone." Vojičić has used an equally typical, but not the same, construction. He has made the second idea, that of hurling stones, equal in length to the first idea. "Nahod Simeun jumped farther than the rest, / And he hurled stones from the shoulder, farther than the rest." The difference is one of line economy rather than of sense. In line 163 Podrugović says "Simeune spade od đogata," "Simeon dismounted from the white horse"; Vojičić has it "Skoči Simo sa konja đogina," "Simo jumped from the white horse." They both mean that Simeon dismounted from his white horse. The line construction is different, but the meaning is the same.

In whatever changes there are between these two texts no change in sense takes place, but the copier on occasion exhibits a preference of his own for one phrase or formula rather than another. When we know that he is a singer in his own right, we can see that his slight changes are in the natural direction of the words and phrases that he usually employs in his own singing.

As an example of Category B I have chosen a somewhat unusual case, a song that was recorded from singing on August 23, 1934. The singer was Ilija Mandarić of Vrebac. His version of the well-known song "Marko Kraljević and Musa Kesedžija" is 312 lines in length compared to Karadžić's 281 lines.[6] In the first hundred lines, which are typical of the whole song, approximately 50 percent are identical or very close to

[6]Parry Text no. 517; Karadžić, 1958, vol. 2, no. 66.

the lines in Karadžić. This figure should be compared with the nearly 99 percent identical in Category C. There are 12 lines of Karadžić missing in the Parry text, and 23 lines of the Parry text that are not to be found in Karadžić. There are 25 lines identical save for orthographic variations in both texts. We can follow the differences (underlined in the Parry text) in detail in the first 50 lines.

Karadžić	Parry
	Oj! Mili Bože, na svem' tebi fala!
Vino pije Musa Arbanasa	Vino pije Musa Keserdžija
U Stambolu, u krčmi bijeloj;	U Stanbolu, u krcmi bijeloj;
kad se Musa nakitio vina,	Kad se Musa napojijo vina,
onda poče pijan besjediti:	Onda poče pijan govoriti
	"Mili Bože, na svem' tebi fala!
"Evo ima devet godinica	Ev' imade devet godin' dana
kako dvorim cara u Stambolu:	Kako dvorim cara u Stambolu;
ni izdvorih konja ni oružja,	Ne izdvori' pare ni dinara
ni dolame nove ni polovne:	Nit' aljine nove ni polovne.
al' tako mi moje vjere tvrde,	A tako mi moja vjera tvrda,
	I tako me ne rodila majka,
	Već kobila neka bedevija,
odvrć' ću se u ravno primorje,	Oj! odvrću se u primorje ravno,
zatvoriću skele oko mora	zatvoriću skele oko mora
i drumove okolo primorja,	i drumove okolo primorja.
	Tud prolazi carevina blago,
	Na godinu po trista tovara.
	Sve ću blago sebi prigrabiti,
načiniću kulu u primorju,	U primorju kuću načiniti,
oko kule gvozdene čengele—	Oko kuće gvozdene čengele.
vješaću mu hodže i hadžije!"	Vješaću mu 'odže i 'adžije."
Što gođ Ture pjano govorilo,	Što je Ture pjano govorilo,
to trijezno bješe učinilo:	To trijezno bješe učiniljo.
odvrže se u primorje ravno,	Pozadvrže se u primorje ravno,
pozatvara skele oko mora,	Pozatvara skele oko mora,
i drumove okolo primorja,	I drumove okolo primorja,
kud prolazi carevina blago,	E prolazi carevina blago,
na godinu po trista tovara:	na godini po trista tovara

sve je Musa sebe ustavio;
u primorju kulu načinio,
oko kule gvozdene čengele,
vješa caru hodže i hadžije.
Kada caru tužbe dodijaše,

Sve je sebi blago prigrabijo.
U primorju kuću načinijo,
Oko kule gozdene čengele,
Vješa caru 'odže i hadžije.
Jali tužbe caru dodijaše,
Sve tužeći Musu prokletoga.
Stade care tražit' megdandžije.
Jal koji je tamo odlazijo,
Već Stanbula nikad ne vidijo;
Sve polomi Musa po
      primorju.

posla na njga Ćuprilić-vezira
i sa njime tri hiljade vojske.

Na njeg posla Ćuprilić vezira
I šnjim vojske dvanajest
      'iljada.

Kad dođoše u ravno primorje,

Kad su došli u primorje
      ravno,

sve polomi Musa po primorju
i uvati Ćuprilić-vezira,
saveza mu ruke naopako,
a sveza mu noge ispod konja,
pa ga posla caru u Stambola.
Stade care mejdandžije tražit',

Sve polomi Musa po primorju
I uvati Ćuprilić vezira,
Pa mu sveza ruke naopako,

Svezata ga posla u Stanbolu.
Oj! Stade care tražit'
      megdandžije,

obećava nebrojeno blago
tko pogubi Musu Kesedžiju;
kako koji tamo odlazaše,
već Stambolu on ne dolazaše.
To se care ljuto zabrinuo;

Obećuje nebrojeno blago.

al' mu veli hodža Ćupriliću:
"Gospodine, care od Stambola,

Al' da vidiš Ćuprilić vezira.
Ovako je caru govorijo:
"He, čuješ me, care
      gospodine,

da je sada Kraljeviću Marko,

Sad da o'đe Kraljeviću
      Marko,

zgubio bi Musu Kesedžiju."
Pogleda ga care poprijeko,
pa on proli suze od očiju:

zgubijo bi Musu Keserdžiju."

"Prođi me se, hodža Ćupriliću!
Jer pominješ Kraljevića Marka?

A govori care gospodine:
"Ne divani, Ćuprilić veziru!

I kosti su njemu istrunule:

Musa Arbanasa was drinking wine

in a white tavern in Stambol;
when Musa had finished his wine,

then, drunk, he began to speak:

"It is now nine years
that I have served the sultan in
    Stambol;
I have not earned a horse or arms,

nor a new or used cloak;
by my firm faith,

I shall revolt to the level coastland,

I shall close the seaports
and the roads on the coast.

I shall build a tower in the coastland,

Around the tower iron hooks;
I shall hang his priests and pilgrims!"

Whatever the Turk said when drunk,

when sober that he had done:

I kosti su ustrunile Marku.
Što spominješ Kraljevića
    Marka?

Oj! Dear God, praise to Thee
    for all things!
Musa the Highwayman was
    drinking wine
in a white tavern in Stambol.
When Musa had drunk his
    wine,
Then, drunk, he began to say:
"Dear God, praise to Thee for
    all things!
It is nine years of days
that I have served the sultan
    in Stambol;
I have not earned penny nor
    pence,
Nor clothing, new or used.
By my firm faith,
May a mother not have borne
    me,
But some Bedouin mare!
I shall revolt to the seacoast
    level,
I shall close the seaports
and the roads on the coast.
There the imperial monies
    pass,
In a year three hundred pack
    loads;
I shall seize it all for myself.
I shall build a house in the
    coastland,
Around the house iron hooks;
I shall hang his priests and
    pilgrims."
What the Turk said when
    drunk,
When sober that he had done;

he revolted to the coastland level,

he closed the seaports
and the roads on the coast,
where the imperial monies pass,

in a year three hundred pack loads:

all Musa held for himself;

in the coastland he built a tower,

around the tower iron hooks,
he hanged the sultan's priests and
    pilgrims.
When the complaints disturbed the
    sultan,

he sent Ćuprilić-vezir against him,
and with him three thousand soldiers.

When they came to the level
    coastland,
Musa destroyed them all on the
    coastland
and captured Ćuprilić-vezir,
tied his hands behind him,

and tied his legs under his horse,
then sent him to the sultan in
    Stambol.

He rebelled to the coastland
    level,
He closed the seaports
and the roads on the coast,
Well, the imperial monies
    pass,
In a year three hundred pack
    loads;
He seized all the money for
    himself.
In the coastland he built a
    house,
around the tower iron hooks;
He hanged the sultan's priests
    and pilgrims.
But the complaints disturbed
    the sultan,
Complaining about the cursed
    Musa.

The sultan began to seek
    champions,
But whoever went out there
Never saw Stambol again.
Musa destroyed them all on
    the coastland.
Against him he sent Ćuprilić
    vezir
And with him twelve
    thousand soldiers.
When they came to the
    coastland level,
Musa destroyed them all on
    the coastland,
And captured Ćuprilić vezir,
Then tied his hands behind
    him,

Sent him bound to Stambol.

The sultan began to seek champions,	Oj! the sultan began to seek champions,
he promised countless monies for whoever would kill Musa the Highwayman; whenever anyone went out there, he did not come back to Stambol. This worried the sultan sorely,	he promises countless monies.
	But then you see Ćuprilić vezir. This is what he said to the sultan:
but Hodža Ćuprilić said to him:	
"Master, sultan of Stambol, Were Kraljević Marko here now,	"Listen to me, sultan, master! Were Kraljević Marko here now,
he would kill Musa the Highwayman." The sultan looked at him askance, and then wept tears from his eyes:	He would kill Musa the Highwayman."
	And the sultan, master, said:
"Forget it, Hodža Ćuprilić!	"Do not speak idly, Ćuprilić vezir!
Why do you mention Kraljević Marko? Even his bones have rotted:	Marko's bones have rotted.

This sample shows us patterns similar to those we have seen in Category C, namely, identical lines (though not so numerous) and very close lines. The novelty here is the number of lines in the Parry text that are not in Karadžić and vice versa. One should notice, however, that the new lines in the Parry text consist of (1) the exclamatory line "Mili Bože, na svem tebi fala," "Dear God, thanks be to Thee for all things!" (twice); (2) a common traditional couplet that is an elaboration of the oath of Musa "I tako me ne rodila majka, Već kobila neka bedevija!," "And may a mother not have borne me, but some Bedouin mare!"; (3) three lines concerning the stealing of imperial treasure, lines that have no counterpart in the Karadžić text at that particular place, *but* are actually found later in Podrugović's text (i.e., Parry lines 17–19 correspond to Karadžić lines 21–23); and (4) Parry lines which concern the fate of those who went out against Musa, namely, that they never returned to Stambol, do not have a counterpart in the same place in the Karadžić text, although once again they are in part to be found later in Podrugović's text (i.e., Parry line 36 equals Karadžić line 36, Parry lines 37–38 equal Karadžić lines 39–40). One should also direct attention to the metathesis of lines 49–50 of Karadžić and Parry lines 56–57. In short, in our sample fifty lines there are no significant additions to the song. What slight novelties there are are exclamatory or elaborative. Elements are found in one place in one text and in a different place in the other. Although the singer is clearly aware of the fixed text and has presumably partly memorized, it is not inviolable and can be departed from.

The remainder of the poem follows in the same pattern of identical, close, and corresponding lines; of omissions and additions; of differences in order. Mandarić changes nothing of significance in the story. He does omit the *vila's* scolding of Marko for fighting on Sunday (a *vila* is a winged female mountain spirit), but both the voice of the *vila* and the hidden knife are there, as well as the heart with three serpents. Mandarić closes his song proper with the comment of the serpent that Marko would have had much more trouble had he, the serpent, been awake. Thus he omits Podrugović's ending in which Marko brings Musa's head to the sultan, who is terrified by it. Instead Mandarić finishes with an address to his audience:

Eto tako, moja braćo draga!	There you are, my dear brothers!
Eto vami pjesma na poštenje!	There is a song in your honor!
Bilo nami od Boga proštenje!	May God forgive us!
Nije više, nit' se. . .	There is no more, nor. . .
Ko me čuo, Bog mu zdravlje dao!	God grant health to him who has heard me!
Ko ne čuje, i on zdravo bijo!	May he also have health who has not heard me!
Nije više, nit' se perom piše,	There is no more, nor is it written by pen,
Jer pisara zaboljela glava,	For the writer has a headache,
A nestalo tinte i papira.	And there is no more ink or paper.

The dependence of the literate Ilija Mandarić on the Karadžić text is clear, yet his song shows a tendency toward expressing the song in the singer's own words and formulas, a tendency more marked than in

Category C, but still not strong enough to free the song from the fixed published text. Category B contains many gradations in relationship to the version of Karadžić. From the example just given, one can range to texts in which there are comparatively few identical lines, less than 10 precent, for instance, and where there is a greater number of corresponding lines with quite different wording, and not only more frequent transference of lines, but the addition of genuinely new material. In other words, Category B is a large and much varied group, covering a full spectrum of variation, leading at last to the independent texts in Category A.

Both the previous singers were literate. The singer of our third example, from Category A, Stanko Pižurica of Rovce in Montenegro, was illiterate. Although he had little voice and even less sense of musical pitch, and although he was awkward with the gusle, he was a fine poet in words, a good storyteller. He sang a version of "Nahod Simeun," the same story we used for Category C.[7] Pižurica's song is, I believe, independent of the Karadžić text. If it has a printed, fixed, songbook version somewhere in its background, that text is not from Podrugović.[8] The first indication of this comes from the fact that Pižurica's song has 305 lines as against the 197 lines of Podrugović's text.

There are no lines completely identical with the version in Karadžić. It is true that in one passage they are somewhat similar. This is the naming scene and the account of the precocious childhood of the hero (variations are underlined in the Parry text).

Karadžić	Parry
Iz sanduka čedo izvadio,	
	Pa nosijo čedo u dvorove,
pokrsti ga u svom namastiru,	
	Povijo ga u bijelu svilu,
	U bijelu crvenu svilu.
	Staviše ga u bešiku zlatnu,
	Založiše medom i šećerom,
	Dobaviše kuma igumena,
	Pokrstiše muško čedo ludo,
lijepo mu ime nadenuo,	E car mu je ime izdenuo,

[7] Parry Text no. 6778.
[8] Karadžić, 1958, vol. 2, no. 13.

nadenuo Nahod Simeune.

Ne šće davat' čedo na dojilje,
već ga 'rani u svom namastiru,
'rani njega medom i šećerom.

Kad je bila čedu godinica,
kolik' drugo od tri godinice!
Kad je bilo od tri godinice,
Kolik' drugo od sedam godina!

A kad bilo od sedam godina,
kolik' drugo od dvanaest ljeta!
Kad je bilo od dvanaest ljeta,
kolik' drugo od dvadest godina!

Čudno Simo knjigu izučio

Aj, divno ime, Nahod
    Simeune.
U odaju na dvorove bjele,

Sve ga medom i šećerom
    hrane,
Mlijekom ga zadojaše često.
Nahodu je napredak pošao.
Kad mu bila godinica dana,
Kano drugo od tri godinice.
Kad mu bile tri godine dana,
Kano drugo od šes' puno
    ljeta.
Kad mu bile šes' godina dana,
Kano drugo od dvanaes' ljeta.
Kad mu bilo dvanaes' godina,
Kano drugo od dvadeset ljeta,
Od dvadeset ljeta i četiri.
Eto care Nahoda nauči,
Na škole ga mnoge naučijo.

He took the child from the chest,

christened him in his monastery,

gave him a fine name,
named him Simeon the Foundling.

He did not want to give the child to be
    nursed,
but fed him in his monastery,

Then he carried the child to
    the house,
Wrapped him in white silk,
In white and red silk.
He placed him in a golden
    cradle,
Fed him on honey and sugar,
Brought a godfather and
    iguman
Christened the little male
    child,
The tzar gave him a name,
Aj, a fine name, Simeon the
    Foundling.

In the chamber of the white
    house,

fed him on honey and sugar.	Ever he fed him on honey and sugar,
	Frequently gave him milk.
	The Foundling progressed.
When the child was a year old,	When he was a year of days,
he was like another of three!	As another of three.
When he was three,	When he was three years of days,
he was like another of seven!	As another of six full years.
And when he was seven,	When he was six years of days,
he was like another of twelve!	As another of twelve years,
When he was twelve,	When he was twelve years,
he was like another of twenty!	As another of twenty years,
	Of twenty years and four.
Simeon learned to read wonderfully well.	Lo the tzar taught the Foundling,
	Taught him at many schools.

This passage is the closest in Pižurica's text to that in Karadžić, as we saw to be true earlier in Vojičić's text of the same song. Yet Pižurica's text is not nearly so close to Karadžić's as was Vojičić's; there are ten lines without equivalents in the Karadžić text, and two of that text's lines are unmatched in the Parry text. Where there are parallels, the wording is quite divergent for the most part, as can be seen from the underlining. The core of this passage, telling of the phenomenal growth of the foundling is a commonplace theme, a well-known run. In fact the correspondences in the entire section quoted do not necessarily indicate a direct relationship between the Karadžić and Parry texts. They simply point to a set of variants of a common theme.

The poem itself, although dealing with "Nahod Simeun," tells an entirely different, though related, story. The Karadžić text, Podrugović's song, concerns a child found in a chest on the shore of the Danube by a monk who brings him up in his monastery. There is nothing remarkable about the child. Pižurica's song concerns a child found in a vineyard by the Serbian emperor Šćepan and his vizier, Todor. In his version the child, when found, has certain marks that set him apart, a star on his forehead, wolf's hair on his shoulder, a sword depicted on his thigh, fire from his teeth. When Šćepan sees these markings, he decides to keep the child, since he has only a daughter, the beautiful Cvijeta.

In both songs the hero has a precocious childhood as evidenced in the

passages quoted. In the Karadžić story other children taunt the foundling for his ignorance of his parenthood, after he has bested them in
various sports. As a result Simeon asks permission to set out to find his
parents. He wanders in vain for nine years, and on the way back is seen
by the Queen of Budim. She summons him to her castle and, when he is
drunk, sleeps with him. When Simeon leaves next morning he forgets
his Gospel book and returns to the castle for it. There he finds the queen
reading the book and weeping. She realizes that she is Simeon's mother.
Simeon goes back to the monastery and confesses his sin to the iguman
(abbot), who throws him into prison and hurls the key into the Danube.
After nine years the iguman remembers Simeon the Foundling. Fisher-
men catch a fish that contains the key, and when the prison is opened,
the sun is shining in it and Simeon is sitting at a golden table with the
Gospel book in his hands.

Pižurica's tale has some points of resemblance to Podrugović's. The
place of the taunting friends is taken by Todor the vizier and the twelve
dukes. They are jealous of the favors shown Simeon by Emperor Šćepan
and plot his downfall. Simeon's wine is drugged and, when he is uncon-
scious, the dukes put him in bed with the emperor's daughter, Cvijeta.
Note the basic similarity of the drink and the bed. In one case, however,
the pair are guilty of mother-son incest.

The emperor condemns Simeon and Cvijeta to be hanged on a leafless
orange tree in the garden. The following morning the tree has blos-
somed, under it is a church, and in the church are the two young people
with crosses in their hands. This is a multiform, of course, of the ending
of the Karadžić text. In Pižurica the story continues with the execution
of Todor and the twelve dukes. On the day following their execution
the orange tree is again withered and beneath it is a lake of blood in
which are the twelve dukes and Todor as well as the cup from which
Simeon had been drugged.

In view of the considerable divergence in the stories of the two texts
and of the common traditional character of their resemblances it is clear
that Pižurica's song has not been influenced directly by the Karadžić text
in question.

Pižurica's song, however, has elements from other stories that were
current in the tradition and combinations and recombinations of them
account for Pižurica's song.[9] It was not the influence of any single text

---

[9]For a study of "Nahod Simeun" in a larger context see Lord, A., 1978, 340–348.

that I have found but rather of the normal workings of an oral-traditional literature.

When an oral narrative song has been written down and in one way or another a fixed text of it is made available to traditional singers, it may affect literate bards directly and others indirectly. Yet even when a singer who can write copies it, he makes changes, tending to express some lines in the formulas to which he is most accustomed in his own singing. Even as copyist he remains to some extent a traditional singer. When a singer attempts to memorize the published text, his basic training shines through and enables him to reconstruct lines according to his own creative habits, to rearrange them in the manner he had learned when he was young.

There are many degrees of relationship to the fixed text. At one end of the scale, at its highest point, comes the song that is independent of the published text. At its best this song represents a pure oral tradition. Its value is great and is becoming ever greater because it is rare. At the other end are the songs memorized from the published fixed text. We have observed a few of the degrees in between those extremes. The memorized texts cannot tell us much more about the pure tradition than the published text of which it is a "copy." From the singers and songs that have been influenced by the printed texts, although not to the point of memorizing them, the scholar can learn much about the life of a tradition as it is affected by cultural changes in the traditional society.

We have been investigating what happens in the last degenerative stages of a tradition, when texts have been fixed by being written down, and when those written texts have been disseminated in a literate, or partially literate, community. I have demonstrated the results of true memorization; they are contrasted with the songs that are "composed in performance" in a living and thriving tradition. The evidence I have presented points up the more remarkable aspects of the tradition in its truly creative period.

CHAPTER II

Notes on *Digenis Akritas* and Serbo-Croatian Epic

This paper was inspired by an article by the eminent Byzantinist Henri Grégoire.[1] Published in 1949, the article, entitled "Le Digénis russe," established the priority of the Russian versions of the Digenis Akritas poem over the Greek versions. Grégoire demonstrated that the two extant Russian texts are drawn from Greek manuscripts earlier than any of those that have survived and also that the Pogodin and Tixonravov texts come from separate Greek originals. In presenting his proof Grégoire brought forth many details that excited my interest because they called to mind details and situations in Serbo-Croatian epic poetry. I have here set down my comments on three of these points.

Aornos

Digenis, enamored of the daughter of the Strategos, breaks into the courtyard of the Strategos's palace and calls to him and to his sons to emerge. When the Strategos is informed of this, he cannot believe that any man would dare to enter his courtyard, where "not even a bird dare approach in flight."[2] This detail of the bird does not occur in any of the Greek manuscripts of the epic of Digenis Akritas, but is in the Tix-

Published in *Harvard Slavic Studies* 2 (1954), 375–383. Reprinted by permission of the Harvard University Press.
[1] Grégoire, 1949.
[2] Ibid., 1949, 142.

onravov manuscript of the Russian version of the story. This was pointed out by Grégoire, who also noted the same detail in one of the Acritic ballads, in which a Saracen boasts that he has been guarding the River Euphrates for forty years, and "not a single bird has flown over it, nor has any man passed it." This is a striking poetic detail, and Grégoire cites it as part of his proof that the Russian Digenis is close to the folk tradition of the Acritic ballads.

A similar passage concerning a place that is so well guarded that not even a bird could pass it occurs in two other folk traditions that are contiguous with the Greek. One of these is Turkish, the other is South Slavic. The Turkish prose romance of Sajjid Battal, according to H. L. Fleischer, was given its present form between the fourteenth and fifteenth centuries A.D., although the hero himself may have lived in the ninth century. In the Turkish romance we read: "He also sent a letter to Sumbath ben Iljun and to Kalb ben Sabah that they should fortify the mountain passes and kill, or rather, send to the Emperor, everyone whom they found. This they did, and so strong were their fortifications that not even a bird could pass." And shortly thereafter we read again:

One day Sajjid was sitting with his friends when Iahja ben Munsir came through the door, and when Sajjid asked him, "Whence come you?" he replied, "From Rumelia. All the mountain passes there that are in the Emperor's possession have been closed and fortified; in each pass he has stationed ten to twenty thousand men and given the order that not even a bird shall pass."[3]

In Serbo-Croatian and Bulgarian epic the same image is found. The song "Marko Kraljević and Musa Kesedžija" in one Bulgarian version has a passage very close to the selection just given from Sajjid Battal. Musa has blocked all the roads to the coastland, so that "not even a bird could pass through."[4]

In a Moslem epic collected by Milman Parry in 1934 in Novi Pazar, the hero, Gol Alija, had become a haiduk and had taken refuge in a cave on Mount Goleš. "Then he put the mountain under his order. No bird even dared to fly across it; how then would any human being dare to

---

[3] Translated from Ethé's German translation of the romance: Ethé, 1871, 135. See also 89 and 191. For further information about the Sajjid Battal romance see Fleischer, 1888, 3:226–254.

[4] Xalanskij, 1893, 90–92.

pass through?"[5] The same theme is repeated twice in the course of the song. A messenger is sent to Alija with a letter, and a sentinel challenges him: "Ill-begotten one, who are you here on the mountain? You know that there is no passing through here. It is now twelve years that even the birds have not flown over here, to say nothing of heroes on this earth."[6] Finally, when the messenger approaches the cave itself, he hides behind a fir tree and cautiously holds out the letter. The haiduk sees it and says to his lieutenant: "Hearken to me, Orlan the standard-bearer! Birds have not flown over here, to say nothing of heroes upon this earth, for twelve years now. Here is a letter behind the dry fir tree. Who has brought it? Who is walking about here?"[7]

Thus in three folk traditions, Greek, Turkish, and South Slavic we find the same ornamental ornithological detail of birdless places.

Such birdless regions are found also in the writers of ancient Rome. In the sixth book of Vergil's *Aeneid* the entrance to Avernus is described as follows:

> There was a wide-mouthed cavern, deep and vast
> and rugged, sheltered by a shadowed lake
> and darkened groves; such vapor poured from those
> black jaws to heaven's vault, no bird could fly
> above unharmed.[8]

From the *apparatus criticus* of R. G. Austin's edition we learn that some of the manuscripts add the line: "Hence the Greeks have named this place 'Aornos'(Birdless)."[9] This is folk etymology, of course. Lucretius in his *De Rerum Natura* gives us further information about the Avernian regions.

> Now attend, and I will explain what nature belongs to those various regions which are called Avernian, and their lakes. In the first place, their name Avernian has been bestowed upon them because of their character, being dangerous to all birds, because when they have come in flight over against those places, forgetting their oarage of wings and slackening their sails, headlong they fall to the ground with soft necks outstretched, if it so

---

[5] Parry, M., 1954, 122; Parry, M., 1953, 107, lines 25–27.
[6] Parry, M., 1954, 124; Parry, M., 1953, 109, lines 165–169.
[7] Parry, M., 1954, 125; Parry, M., 1953, 150, lines 254–259.
[8] Vergil, *Aeneid* 6.237–242. Translation, Mandelbaum, A., 1971.
[9] Line 242 is bracketed by Mynors (Vergil, 1969).

happens that the nature of the place allows it, or into the water, if it happens that a lake of Avernus lies below. Such a place is close by Cumae, where mountains, filled with black sulphur, smoke, all covered with hot springs. There is another within the walls of Athens, on the very crest of the citadel, by the temple of fostering Tritonian Pallas, whither hoarse crows never wing their way, not even when the altars smoke with offerings; so carefully do they flee, not as the Greek poets have sung from the bitter wrath of Pallas because of that vigil of theirs, but the nature of the place does the job itself.[10]

In Vergil and Lucretius, then, Avernus means "Aornos," "Birdless." Yet it is from neither of these authors that we might expect the idea to have entered Greek, Turkish, or Serbo-Croatian oral tradition, although it seems clear that they all reflect a belief that "aornos," "birdless," means "unapproachable."

The Greeks applied folk etymology to a Sanskrit word *avarana*, which was the name of an impregnable rock fortress in India on the Indus River. The men of Alexander of Macedon called it Aornos when they laid siege to it in 326 B.C., and legend had it that even Herakles had not been able to take it.[11] We can carry back the idea that an "impregnable" and "unapproachable" place is "birdless" to at least the fourth century B.C. The idea may be traced still further back, however. It may be that in Alexander's time it was already known to Greek oral tradition.

In Homer's *Odyssey* Circe advised the hero of the dangers that would beset him and his men when they leave her island; first they will meet the Sirens, and then,

After your men have brought the ship past these, what is to be your course I will not fully say; do you yourself ponder it in your heart. I will describe both ways. Along one route stand beetling cliffs, and on them roar the mighty waves of dark-eyed Amphitrite; the blessed gods call them the Wanderers. This way not even winged things can pass—no, not the gentle doves which bear ambrosia to father Zeus; but one of them the smooth rock always draws away, though the father puts another in to fill the number.[12]

[10] Lucretius, 1943, *De rerum natura*, 6:738–755. Translation, W. H. D. Rouse, 1924. For further commentary on the passage see Bailey, 1947, vol. 3, 1665–1668.

[11] Arrian, 4.28–30.

[12] *Homeri opera*, 1976, *Odyssea*, 3:12, lines 55–65; translation, G. H. Palmer, 1912, 186–187.

There was clearly something more than a natural phenomenon embedded in the traditional image of the place so awful that not even a bird could fly over it to account for its appearance in an Homeric poem, in Vergil and Lucretius, in Byzantine and modern Greek, Turkish, and South Slavic. Perhaps Vergil has given us the clue in indicating that the birdless place marks the entrance to the realm of death and of the dead. There is a continuity here from ancient times to the present and, even in our brief sampling, a geographical distribution from India to the Near East and the Mediterranean.

Griffins

The Serbo-Croatian epics are rich in details of clothing, arms, and horses. It is reasonable to suppose that this richness is in no small part due to Byzantine influence. In the Moslem Yugoslav poems such descriptions, of course, have been elaborated by addition of details that belong specifically to the life of the Sublime Porte. The number of words of Turkish origin in these passages bears witness to this fact. But underneath even these the ceremonial ornateness of Byzantium and its love of vestiture almost literally shine through. Have the Yugoslav generations of singers devised these passages of description from what they saw in Byzantium or from what was brought from Byzantium into the Balkans? Or have they taken over at least some details from a contact with Byzantine folk epic? The answers are, of course, affirmative in both cases, but the second question deserves special attention.

In the poem of Digenis Akritas, after his youthful "initiatory" hunt and a bath, the hero is prepared by his father for return to his mother. In his analysis of the verses that tell of the ritual dressing of the hero at this point, Grégoire discusses the parts of his vestment that are described in the Russian version and in the Greek manuscripts.[13] First the young Digenis puts on a light undergarment against the cold, and then a red (or black in the Russian version) vest or doublet with golden sleeves that are encrusted with pearls (or precious stones). His collar is decorated with amber and sea shells, the buttons are large pearls, and the buttonholes are embroidered with pure gold. He then puts on breeches of fine brocade ornamented with griffins; his boots are decorated with gold and

[13] Grégoire, 1949, 145–150.

precious stones, and his spurs shine with emeralds. This is a composite picture.[14]

Compare with this the raiment of another youthful hero as he is prepared by his mother to appear before his father for his parental approval on setting out on his first important mission. The South Slavic hero is Smailagić Meho, and the song is the tale of his wedding.

First of all his mother put upon him linen of finest silk cloth. Every third thread in it was of gold. Then she gave him a silken vest, all embroidered with pure gold. Down the front of the vest were buttons fashioned of gold pieces, a row which reached to his silk belt. There were twelve of them, and each contained half a liter of gold. The button at his throat shone even as the moon, and in it was a full liter of gold. The vest had a gold-embroidered collar the two wings of which were fastened by this button. At the right side of the collar, above the button, was the likeness of Sulejman the Magnificent and on the other side was that of the imperial pontiff of Islam. Then she gave him his breastplate. It was not of silver but of pure gold and weighed full four oke. On his back she fastened it with a buckle. Then she put on him his silken breeches, which had been made in Damascus, all embroidered in gold, with serpents pictured upon his thighs, their golden heads meeting beneath his belt and beneath the thong by which his sword was hung. . . . [here follows a description of his pistols and sword] Upon his shoulders was a silken cloak, its two corners heavy with gold. Gilded branches were embroidered round about and upon his shoulders were snakes whose heads met beneath his throat. Down the front hung four cords, braided of 'fined gold, all four reaching to his belt of arms and mingling with his sword-thong, which held his fierce Persian blade.

Then with an ivory comb his mother combed out the sheaf-like queue and bound it with pearl. She put on him his cap of fur with its twelve plumes, which no one could wear, neither vizier nor imperial field marshal, nor minister, nor any other pasha save only the alaybey under the sultan's firman. . . .

[Finally she] put on him his boots and leggings and sent him to his father.[15]

This same amazing song from a Yugoslav Moslem begins with a gathering of the lords of the Border. The singer describes them as they sit and boast.

[14]Ibid.
[15]Međedović, 1974a, 100–101; 1974b, lines 1596–1624, 1645–1663, 1677–1678.

About their necks were collars of gold fastened beneath the throat by a clasp, and all the clasps were of 'fined gold. . . . Each man's cap upon his brow was of sable, and on his heroic shoulders was gold embroidery like branches, and along his arms were braided snakes whose heads met beneath his throat; one would say and swear that they were living. . . . They wore breeches of finest make; the cloth was dark, and the gold shone brightly. Along their legs golden branches glistened, and on their thighs were braided snakes whose heads met beneath the belt of arms.[16]

In another passage from a different singer the snakes' heads are placed below on the knees and their effect is described:

When he gave her the richly made breeches, there were serpents braided along the legs, their heads resting on the knees. When he walked, the serpents opened their jaws. One would say that they were living. When he walked the serpents clamped their jaws, and anyone who was not of strong mind would have lost his reason.[17]

These snakes are, of course, the griffins of the Byzantine epic, elaborated and made dramatic. The light undergarments, the vests with embroidered sleeves, the collar, and the buttons are Byzantine also. Everything is adorned with pure gold (od suhoga zlata or od čistoga zlata in Serbian, καθαροῦ χρυσοῦ in Greek; suxim zlatom in Russian).

Weddings and Rescues

The two preceding sections have concerned themselves with ornamental details in the Digenis Akritas and in Serbo-Croatian epic. They show, I believe, a close relationship between the two epic traditions. The number of such details could be multiplied, and the number of traditions could be broadened to include other Near Eastern and Middle Eastern traditional epics. Other parallels in the story elements and in their structure can be adduced as well.

Songs of bride stealing and of rescue from captivity are the warp and woof of many oral epic traditions. In essence, of course, they are merely two sides of the same coin. The hero sets out to obtain something; in one case he wishes to capture a maiden; in the other he wishes to free

[16] Međedović, 1974a, 81; 1974b, lines 138–150, 156–160.
[17] Parry, M., 1954, 255; Parry, M., 1953, 237, lines 713–720.

someone from captivity. In both cases there are opponents. Nothing could be simpler; yet the possibility for variety is great.

The Digenis Akritas poem contains several instances of bride stealing and of rescue. The exact number depends upon the text used and upon the scholar's interpretation of a few of the episodes. The two most obvious wedding songs in the compilation that makes up this poem are the story of the emir and the tale of the wedding of Digenis.[18] Somewhat hidden are the wedding themes in the encounter between Digenis and Maximo, the Amazon, and in the Philopappos episode, if one considers the latter as separate from the hero's wedding song.[19] The rescue theme is clear in the story of the daughter of Haplorrhabdes, told by Digenis, but it is also to be found in the story of the emir.[20]

The emir's story, indeed, is instructive, because it is a wedding song of bride stealing that becomes a rescue tale with a peculiar twist. The emir is a worthy man even if not a Christian and his capture of the maiden begins like a Moslem wedding song as told by a Christian. The point of view is only partly that of the emir. Very soon, however, the perspective becomes fully Christian and attention is focused on the girl's mother and on her brothers and their pursuit. We are in a rescue song. It is clear that the brothers must save their sister from falling to the lot of a Moslem. In the single combat scene the situation is ambivalent. Neither side must lose; both sides must win. This is accomplished by the conversion to Christianity of the emir and all his men. This ambivalence and the change of faith of the bridegroom make this a very strange tale from the standpoint of the Serbo-Croatian epic wedding songs. It is strengthened by the sequel of the conversion of the emir's mother. This is, or at least becomes, a nonheroic episode.

I know of no parallel to this story in South Slavic epic. There the characters are either good or bad—yet the stories are quite complex. South Slavic epics frequently combine wedding and rescue songs. The hero sets out to rescue his friend from captivity and is helped in this by the captor's daughter, whom he takes with him and later marries. This is true, for example, in the story of "Hasan of Ribnik Rescues Mus-

---

[18] The emir's story is told in Mavrogordato, 1956, 1.30–3.980, 5–65. The courtship and wedding of Digenis Akritas are related in 4.1323–2034, 89–133.

[19] Maximo enters the poem at line 2835 and she is slain by Digenis, in the Grottaferrata manuscript alone, at 6.3300–3301, 185–215. For a discussion of the Philopappos episode see Grégoire, 1949, 152–155.

[20] The story of Haplorrabdes's daughter is told by Digenis himself in Mavrogordato, 1956, 5.2190–2461, 143–161.

tajbey."[21] Sometimes there is a double wedding in the Moslem songs, in which the hero gains two wives, as in "The Wedding of Ćejanović Meho."[22] Here one wife is gained without any opposition, whereas the other must be fought for. There are frequent conversions in these songs but they are on the part of the bride, never on that of the bridegroom. Moreover, the pursuers are always worsted, killed, or put to flight.[23]

Similarly, in a rescue song there is never any ambivalence. The pursuers overcome the captors, never come to terms with them. There are many instances of brothers rescuing a sister. This is especially true in the Moslem tradition, in which the famed brothers Mujo and Halil Hrnijičić often set out in pursuit of their much sought-after sister.[24]

The story of the emir reflects a period of expansion of Christianity, an era of mass conversions. Many of the South Slavic Moslem epics are set in the reign of Sulejman the Magnificent, and are thus pictured as coming from a time when, as the poems themselves say, "the empire of the Turks was at its height, and Bosnia was its lock, its lock and its golden key."[25] The conflict was waging back and forth across the borders. The tone of the Byzantine epic is closer to that of Sajjid Battal, except that the stories are told from the Christian point of view.

These three analyses provide a modest demonstration of how fruitful the comparative study of Byzantine Greek and Serbo-Croatian oral epic traditions can be.

[21] Parry, M., 1954 and 1953, no. 18.

[22] Parry, M., 1954 and 1953, no. 12.

[23] Several rescue tales in the fifteenth-century Turkish *Book of Dede Korkut* (*Dede Korkut*, 1974) are not unlike those in the South Slavic tradition.

[24] Parry, M., 1954 and 1953, no. 13.

[25] Part of the preamble to "The Wedding of Smailagić Meho," Parry, M., 1974a and 1974b.

CHAPTER 12

Narrative Themes in Bulgarian
Oral-Traditional Epic and
Their Medieval Roots

The core of this paper consists of the examination of several narrative themes in Bulgarian oral-traditional epic, particularly in the songs about the hero Krali Marko, with the hope of discovering possible medieval roots for them. It is necessary to stress at the beginning that the medieval roots I am seeking are not to be found only, or even mainly, in literary documents, but also in oral-traditional literature.

While the monks and scribes were busily translating, copying, and writing, laying the foundations for Bulgarian written literature, what kind of oral-traditional literature were the Bulgarian people in the Middle Ages creating and listening to outside the monasteries? What stories were they telling and singing during those centuries when their written literature was beginning to develop? Was there any connection between the two kinds of literary activity?

One theme, or a detail in it, has directed me to the Armenian Paulicians and Bulgarian Bogomils and to larger patterns of traditional narrative. Another has led into newer areas, to which considerable attention is now being given in scholarship dealing with oral-traditional literature, namely shamanism.

A people's past can be read in its songs and stories that have been bequeathed to each generation from its elders since the time when the

This paper was read at a meeting in 1981 at Dumbarton Oaks, Washington, D.C., celebrating the thirteen-hundredth anniversary of the Bulgarian state. It was published in *Byzantino-bulgarica* 8 (Sofia, B'lgarska akademija na naukite, Institut po istorii, 1986), 102–111.

community first came together to share common concerns. History of a particular sort, not political or military or diplomatic history, but what might be termed "spiritual," or even intellectual history, can still be heard on the lips and in the voices of the truly traditional singers in any country. Bulgaria's past has been blessed with an abundance of that kind of history which is embodied in its literature both oral and written. Since oral-traditional literature is older than written literature, its themes may go back to the oldest times. Much of common Slavic provenience was in the tradition when the Slavic peoples came into the Balkans; and much also was taken from the Greeks at various times. The Slavs brought the living forms of the tradition, the language and the metrical patterns in which we still listen to and read the record; perhaps the earliest Indo-European elements in Bulgarian oral-traditional literature came from them, sometimes reinforced and increased by other Indo-European themes when they met with the Greek population of the Balkans. The evidence is in details, but they are suggestive of larger landscapes.

It is always difficult to talk with any degree of precision about the roots of any single oral-traditional narrative song. The streams of narrative in Bulgaria in the Middle Ages sprang from wells of stories told and sung rather than written and read. And it is important that some at least—probably more than is usually thought to be the case—of the written stories that were brought to Bulgaria in Greek from Byzantium and translated into Bulgarian, had themselves come eventually from oral-traditional sources. It is a moot point, therefore, whether some of the narrative songs collected in the nineteenth and twentieth centuries stem from medieval documents or from continuous oral tradition. If they stem from the written narratives from medieval times that we possess, it is not easy to determine exactly what the process was by which they came into oral tradition. If they were read aloud from the manuscript to "people," or if the stories were read or recounted by the monks or priests in sermons, then the effect on oral tradition would most likely have been much the same (but not quite) as if someone had told the story in the tradition itself. The book transmitted it from one culture or from one region to another in the manner in which a traveler or traveling storyteller might have transmitted it. The story, not the text, is passed on. I shall, therefore, speak more about stories than about manuscripts, although they too have a place.

One of the narrative themes that seems to have appealed to people on various levels was the creation of the world and its organization. Joan Exarch's *Šestodnev,* the "Six Days of Creation," a translation of Basil the Great's *Hexameron,* with many additions of the Exarch's own, including a famous description of Simeon the Great and his palace, represents Orthodoxy.[1] Joan was reputed to be one of the most learned men of his time in Bulgaria.

On the level of dualistic heresy, or of the "unofficialdom" represented by apocryphal works, originally in Greek, some of which have survived to us only in Slavic translation, stemming even from the early period of Church Slavonic and Bulgarian letters, the creation of the world was also a recurring topic.

The apocryphal and similar works that were apocalyptic or visionary in nature, or that dealt with the creation of the world and with the role of Satan as well as of God in a dualistic universe, were, understandably enough, popular with Bogomils, even though it may be an exaggeration to say that these works were "their" books.[2] The *Tajna kniga,* the "Secret book," contained a dialogue between the apostle John and Jesus. In answer to John's questions Jesus recounted how the primeval world was different from the present one, and how Satan had created this our earth and men and women on it. He told also what His mission was to this sinful world and how in the end, at the second coming of Jesus, the world would perish.[3] This in brief was its content. Cosmology and the creation of mankind were some of the subjects that were most significant for the Bogomils and the highly important *Tajna kniga* fitted so

[1] The manuscript is preserved in a copy of A.D. 1263 in Hilendar Monastery on Mount Athos, Greece. For more on Joan Exarch (ninth and tenth centuries) and his "Šestodnev" see Konstantinov, 1946, 101–107; Elevterov, 1978, 148–151.

[2] The best source for the texts associated with the Bogomils is Ivanov, 1925. For more on the Bogomils see Obolensky, 1948.

[3] The *Tajna kniga* is discussed and summarized in modern Bulgarian in the 1970 photocopy of Ivanov, 1925, 61–87. According to Ivanov, the Slavic text has been lost, but a Latin translation exists in two manuscripts. One, now in Paris, was found in the Archives of the Inquisition in Carcassonne; the other is in a parchment codex of the fourteenth century, no. 1137, in Vienna. The Carcassonne text was first published in Paris in 1691 by the Benedictine Benoist, in his *Histoire des Albigeois et des Vaudois ou Barbets,* 1:283 ff. It was reprinted in *Fortgesetzte Sammlung von alten und neuen theologischen Sachen,* 1734, 703 ff., and by J. C. Thilo, *Codex apocryphus Novi Testamenti* (Leipzig: n.p., 1832), 1:884 ff. The latest printing listed by Ivanov was by M. I. Sokolov', *Slavjanskata kniga Enoha Pravednoga* (The Slavic Book of Enoch the Just) (Moscow: n.p., 1910), 165 ff. The Vienna text was first published by Johann Joseph Ignatius von Döllinger in *Beiträge zur Sektengeschichte des Mittelalters* (Munich: C. H. Beck, 1890), 2:85 ff. Both Latin texts are published in Ivanov, 1925, 73–87.

well that it is not surprising that it was even thought to be one of their own works.

But the *Tajna kniga* was not the only work concerned with Creation. *The Sea of Tiberias* falls into the same category.[4] It contains a dualistic myth of the creation of the universe. In it God sees a duck, which is Satan, swimming on the sea and orders it to dive and bring up a rock, which God then breaks into two pieces, one of which He gives to Satan and from the other He strikes sparks, which become the archangels, Michael and Gabriel, and all the other angels. The Bulgarian text is short; it is worth quoting in its entirety.

The Creation of the World

The Lord of Sabaoth lived in three layers of the sky before Earth existed. And the Lord of Sabaoth, the eternal Father, thought and brought forth from his heart and gave birth to his beloved Son, our Lord Jesus Christ, and from his mouth came out the Holy Spirit in the form of a dove. And the Lord said, "Let the crystal heaven be on iron columns resting on seventy myriads, and let there be lakes, clouds, stars, light and wind." And after he blew in his bosom, he planted paradise in the east. The frost is of the Lord's face; the thunder is the Lord's voice, hardened on an iron chariot; lightning is the Lord's word, which comes out of the Lord's mouth; the sun is from the inside of the Lord's garment, and the moon from the Lord's face, because the Lord wiped his face. And the Lord said, "Let there be a Sea of Galilee on the earth, salty water; let there be myriads of columns in the air." And the Lord descended through the air to the Sea of Galilee and saw a grebe swimming on it. Standing above it, he said, "Grebe, who are you?" The answer came, "I am Satan." And the Lord said to Satan, "Dive into the sea and bring out some soil and a stone!"

And the Lord, after breaking up the stone into two halves, gave with his left hand one half of the stone to Satan, and struck the other half with his scepter. Out of the fiery sparks from the stone God created the archangels Michael and Gabriel, and the angels flew out. Satan made from the stone myriads of satanic powers for the gods. And the Lord said, "Let there be thirty-three whales in the Sea of Galilee and let earth stand upon these whales."[5]

This reads like oral-traditional literature, and the concept of the "earth diver" is a very widespread motif in the lore of many parts of the world.[6]

[4] Ivanov, 1925, 287–311.

[5] Nicoloff, 1979, 103.

[6] Oral-traditional versions of Creation have been collected and published in *BNT,* vol. 11.

On both the official Orthodox level of Joan Exarch and on the hereti-
cal and apocryphal level the story of Creation was important. It can still
be found in oral-traditional literature.

There have been collected in the nineteenth and twentieth centuries
tales of the Creation that seem to derive to some degree from these
medieval stories, which must have entered into the repertory of the
people and to have survived among them. These are not oral-traditional
epic songs, but they belong among the prose narratives with medieval
roots. They may have been known to the singers of oral-traditional
epos, but we do not have any epic texts of them. Here is a small part of
such a tale, published in 1914, reflecting the incident of the "earth diver"
to which I just referred in *The Sea of Tiberias*.

> In the beginning there was no earth nor people. There was water every-
> where. There were only the Lord and the Devil who were living together
> at that time.
>
> Once the Lord said to the Devil "Let us make earth and people."
> "Let's," answered the Devil, "but where will we get some dirt?" "There is
> earth under the water," said the Lord to the Devil. "Say 'With the power
> of God and mine,' then you will reach the bottom and find dirt."
>
> The Devil set out, but he didn't say first "With the power of God and
> mine," but "With my power and that of God." That is why he did not
> reach the bottom. He did it again a second time, and again he did not
> reach the bottom. But the third time he said, "With the power of God and
> mine." And then he reached the bottom and with his nails picked up a
> little dirt.
>
> The lord cast this dirt into the water and there came into being a little
> earth.

Thus, in the case of Creation stories, we seem to have an amazing
continuity of popularity from written to oral literature.

Some themes that are prominent in the written literature and that one
might expect to find in Bulgarian oral epic tradition, however, are not
well represented there. One of these is the taking of cities, the subject of
the Trojan cycle in ancient Greek epic. As far as I can see, the medieval
Slavic translations or adaptations of the Trojan story, stemming from
Dares and Dictys and very widespread in medieval European literature,
including Bulgarian, had no influence on Bulgarian oral-traditional epic.

The theme of the return of the hero after a long absence to find his
wife about to marry again, the *Odyssey* theme, is also rare in Bulgarian

oral tradition, although it can be found.[7] In the Slavic world outside the Balkans it is exemplified best, of course, by the Russian *bylina* of Dobrynja and Alyosha and its many variants.[8]

On the other hand, songs about dragon-slayers are numerous in the Bulgarian repertory. In addition to real dragons, there are dragon substitutes such as Musa the Highwayman and the three-headed Arab. Since Musa has three snakes in his heart and the Arab has three heads, there is no difficulty in classifying them as unusual and dragon- or monster-related.

Such themes certainly go back to the Middle Ages, to the time when the present repertory of themes was being formed, and they belong in the cultural continuum of East and West. In fact the basic story patterns of epic dragon-slaying, in which the hero fights the dragon who blocks the roads or guards treasures (as distinguished from the dragon-slayer type in the folktale, in which the hero saves a maiden about to be sacrificed to a monster) are very ancient shared cultural characteristics, for they represent the constant renewing of the primeval establishment of order in the universe. Dragons should be taken seriously. Strangely enough, most dragon stories in oral-traditional epic narrative do not seem to have any relationship to the dragon stories in the medieval Slavic documents. I am thinking in particular of the Life of Saint George as told in the medieval Slavic texts, which is the usual tale found also in the Golden Legend of Jacobus de Voragine.[9] No epic hero defeats a dragon by praying, thus making the beast submissive enough to be led by a halter by the freed maiden to the city, there to be killed by Saint George. This is a distortion of the folktale type of dragon-slayer rather than of the epic one. These stories keep the outward form of hagiography, but are really traditional tales in saints' clothing. A new and highly original example of this phenomenon is found in the medieval Bulgarian text of Mihail Voin, Michael the Warrior.[10]

Its manuscripts are of the fourteenth century, but it belongs to a somewhat earlier date, by at least one century, coming perhaps at the very beginning of the second Bulgarian empire. This apocryphal life of

[7]Lord, A., 1978, 348–355.

[8]See, for example, Rybnikov, 1909, vol. 1, nos. 26 and 41; vol. 2, nos. 129, 155, 160, 178, and 193.

[9]*The Golden Legend*, 1969.

[10]Ivanov, 1935, no. 25, 184–186, Text, 211–212.

Saint Michael of Potuk, who lived in the time of Boris, is built around the well-known type of tale of the slaying of a dragon, an almost ageless story with myriad ramifications. Saint Michael of Potuk's encounter with a three-headed *lamja* varies from many other such encounters, however, because Saint Michael died from a blow of the dragon's tail after he cut off its three heads in fair fight. The tail struck him on the right cheek and the left arm and wounded him. Michael, nevertheless, rose to his feet again immediately. His servant ran to the city to tell what had happened, and the citizens went out to meet Michael with candles and blessings. He gave the girl whom he had saved back to her parents, went home, and a few days later died. His relics performed many miracles and gave healing to all who came to them with faith.

The life depicts the saint as being born to a good family; he was a saintly youth who fought against the Ethiopians and heathen at Carigrad. When all the Romei were fleeing in defeat, Michael prayed, rallied and encouraged the troops, and they were victorious. It is on the return from this war that the saint stops to rest by a large lake. His servant learns about the dragon (*lamja*) and Michael undertakes its annihilation.

Michael is a fine and tragic hero, yet I know of no oral-traditional epic in Bulgaria in which the hero is killed by the dragon, or of any other saint—though I have not searched for one—who was thus martyred. I must confess that I am also fond of this story—attractive enough in its own right—because it reminds me, as I am sure that it has reminded many, of the Anglo-Saxon Beowulf. I do not suspect any connection.

The treatment among the Balkan Slavs of such ancient and well-known themes as that of the Oedipus myth is noteworthy.[11] The medieval South Slavic texts (both Serbian and Bulgarian) of the life of Paul of Caesarea emphasize the prophecy of incest and its fulfillment. It is found in a document that, according to Jordan Ivanov, is preserved in Middle Bulgarian copies of the sixteenth century and in modern Bulgarian *damaskini* of the seventeenth-nineteenth centuries, but all these are presumed to go back to a Byzantine Greek original now lost.[12]

The essential story begins with the marriage of a brother and sister for the purpose of eventually keeping whole the kingdom of their father, a

[11] A companion piece to this article, "The Ancient Greek Heritage in Modern Balkan Epic," treats the relationship of the ancient Greek Oedipus myth to some of the same material that is discussed in this paper. See Lord, 1978a, 340–348.

[12] Ivanov, 1935, no. 23, 177–179, "K'rvosmeštenie."

half of which was to be inherited by each child. When they had a son, he was put in a chest and set in the sea with a note that he was of incestuous birth. The brother died and the sister became queen of the whole kingdom.

The boy Pavel—the name is given to him later—was found by a monk, who hid the letter and brought him up, and Pavel became emperor of *irodskata zemja,* "heathen country." The Empress Egazia (his mother) heard of him and said she wanted to marry him. He would thus become emperor of all Caesarea. The monk told Pavel that he was not worthy of even living, to say nothing of becoming emperor, and he gave Pavel the letter that he had found with the child. But Pavel gave it to a servant and forgot about it. Thus he married his mother.

But—to shorten the story—he finds the letter again, forsakes his wife's bed, she finds the letter (through a servant), and the truth comes out.

The incest theme is avoided or at least not found in my experience in the Bulgarian oral-traditional versions of the Oedipus story. On the other hand, the prophecy of patricide and its fulfillment are interestingly worked out in the Bulgarian traditional songs, which seem to have no connection thus with Pavel or Paul of Caesarea. Why this is so is not entirely clear, but it is to be noted that the Bulgarian songs of patricide are attached mainly to Krali Marko, whose relations with his mother were impeccable while those with his father were far from amicable. It should also be noted that in the Bulgarian songs Marko does not actually kill his father. He simply beats him, or as one song says, "he crushes his father's bones." They are indeed in the tradition of the Oedipus theme because of the connection with fulfillment of a prophecy, and because in the battle between father and son the contestants do not know each other's identity. The exception to these songs of Krali Marko in the patricide tradition is one about Porče ot Avale, in which the father is actually killed.[13]

In this extraordinary song Porče ot Avale tells his wife that he will send her home because she has borne him no children, although they have been married nine years. She tells him he should take three loads of money and go to Venice to buy swaddling clothes since she is pregnant with a boy child. In joy Porče does as she bids and when he is on his way back, at a place two hours away from home, he hears a child crying, and

[13] "Porče ot Avale," 1891.

its voice reaches to heaven. Porče realizes that this child is his and it will become a great hero who will kill him. So Porče returns to Venice and buys a gypsy child. When he arrives home he finds his wife nursing their son. He steals the baby boy, putting the gypsy child in its place, wraps his son in a sheaf of rye (?) and casts him into the Danube. An old woman hears the child crying when she goes to draw water from the river and she keeps him until he is a handsome hero of twenty.

At that time the king of Buda gathers an army and takes a hero from each house. The young man hears the old woman cursing the Austrian Empire as she sweeps the house, and tells her that he will join the army. He orders her to bring him the hidden arms and prepare his horse. The young man then goes to Buda, where he comes upon a turbulent river that is impassable. On the other side is a mighty Turkish army (which the poem describes very vividly). The youth is afraid, but his horse advises him to tie his shirt over his eyes so that they will not get wet when he leaps over the river. The horse comes down in the midst of the river and then leaps up again onto dry land. The hero, again at his horse's advice, unbinds his eyes, draws his sword, and attacks the Turks.

The young hero is about to return from the battle when he sees seventy kings sitting under an olive tree drinking raki. He greets them and Porče (evidently in the company of the kings) declares that the great hero is his son. He repeats the story told previously about his trip to Venice. The young man is so angry at his father for what he has done that he draws his sword and cuts off his father's head. He says farewell to the kings and takes his mother to live with him and the old woman who had brought him up. This last may be a vestige of mother-son incest.

This brings me to a consideration in greater depth of another song, more typical than "Porče ot Avale," in which the theme of patricide occurs. The song tells, among other things, of the childhood deeds of Krali Marko.[14] In it the foundling Marko is brought up by a shepherd, and when he is old enough he is given the task of pasturing the village calves. He pastured them three days and three nights and on the fourth he beat them to death and went home. His foster father sent him away to live by the River Vardar where he had found him. The story continues, and is the same as that in which Marko "crushes his father's bones."

---

[14] "Marko i tri narečnici," "Marko and the Three Soothsayers," BNT, 1:116–123.

The pattern of miraculous birth, absenting, and precocious childhood has a long and impressive history. The element of beating the calves fits into this pattern of precocious and unusual childhood, and is a recognizable and characteristic trait in the sequence of story elements. Irrational, frenzied behavior seems in these cases to be a mark of special powers, of an otherworldliness.

Whence comes the incident of the beating of the calves? Two parallels come to mind. One is found in the Kullervo songs in the Finnish *Kalevala,* the other in the childhood deeds of the Armenian hero David of Sassoun.[15] Both parallels point to the East. An Armenian connection is not beyond the realm of possibility. In the Middle Ages on at least two occasions large groups of Armenian Paulicians were resettled from eastern Anatolia to Bulgarian Thrace. I cannot prove that those people knew the Armenian epic songs, but it is thoroughly possible, and even likely. Although the first Armenian epics were written down in 1873, at least one Armenian scholar (Shalian) states that the songs must have been formulated not later than the tenth century; there is no doubt that the songs were much older than that. According to Obolensky, Constantine V transferred Armenians to Thrace as early as A.D. 757.[16] During the crucial period when Bulgars and Slavs were gradually being assimilated, one can assume that traditional songs and stories were being formed and reformed. It must have been a creative period for epic. It is thoroughly possible that the episode of Marko's childhood—without Marko, of course—came into the Balkans at that time. His name would have been associated with it later.

But that is only one of the possibilities. The incident is also reminiscent of apocryphal stories of Jesus. These are found in the Gospel of Thomas, with two Greek forms and one Latin, and the Arabic Gospel of the infancy of the Savior. The Gospel of Thomas was translated into Slavic.[17] All of these contain narratives of the strange childhood deeds of Jesus.

It is true that none of the incidents in either the apocryphal texts or the Armenian epic corresponds exactly to the incident in the Bulgarian oral-traditional song of Krali Marko. In the case of the former, the apoc-

[15] See Lord, A., 1976, 349–358. For the story of Kullervo see Lönnrot, 1963, Poems 31–36, 223–255. For David of Sassoun see Surmelian, 1964, 104–128. A similar incident is told of David's father, Great Meherr; see Surmelian, 77–78.

[16] Shalian, 1964, xviii–xxi. Obolensky, 1948.

[17] For translations of "The Infancy Story of Thomas" and extracts from the "Arabic Infancy Gospel" see Hennecke, 1959, 388–401.

ryphal texts, it is clear that the documents themselves that were involved had no direct influence on the tradition. Put simply, I do not
believe that any "carrier of the tradition" read or had read to him or her
any apocryphal gospel. But it does seem that Krali Marko took unto
himself, or his name was attached to, stories typical of the lives of a
special type of hero. It is also to be noted, although here one must be
cautious, that such apocryphal texts, or the stories in them, were possibly known to the Armenian Paulicians, or at least the Bogomils, and
thus our two threads may be tied together. The incidents in the Armenian epic of David may also have been influenced directly by apocryphal
gospels like those cited.

This final section concerns the way or ways in which the Krali Marko
of the Bulgarian oral-traditional epic gained his unusual qualities, his
strength, his horse, his relationship with the "other world" of the
supernatural.

A traditional song will serve as a transition.[18] It begins with the
prophecy that Marko will be a hero and that he will crush his father's
bones. His father, V'lkašin, puts the baby into a basket and casts it into
the Vardar River. Marko is found and brought up by a shepherd, and
when he is old enough he pastures the village calves. The song begins,
therefore, like the one already cited.

No more is heard of this theme in the song in question, however, but
a second subject is taken up. In the mountains Marko finds a cradle with
two children whom he shades from the sun. Their mother is a *vila* (a
winged female mountain spirit) and in gratitude for his kindness to her
children she gives him suck and from her milk he receives his strength.
In a third section of the song the *vila* tells him how to capture a wondrous horse, which he mounts from ambush. The horse had many
wounds and came to a tree, in which Marko was hidden, to scratch his
wounds. After Marko was on his back, the horse in fright flew off as fast
as he could, but Marko was not afraid and hung on until the horse spoke
and admitted that Marko was more of a hero than he and so would be
his master. Marko asked him then why he had been afraid and had fled,
adding: "I will be your master and you will be my faithful servant. Let's
go and fight the Turks and guard the highways from evil!"

Leaving aside Marko's final speech, let me begin to analyze the back-

---

[18] *B'lgarski junaški epos,* no. 143.

ground and meaning of the second and third parts. Are they simply fantastic tales of the supernatural, or is there more to them? Can we tell from where they may come and possibly speculate as to when?

The first step in our archaeology of a song is to ask what its meaning is and why it would ever have come into being. Some songs cry out for an explanation. For example, there is a short song in which Krali Marko saves the young of a falcon and later when he lies wounded and dying the falcon brings him water in its beak and saves his life. Usually such songs are ignored by critics, or it is implied that they are intended to show how the great hero was kind to animals. The folk have composed, as it were, a character study for their beloved hero. Or one could say simply that it is a nice little folksong. I do not find these answers satisfactory and, as I have said earlier, I have a conviction that most oral-traditional songs have a long history and deeply embedded meanings.

This song is widely known in both Serbo-Croatian and Bulgarian and has many variants.[19] The bird can be a falcon, a raven, or an eagle. In the Bulgarian versions it is usually an eagle. It is an easy jump from the song about the eagle to the one in which young Marko the calf-herder shaded the children of a *vila* (or *samodiva* in Bulgarian lore), who then suckled him and gave him strength and showed him how to gain his wondrous horse.

These stories explain how Marko obtained an animal helper in the form of a bird, how he is transformed in strength by the milk of a supernatural substitute mother, and how he obtains another animal helper and alter ego. Both animal helpers, as well as the supernatural female, are a means of conveyance in either air or on the ground, although Marko's horse is also aerial, as we see in other songs. These characteristics, animal counterpart spirits and means of air travel, suggest a shamanistic background as the proper sphere in which these elements will be found to be at home. Are there, in short, parallels in shamanic epics among peoples of a culture that had connection at some time with the Balkans? There are some central Asiatic narratives similar to what the proto-Bulgars might very well have known, and they provide us with evidence that points to more important meanings for these tales than a trite "character study" of Marko!

There is an incident in the Turkic Kirghiz epic of Er Töshtük, a part of the Manas cycle collected by Radloff and others later, and noted by

[19] See, for example, Karadžić, 1958, nos. 53 and 54, "Marko Kraljević i soko" (Marko Kraljević and the Falcon).

Hatto in his translation of *The Memorial Feast of Kökötöy Khan*, parts of which are strikingly like elements in our Marko songs.[20] The hero Er Töshtük encounters in the Underworld, where he has gone on a quest, a giant black eagle, which carries off in its talons the just-born foal of the spotted mare. The hero pursues the eagle to the base of the giant World Tree in the crown of which are the eaglets of the giant black eagle. They are threatened by the serpent at the foot of the tree. Er Töshtük cuts this dragon in two and then into six pieces, which he ties to himself and climbs the tree to feed the eaglets. The head of the dragon is left for the mother eagle. The eaglets tell the hero that it had been foretold they would be saved by Er Töshtük. "Are you he?" "I am." They tell him that they will save him whenever he wants to escape from this world; they say that whenever he has difficulties they will appear at his side. For forty years the dragon has killed the eagle's young and she has vowed this year to leave the world if it happens again. She returns amid great winds and cosmic disturbances and is surprised and rejoices to find her eaglets alive and happy. The mother eagle gulps down the dragon's head and the eaglets explain what happened, uncovering Er Töshtük from under their wings. Mother eagle immediately swallows him, too. The eaglets attack their mother, but she explains, "Mon intention, en avalant Töštük, est de lui arranger les os, en les faisant refondre, aussi solide que l'acier. . . . Ainsi Töštük sera invulnérable; il ne se noiera plus si on le jette à l'eau, l'épée ne pourra plus le transpercer si on l'enfrappe."[21] "My intention in swallowing Töštük is to rearrange his bones and to forge them anew, making them as solid as steel; he will no longer drown if he is thrown into the water, a sword will no longer be able to pierce him if he is struck." The mother eagle ends with, "Tenez! le voilà, votre Töštük!" "So, here is your Töštük!"

The mother eagle gives Er Töshtük a feather from her wing. If he is in danger he has only to burn the feather and she will appear before him. Later when he is in trouble she appears and carries him on her wings out of the Underworld, thus restoring him to the land of the living. One may recognize a not uncommon folktale element in this last flight.[22]

The striking shamanistic elements in this tale are significant. The first overall motif is that of the quest of the hero to the Underworld, and the

[20] Hatto, 1977, 1 n. 2. Boratav and Bazin, 1965, 162–168.
[21] Boratav and Bazin, 1965, 167–168.
[22] Thompson, 1955, vol. 1, B.450, Helpful birds; B.455.3, Helpful eagle; B.542.1.1, Eagle carries man to safety.

second is his acquiring of an animal or bird sponsor in that world, who gives him a talisman or support as a spirit counterpart to save his life and restore him with new powers to the world of living human beings. Very shamanistic indeed is the swallowing of the hero by the giant black eagle and the regurgitation. Her intention, she said, was to rearrange his bones and to forge them anew that he may be strong as steel and invulnerable! Anyone who has read Eliade's book on shamanism will recognize in this story the initiatory experience of a shaman.[23] In our South Slavic songs Marko has been transformed and has acquired vestiges of the age-old shamanistic concepts of being born again with new and otherworldly powers.

The elements are especially clear in the following strange and wonderful Bulgarian songs.[24] One of them is not about Krali Marko but concerns Ilija the hunter, who had gone hunting without success with his uncles and had become separated from them. Soon he came upon a three-headed serpent which had swallowed a stag up to its antlers. The stag asked Ilija to cut the serpent in two, promising him three loads of gold. The serpent asked him to cut off the stag's antlers so that the serpent might swallow him. But when Ilija discovers that the serpent's sisters are fierce snakes (what had he expected?) he cuts the serpent in two and releases the stag, which takes him to its house. After three days and three nights they are met by the stag's grooms (*konjari*) who tell the hunter Ilija to draw his sword and "break the green mountain wood (*da polomiš gora, bre, zelena*) so that it will be impossible to return afterwards (*oti ne mož posle da se varneš*)." Two days later they arrive where the stags are, where they stay for three days and three nights. The grooms advise Ilija to ask for the six-month-old foal, which he can take home with him, as a reward. The stag offers instead three loads of gold, but Ilija does not want anything but the six-month-old foal, because the foal is winged and can carry him home. The stag curses the grooms who taught Ilija the method of taking away his black winged horse.

This is an astonishing and extraordinary song, but some of its mystery, if not all, can be dispelled by reference to narratives like that I adduced from Er Töshtük. For example, the death and rebirth elements seen in the shallowing of the stag by the serpent and his eventual release are apparent. They are mingled with the straightforward element of slaying the dragon, like Er Töshtük's killing of the serpent at the foot of

[23] Eliade, 1964.
[24] *B'lgarski junaški epos*, 1971, nos. 162 and 163.

the World Tree. The hunter seems by chance to have penetrated to another world, as shown by his being lost. The boundaries of the other world are indicated (1) by the deserted glade (sunny place) where Ilija finds the serpent; (2) by the enigmatic statement of the grooms that he break the mountain woods because he will not return; and (3) by Ilija's flying off on his winged horse. These elements, including the helper role of the grooms, have shamanic overtones. The hero acquires his otherworldly horse, one of the several boons such heroes receive in addition to supernatural strength or invulnerability.

Another swallowing song tells how Marko has hunted a stag for three days and three nights, but all in vain. He cannot catch it. When he arrives at the Danube he finds women bleaching cloth and with their help he captures the stag which he presents to the sultan and is richly rewarded. On his return he shares the reward with the women who helped him and when he discovers that they are the captives of Filip the Hungarian, he frees them.

After three days and three nights in captivity the stag escapes by leaping over the high fence and seeks clover. When he has cropped his fill, he approaches a lake and after drinking his fill of the cold water, he falls sound asleep. A serpent comes and swallows him as far as his antlers, but can not swallow any further. Ilija the hunter passes by and the serpent asks him to cut off the stag's antlers so that he may swallow the rest of him. (It is not clear how he can talk with his mouth full.) The stag tells Ilija that if he cuts off the antlers his hand will wither, and then the serpent will swallow the stag, and then Ilija, and then whomever else he finds. "Rather, cut open the serpent and pull me out of him." This Ilija did.

A strange song, but actually somewhat simpler than the first. At least two provocative questions arise: What does it mean? Where does it come from? And one might add, when?

The notes to the 1971 text suggest that the stag represents all that is good and the serpent all that is evil. They tell us that Ilija is unknown as a hero of epic, and say that the song is a contamination of two songs into which the motif of Filip Madžarin has been injected from still a third.

For us the second part of the song is especially interesting. One might suggest that the capture of the stag and its escape is a multiform of the swallowing of the stag and its rescue by Ilija; the tradition has thus put together two multiforms of the same basic idea. On the surface the first part is a simple vignette of a stag hunt for which Marko is rewarded by the sultan. One might be puzzled by the role of the women in the stag's capture and by the fact that it is captured alive and not killed, and one suspects that it is not really a simple tale at all. Of course, if it were that kind of hunt, the second part of the song would not have been joined to the first.

The essence of the second part is the attempted swallowing of the stag by the serpent. This act links this song also with the episodes in Turkic epic in which the hero is swallowed by a monstrous creature and then regurgitated. The Bulgarian song in question, no. 162, is only a dim reflection.

The shamanic keys to this narrative and others like it might have come into Bulgaria and thence to other parts of the Balkans with the Osmanli Turks or simply—if any such avenues are straight and simple—through travel of Bulgarian merchants or soldiers to and from the Near East. My belief is, however, that if that were so, the "Turkish," as against Turkic, elements would be closer to the surface. There would be less of the enigmatic, and so a naive or tendentious reinterpretation would be unnecessary. For these reasons I believe that there is a distinct possibility that the elements in these songs came with some earlier Turkic people, perhaps even the proto-Bulgars. The Middle Ages gradually transformed these narrative elements from old beliefs, codified them in Slavic oral-traditional lore, and bequeathed them to us in many changing forms as jewels of many colors and facets across centuries, marked by the movements of armies, the rise and fall of dynasties, the investing and divesting of religions and heresies.

Let me end with Krali Marko, however, who has played a crucial role in the last stages of the process. It is not surprising, although somewhat paradoxical, that Krali Marko, pictured in the poetry later as the fighter against the Turks, and eventual defier of their overlordship, liberator of captives and slaves, should be the inheritor of one of the oldest layers of Bulgarian tradition. In them the mystery of the origin of his supernatural strength is plumbed, giving him the qualities and attributes that make it possible for him to fight with monsters and disturbers of order in society and the world, to free the stag from the serpent, and his people from tyranny.

CHAPTER 13

Central Asiatic
and Balkan Epic

A musical instrument, a story, a hero and his horse, horse culture, these and other items of narrative and social context unite the epics of the Balkans with some of those of Central Asia. It is possible that certain particulars actually came into Balkan epic from Central Asia, following the migrations of peoples as well as the caravan routes north of the Caspian and either skirting the northern shores of the Black Sea or crossing Asia Minor. Those are the logical ways, but there could have been others, depending perhaps on the kind of influence. A story and a musical instrument do not necessarily travel by the same path, although they might. In this paper I wish mainly to discuss some of the items of resemblance. I shall not pretend to do more than speculate on the reasons for the likenesses.

Let me begin with the musical instrument. The four instruments that are used in the Balkans to accompany story song are the *gusle,* the *g'dulka/lira,* which I class together as one, the *tambura,* and the *violin.* Of these, the instrument par excellence for the accompaniment of epic song

Published in *Fragen der mongolischen Heldendichtung,* Part 4, Vorträge des 5. Epensymposiums des Sonderforschungsbereichs 12, Bonn 1985, edited by Walther Heissig, *Asiatische Forschungen: Monographien zur Geschichte, Kultur und Sprache der Völker Ost- und Zentralasiens,* published by the Seminar für Sprach- und Kulturwissenschaft Zentralasiens der Universität Bonn, edited by Walther Heissig, Klaus Sagaster, Veronika Veit, Michael Weiers et al., Band 101 (Wiesbaden: Otto Harrassowitz, 1987), 288–320. Reprinted by permission of Otto Harrassowitz, Wiesbaden.

is the one-stringed *gusle*. It is not properly used for any other purpose, whereas the other three are used for other types of song as well.

In the musical *Atlas* (by Vertkov et al.) I found only one bowed monochord in any way like the *gusle*, namely the *dúč'k'* from the Panajci people, which is said to be like the two-stringed *hučír* of the Buryats.[1] According to the pictures, however, these do not look very much like the *gusle*, because the resonance bowl is a small round drum with a long neck. It is clear, on the other hand, that many of the two-stringed bowed instruments look more like the *gusle* than does the *dúč'k'*. I noted more than twenty such instruments in the *Atlas*. They are found in the Caucasus, along the southern regions of the Soviet Union from the Turkmen to the Buryats, and in the northern areas from Mari to the Nenets, the Hanti-Mansi, and even as far as the Čukči of the far northeast. The spread of these instruments covers Asiatic Russia, but they are concentrated in the Caucasus and the southern areas. In many regions these instruments are mentioned specifically as being used to accompany oral-traditional narrative song. Since it seems unlikely that the *gusle* traveled eastward from the Balkans, because the migrations of peoples were in the opposite direction, we may conclude that the *gusle* came from Asia. The word *gusle* is apparently Slavic, and this fact may indicate that the instrument was adopted by the Slavs, presumably fairly early, since the name is found in Russian as well, *gusli*, for a musical instrument of the zither type, similar to the Finnish *kantele*.

When one passes from extensive reading in the South Slavic epics, including the Moslem cycles from South Serbia, Bosnia, and Hercegovina, to a perusal of the epics of Central Asia, such as *The Book of Dede Korkut, Er Töshtük, Alpamyš, The Memorial Feast for Kökötöy-Khan,* or the various parts of the Gesar cycle from Mongolia and Tibet, one finds oneself in a familiar world—except that there seems to be more of the shamanistic, the fantastic, and of otherworldliness in many of the Asiatic stories than in those in the Balkans. As someone has remarked, in the South Slavic epics the heroes do not change shape, they change clothes. Changing clothes actually takes place in both epic traditions as a matter of disguise, which is of importance in the return stories, as we know from the *Odyssey*. It is perfectly true, also, that there are some South Slavic songs in which the hero changes shape! One is entitled

[1] *Atlas*, 1963: *dúč'k'*, 148, Ill. no. 746; *hučír*, 144, Ill. nos. 728–730.

"Zmija mladoženja" (The Serpent Bridegroom), which is admittedly a ballad rather than an epic.[2] The other is "Sekula se u zmaja pretvorio" (Sekula Transformed Himself into a Serpent).[3] The element of the shamanic and fantastic, I suggest, may be beneath the surface in some of the Balkan Slavic narratives. The epic stories of the two areas do indeed have a great deal in common and I shall attempt to illustrate that fact in what follows.

Return Songs

Much of the history of the "return song" embodied in *Alpamyš* and in "Bamsi Beyrek of the Grey Horse" in *The Book of Dede Korkut,* which I mentioned in the beginning of this paper, has already been written by Viktor Žirmunskij, and only its Balkan relatives need to be brought into connection with it. In addition to those two epic tales, I shall consider three South Slavic epics, "The Captivity of Janković Stojan," "Marko Kraljević and Mina of Kostur," and "The Captivity of Đulić Ibrahim."[4]

The first feature that strikes one in comparing the South Slavic songs with *Alpamyš* and with "Bamsi Beyrek of the Grey Horse" is that the Central Asiatic tales begin before the birth of the hero and tell the story of his life through his marriage. On the other hand, it is at the time of, or shortly after, the wedding of the hero that the South Slavic narratives pick up his adventures.[5]

This does not mean that there are no South Slavic accounts of the birth and early deeds of heroes. Although a number of songs recount early deeds, there are not many songs of birth, and they are not always associated with the heroes of return songs. The beginning of the first part of *Alpamyš,* for instance, in which two brothers are childless and ask for divine intervention to correct the situation, reminds one of the story of Smailagić Meho's birth in *The Wedding of Smailagić Meho.*

[2] E.g., Karadžić, 1958, nos. 11–12.
[3] Broz and Bosanac, 1896, no. 74.
[4] *Alpamyš,* 1949; *Dede Korkut,* 1974; Žirmunskij, 1960. I have included in Appendix 1 of this chapter synopses of these five return songs.
[5] Sometimes the narrative begins when the hero has been absent from home for many years, but the story of his departure at the time of his wedding is told in flashback. For a fuller study of the biographical pattern in Turkic and Central Asiatic epics see Laude-Circautas, 1979, 113–126.

Meho's uncle explains to him in the first assembly, when the young man is sad because he is not allowed to undertake great things:

> Your father married three times and your uncle four. God gave issue to neither of us, not even to your father, Hadji Smail—God preserve him!—except you alone. I, my son, have none. . . . We can scarcely wait to see that fulfillment of our desires, that we give the command over to you, that you take your place at the head of the thirty captains. We have been waiting to find a wife for you. We pray God that we both may see this, dear son, with our own eyes.[6]

There are many songs about weddings as well as about returns, yet I do not know of any return songs of which Smailagić Meho is the hero, nor do I know of any separate songs telling of the birth or, indeed, the early deeds or wedding of Đulić Ibrahim. On the other hand, there are separate songs in South Slavic of the birth of Marko Kraljević, of his early deeds, and even of his marriage, although they are not of the same kind as the other wedding songs in the South Slavic tradition.

I am acquainted with birth stories of two Christian heroes, Marko Kraljević and Zmaj Ognjeni Vuk, but I do not recall any concerning the birth of any of the Moslem heroes, other than the information just given about the birth of Smailagić Meho. This lack is strange, because of the strength of the Central Asiatic Turkic tradition. In one song, Marko's father, King Vukašin, marries a *vila,* a supernatural winged female, who lives in or near mountain lakes, and Marko was their child.[7] This gives him magical strength. That great strength is also accounted for in other songs by saying that he was suckled by a *vila.* In this way Marko's superhuman characteristics are explained.

The birth of Zmaj Ognjeni Vuk is also recounted in song.[8] He was born with the day-star on his forehead, the shining moon on his chest, a sword depicted on his arm, and, according to some versions, a tuft of wolf's fur on his shoulder. He grew rapidly, and when he was twelve, he was taller than a young man of twenty. In the case of both Marko and Zmaj Ognjeni Vuk there are also traditional songs of their weddings, but the songs of birth and wedding were never joined together, as was apparently the case with *Alpamyš* and "Bamsi Beyrek of the Grey

---

[6] Međedović, 1974a, 88.
[7] Bosanac, 1897, no. 1, "Rođenje Marka Kraljevića" (The Birth of Marko Kraljević).
[8] Broz and Bosanac, 1896, no. 66.

Horse."[9] A Bulgarian song tells of the life of Marko from his birth to the fulfillment of a prophecy at that time that he would "crush his father's bones," but this is in reality a story of his early deeds, not of his birth itself, and it ends with recognition between father and son, not with wedding. It is an integrated song, not the concatenation of separate songs.[10]

There is little need here to give further illustrations of the many wedding songs in both the Christian and the Moslem traditions. This group of songs is undoubtedly the largest and best-developed category in the tradition.

In some Central Asiatic traditions, I believe, there are also separate songs of birth and wedding, which have an independent existence outside of any long epic poem. This matter has been discussed convincingly by A. T. Hatto in respect to the Kirghiz epic. He writes:

> Generalisations as to the essentially "biographical" pattern of hero-tales anywhere from Turkey to the Chinese frontier narrating from the hero's birth, or even conception, to his achievement of earthly felicity, conflict with the facts of earlier Kirghiz tradition, which deals in self-contained actions excerpted mostly from the youth or maturity not of a hero or pair of heroes but of a whole group of heroes from both sides of a divide. . . . Indeed, Radlov especially notes that his recording of "The birth of Manas" rests on an improvisation undertaken at his request. The births of Manas's son and grandson, Semetey and Seytek, though narrated in the two *Semetey* poems, do not launch these poems, nor are the careers of these two heroes co-extensive with the two poems.[11]

The presence of independent birth songs and wedding songs in both the Balkan and the Central Asiatic traditions raises the question in my mind, therefore, as to whether the first parts of *Alpamyš* and of "Bamsi Beyrek of the Grey Horse" are in reality made up of one or more separate songs that have been put together, perhaps by the singing tradition itself, that is, by the traditional singers themselves, or by collectors and/or editors. "Bamsi Beyrek of the Grey Horse" may be in a

[9] For songs of Marko's wedding see, e.g., Bosanac, 1897, nos. 19–21, and Karadžić, 1958, no. 55; for the wedding of Zmaj Ognjeni Vuk see Karadžić, 1932–36, vol. 6 (1935), no. 35.

[10] *BNT*, vol. 1, 1961, "Krali Marko i tri narečnici," "King Marko and the Three Soothsayers," 116–123.

[11] Hatto, 1979, 95–96.

different category because of its position in *The Book of Dede Korkut,* but I wonder whether the length of the *Alpamyš* epic may be the result of the concatenation of separate oral-traditional songs, in a manner similar to that in which the Finnish *Kalevala* came into existence.

The wedding song proper, that is, the second part of the Central Asiatic epics, with which we are concerned here, and the first part of the South Slavic epics, contain the following items.

1. *The hero is captured with a companion, or companions, at the time of his wedding, or soon thereafter.* The only exception is the song of "Marko and Mina of Kostur," in which nothing is said of how long Marko has been married. Moreover, Marko was not captured. He went away to war at the summons of the sultan. It is true also that Alpamyš is not captured immediately after his wedding.

2. *The hero is in prison for a long time and is presumed dead.* Prison is not a proper term for the situation of Janković Stojan and Smiljanić Ilija in "The Captivity of Janković Stojan." In "Bamsi Beyrek of the Grey Horse" the presumption of death is aided by Yaltajuk's presenting of false evidence of Beyrek's death.

3. *The hero receives news that his wife is about to be married again.* The only exception is "The Captivity of Janković Stojan." In "Marko Kraljević and Mina of Kostur" Marko's wife has been captured and his old mother trampled on; later Mina asks Marko, disguised as a monk, to marry Marko to the captured wife.

4. *The jailer's daughter helps the hero to escape.* The exceptions are "The Captivity of Janković Stojan," and "Marko Kraljević and Mina of Kostur," that is, the South Slavic Christian tradition as represented by those songs. In "The Captivity of Đulić Ibrahim" the hero is actually released by the governor of Zadar, but at the instigation of the governor's wife. For that, perhaps not very cogent, reason I have classified it in this respect with the Central Asiatic versions.

5. *The hero encounters several people before reaching home.* Sometimes they are at the border, sometimes they are near his house. Only in "Đulić" is he accosted by border guards, whom he kills if they do not respect the passport given him by the governor. Such border guards are important in the story, because they represent boundaries between the world of the enemy and one's home world, perhaps even boundaries between a world of death and the real world. In "Janković Stojan" and in "Marko" the hero meets no one until he is close to home, where Stojan meets his mother in the vineyard, and Marko his wife at a spring.

Beyrek meets first a minstrel with whom he exchanges clothes and lute for his horse(!), and then he encounters shepherds making piles of stones to throw at the usurping bridegroom. These two incidents are within Oghuz territory but are not near his own tent. It is worth noting that in one version of Ugljanin's "Đulić Ibrahim" the singer represents Đulić as killing the third border guard who challenges him and as changing clothes with the dead man. When Bamsi Beyrek reaches his tents, he meets first his little sister at a spring and then his older sisters. Alpamyš meets his enemy Ultan's caravan drivers, who tell him of the usurper's actions, and he kills them. In the *Alpamyš* epic these men are not guarding the border, as are the men in Đulić's song, but there may be some correspondence here. Alpamyš then meets his sister with the camels, one of which recognizes its returned master, and she almost recognizes him. And after that he meets up with Kultaj, his old servant, with whom he changes clothes. This reminds us, of course, of Beyrek and of Đulić in one version, as just mentioned. The changing of clothes is significant for disguise, as I have mentioned earlier. Without disguise of some sort there would be no testing or recognition. Alpamyš finally meets some simple women just before getting to the feast and he plays a trick on them. I do not really understand this incident, but it is in the same position in the return pattern as Marko's wife at the spring, Stojan's mother in the vineyard, and Beyrek's sisters, young and old.

6. *In the hero's house, or at the wedding feast, he meets an old retainer, his mother, his sister, his horse (or other animal), his wife, and the usurping bridegroom and his company of wedding guests.*

a. Only in "Đulić" does the hero meet an old *retainer*, Huso the steward, who answers the gate when Đulić knocks, and with whom he has his first conversation upon reaching home. In *Alpamyš*, the hero meets Kultaj, who would fit the pattern, but this was on the way home, not actually in the house itself or at a feast. One is, of course, reminded of Eumaeus in the *Odyssey*.

b. The hero's *mother* is met first outside in the vineyard in "Stojan," but she comes into the house later, recognizes her son and dies. In "Đulić" mother and sister together listen to the hero's song during which recognition takes place, and the mother dies. In "Beyrek" the mother is not singled out from "Beyrek's parents" on his return, although his father is. In *Alpamyš*, the hero sees his mother, his father, and little Jadgar doing menial tasks or being mistreated when he returns, but no recognition takes place. Strangely enough, the mother plays no great role in the scenes with the returning hero in the Turkic (that is, Uzbek and Oghuz) songs considered here, but she plays a large role in both "Stojan" and "Đulić." The Marko song is somewhat different from the others that we have been looking at, and the hero's return is not to his own house but to Mina's, where his wife is being held captive.

c. The *sister* in "Stojan" plays an intermediary role. When Stojan's wife recognizes her returned husband from the song he sings, she tells his sister, who greets her brother. In "Đulić" the wife's role is very important. Together with his mother she recognizes the returned hero when he sings his song, and she helps him in arranging other events. In the Central Asiatic epics the sisters are not met in the house, it seems, and they have been considered in the previous section.

d. One of the most interesting characters in the recognition scene is an *animal*. Only in "Đulić" does the hero's recognition by his horse occur during the series of recognitions at home. Marko's Šarac comes home from the army with him, but it is the horse who is recognized by the hero's captive wife. This is a different, although perhaps related, motif. In "Beyrek" the gray horse recognizes its master after the hero has escaped with the help of the jailer's daughter. Alpamyš is recognized by an old camel herded by the hero's sister Kaldyrgač, but this occurs on the way home and not in the main recognition scene; and the sister's near recognition of her brother is not encouraged by Alpamyš. Recognition by an animal, whether at home, or on the way home, or at the time of escape, is present in three of the five songs considered here, and recognition of the animal itself, is present in one other. The two Central Asiatic texts and the Moslem South Slavic text contain it. This may be significant, especially in view of other evidence for the importance of the hero's horse in the traditional cultures of Central Asia and the South Slavic regions, as I shall soon demonstrate.

e. Recognition by the *wife* is crucial to the story, and is found in all five of our texts, and, of course, in the *Odyssey*.

7. *The returned hero mingles with the wedding guests and takes part in activities with them before recognition.* In "Stojan" he sings his song to them, and his wife overhears it. Marko goes to Mina's tower, drinks with him, and cuts off his head. Đulić, disguised as a prisoner, asks alms to be used for ransom, and after various recognitions, he puts on his best clothes and appears to the wedding guests. He insults Mujo and Halil, who is about to attack Đulić, when Tale intervenes and reconciles them. Disguised as a minstrel Beyrek joins the wedding feast, sings, and picks

out Lady Chichek from other ladies. Alpamyš too joins the feast in disguise, observes the woes of his family and friends, and engages in a contest with the bow, which he wins using his grandfather's bow. This item is, of course, very much present in the *Odyssey*.

8. *The suitor receives the hero's sister for his bride, or receives justice.* The former is true in "Stojan" and "Đulić," the latter in "Marko," "Beyrek," *Alpamyš,* and the *Odyssey*.

9. *The hero returns to the place where he was held prisoner, rescues his companions who are still there, and destroys the city.* This does not apply to Stojan, because his fellow captives escaped with him, and they were not really in prison to begin with. It does not apply to Marko either, because it was his wife who was captured, not he. It does apply to Đulić, who returns with Halil—who was part of the ransom price—to Zadar. They kill the governor, and rescue the other prisoners. It applies also to Beyrek, who, with the Oghuz, killed the leaders of the Infidel, stormed Bayburt Castle, and destroyed the church. They also freed the other prisoners who had been with Beyrek. In *Alpamyš,* after full recognition of the hero Alpamyš, and the meting out of justice to Ultan and his supporters, Bajsary returns from the land of the Kalmyks. This return might well be considered as the return of prisoners. But the clearest correspondences are between Đulić and Beyrek, as one might have expected.

Although many correspondences exist between the South Slavic traditional return songs and Homer's *Odyssey,* there are also more than a few similarities between them and epics from Central Asia. Both the capture of the hero and the timing of it, namely on the occasion of his wedding, are shared with Central Asiatic epic rather than with Homer. The presence of the hero's sister in the epic, and the role that she plays, are not Homeric. The horse as the animal in the story is Central Asiatic, although the camel in *Alpamyš,* which has been lying around for seven years and jumps up to circle around the hero, is faintly reminiscent of the dog Argos in the *Odyssey,* who, however, can do nothing more than wag his tail. One must study the texts more carefully before coming to anything like a conclusion, but one might suggest that in the Slavic Balkans there took place a meeting of stories and story elements telling about the return of a hero as old as the Homeric poems with newer arrivals in the peninsula, probably also of great age. What I have tried to stress in my consideration of return songs in this paper is the existence of a cultural continuum, of which these tales and the manner of their telling are a part, stretching from Mongolia to the Balkans and beyond.

Bride Capture and Rescue Songs

The return song is by no means the only type of story shared by both central Asiatic and Balkan epics. Another notable tale concerns obtaining a bride. This is, as we have seen, related to the return songs, of which it may be a part, but it also has a life of its own. In reading *Ostjakische Heldenlieder* I was struck by several of its stories of bride capture.[12] *The Book of Dede Korkut* has three tales of the capture of a father who is rescued by his son, one of the capture of son, mother, and wife who are rescued by their father, a wedding song, and the famous return song of "Bamsi Beyrek of the Grey Horse," which we have already discussed. All these types are common in the Balkan Slavic epic traditions. Rescue songs form a very large group in both Christian and Moslem traditions in the Balkans.[13]

In the Uzbek epic of *Rawšan* (which belongs to the Kurroglou cycle, since Rawšan is Kurroglou's grandson) the first part of the story tells of Rawšan's wedding and the second part relates how his father rescued him and his comrades from captivity just at the moment when Rawšan is about to be executed because he will not change his faith.[14] In this epic a song of gaining a bride has been merged with a song of rescue. The motif of execution when a Moslem will not become a Christian is common also in the Moslem Balkan songs. In the song that tells of Bojičić Alija rescuing the children of Alibey, the two sons are to be

[12] Erdelyi, 1972.

[13] I have written elsewhere of rescue songs in the Bulgarian tradition, and there is a listing, with synopses, in Appendixes III and IV of Lord, 1960, of return and return-rescue songs in the Parry Collection. One of the best of the songs in which a son and nephew rescues his father and uncle is "Omer Hrnjičić Rescues His Father and Uncle." For a study of the relationship of this song to medieval and modern Greek ballads see my article "La poésie orale des peuples du sud-est européen entre le passé et le présent," which was read at the Fifth International Congress for the Study of Southeastern Europe, Belgrade, September 11–17, 1984.

[14] Reichl, 1985a; see especially 23–29; he mentions the work of Matija Murko and South Slavic epic on page 27. Reichl has pointed out that many of the motifs in *Rawšan* have parallels not only in other Asiatic epics and in folklore, but also in medieval European epic and romance. Walther Heissig of the Seminar für Sprach- und Kultur-Wissenschaft Zentralasiens der Universität Bonn, in an earlier article, has indicated parallels between central Asiatic epic and medieval Germanic epic. See Heissig, 1983b, 17.

impaled because their sister will not become a Christian.[15] Bojičić Alija arrives just in time to prevent the execution, and he is aided by the timely arrival of an army from the Bosnian Border.

Catalogues in Central Asiatic and Balkan Slavic Epic

Catalogues are characteristic of oral-traditional epic, although they may be found elsewhere also. One of the most common forms of them is the catalogue of people invited to a meeting of some sort. In its fullest form it has three parts. In the first, the summoner gives the message to a messenger; in the second, the messenger delivers the message to each of the designated recipients; in the third part, the invited people arrive at the scene of assembly.

In Međedović's *The Wedding of Smailagić Meho*, Hasan pasha Tiro writes (or dictates) invitations to a series of leaders of the Bosnian Border to come to Kanidža for the wedding of Smailaga's son. A section at the end of this part of the catalogue is devoted to the inviting of a special person, Tale of the Lika. The second part of the theme, the delivering of the messages, is missing, but the distribution of the letters had been taken care of at the beginning of the letter writing as follows: "Then the twelve imperial scribes knelt at the tables among the beys. . . . And the pasha ordered his fifty warriors to prepare their fifty Bedouin mares and the imperial captains to distribute the letters."[16]

In the third part of the sequence of elements in the catalogue, the chief men arrive with their contingents, and they are described in great detail as they descend from the surrounding mountains. At last all are gathered except for Tale of the Lika. The leaders decide to wait for him, and special treatment is given to his arrival.

A similar type of catalogue series occurs in the Kirghiz epic about the memorial feast for Kökötöy-Khan.[17] First, Bok-murun gives instructions to Jaš-aydar as to whom to seek and what to say to each of the heroes being invited to the memorial feast. There are special instructions on how to approach the next to the last hero named in the catalogue, Er

---

[15] Parry, 1954, no. 24, "Bojičić Alija Rescues Alibey's Children," Parry Text no. 670, recorded November 22, 1934, in Novi Pazar (Milman Parry Collection, Widener Library, Harvard University, Cambridge, Mass.).

[16] Međedović, 1974a, 166–167.

[17] Hatto, 1977, 17–35.

Manas: "Lest he put you to death and slaughter Maniker [Manas's steed], be sure to greet him on foot, taking care to dismount before approaching him, and salute him with a lowered voice!"

In the second part, we see Jaš–aydar go to each of the chieftains and deliver the message, beginning with Er Košoy and ending with Er Manas, although there are lacunae in the manuscript in this second list. The encounter of Jaš–aydar with Manas is special, since Manas's retinue is about to kill the messenger at the hero's bidding, when Jaš–aydar tells him: "From the nest on the thundering cliff I was the Only One—why are you going to kill me, why do you press on your mark? Do not cut my body to pieces, spare my fair life, fragile as a hair! If you slay me, my wrong will stab your eyes! From the nest I was a One-and-only One, whiter than an egg!" Manas replies: "Of late, when I overpowered the ten sons of Urus-khan and made them captive I was reminded of what it means to be an Only One. Never slay Only Ones, never put out their fires!"

The third part of the series of catalogues, namely the arrival of the guests, is shortened in the Kirghiz text, as follows:

> They were announcing the beginning of milking, and with the coming of the dappled snow-and-thaw of early Spring, all-sorts-of-heroes and all-sorts-of-steeds were arriving in an unbroken stream. The Infidel numerous as hairs in a cow's coat, followed by the Faithful, arrived at the trot. Bok-murun there was thinking "How could Manas not come?" and stood there with downcast gaze. "Will not Manas in his rage come and make my children cry, come and make my mares run wild? I'll go out and meet Manas, I'll waylay him with gifts of honour!"

There follows a lengthy description of the meeting with Manas. These series of catalogues, in spite of their cultural differences, are built on the same frame, including the special treatment of the most significant of the heroes invited.

The Hero and His Horse

At the beginning of this paper I mentioned that one of the items that would take our attention consisted of a hero and his horse. I was thinking of Marko Kraljević and his horse Šarac, who could fly and talk, and who was in reality the alter ego of the hero. Marko is a Christian hero, although he is in the service of the sultan, but he has a counterpart in the Moslem tradition, Mujo Hrnjičić of Kladuša, the *sirdar* (commander-in-chief) of the Border, who has a winged white horse (a *đogat*), which also has the power of speech but does not have a special name. These two horses, as you have already surmised, have a number of illustrious counterparts in Central Asiatic epic.

In her study of the subject, Veronika Veit considers the concept of the hero–horse-as-alter-ego on three levels, (1) the economic, or the real level; (2) the poetic, or the literary level; and (3) the religious, or the cultic level.[18] Marko's steed has existence on both the poetic and the cultic level, in that the horse Šarac not only inhabits the oral-traditional poetry, but also plays a role in Marko's life which, to my mind, has cultic overtones. For example, when the time came for Marko to die, his death was foretold by his horse's stumbling, and Šarac was with him when he died.[19]

One of the characteristics mentioned by Veit, the simultaneous birth of hero and horse, does not seem to hold for the South Slavic horses with which I am acquainted.[20] She also adduces the praises of the horse, which are a topos in the Central Asiatic epic, and which do not, to the best of my memory, exist in the South Slavic traditional poetry. The closest to them in the Balkan Slavic songs is the description of the horse at the time of its being prepared for the hero, or when it is led forth for him to mount.

Perhaps the closest parallel to Marko is the Turkic hero Kurroglou. Marko's bushy eyebrows, his long black moustaches, his prodigious appetite for food and drink, his enormous strength, his mace, all remind us of Kurroglou, and Šarac makes us think of Kurroglou's chestnut horse Kyrat. Another hero and horse pair that immediately comes to mind is Alpamyš and his winged Bajčibar, like Šarac, piebald. Both Kyrat and Bajčibar were unpromising foals. Kyrat's extraordinary qualities were understood by Kurroglou's father. One cannot forget the scene in the Uzbek version of *Alpamyš* in which the hero, under the direction of Kultaj, chooses, against his better judgment, the horse which fate had three times indicated to be his. It was his sister, Kal-

---

[18] Veit, 1985.

[19] Karadžić, 1958, no. 73, "Smrt Marka Kraljevića" (The Death of Marko Kraljević).

[20] There is something similar, however, in Old Welsh tradition. See Ford, 1977, 52–56, concerning the birth of Gwri Golden-Hair, son of Pwyll, Prince of Dyfed.

dyrgač, who confirmed the excellence of the unlikely Bajčibar. Great Meherr, the father of David of Sassoun, in the Armenian epic, also chose an unpromising foal who was later to become the great horse Jalali. In South Slavic epic the horses of Marko and Mujo Hrnjičić belong in the same category, and their tales are similar to those of some of the most famous Central Asiatic steeds.

Another South Slavic Moslem hero with a winged chestnut horse (a *dorat*) is Đerđelez Alija of Sarajevo. I note, by the way, that Geser's horse in all parts of the Mongolian Geser cycle is—to quote Walther Heissig—a "magischer Rotbraune" (a magic chestnut).[21] The story is told that when Đerđelez Alija was a youth, he had saved the young of a *vila* from the heat of the sun (a similar story is told of Marko Kraljević), and she had rewarded him by telling him to buy a certain mare with an unpromising looking chestnut foal on the next market-day. This he did and kept it in the stable with his master's stallion. When the foal was one year old it looked like a three-year-old. As the foal grew bigger and stronger, the master's stallion grew weaker. One night Alija watched in the stable and saw that his foal had wings, one of which he would rest on the back of the stallion, which could not stand the weight. The next day Alija moved his horse to another place, and the stallion regained its former strength.[22]

Other stories and songs tell how Marko Kraljević and Đerđelez Alija met and became blood-brothers; these stories emphasize a lasting similarity between the two heroes. As one might have expected, similar stories are told of the provenance of Marko's horse Šarac. In a Bulgarian epic a *samodiva,* the equivalent in Bulgarian lore to a *vila* in Serbian and Croatian, tells Marko to climb a leafless tree and when a mangy horse comes and scratches its sores on the tree, he is to mount him. The horse takes Marko flying in an effort to unseat him, but finally tells Marko that he (the horse) is a hero but that Marko is a greater hero and he will obey him as his master. This was the horse Šarkolija.[23]

Horses and Horse Culture

The *Memorial Feast for Kökötöy-Khan* provides also excellent descriptions of horses and of groups of horses, because the main event of the

[21] Heissig, 1983a, 461.
[22] Hörmann, 1933, 1:589–591.
[23] *BNT,* vol. 1, 1961.

feast is to be a horse race, or horse races.[24] Although South Slavic really has nothing quite comparable to the accounts in that extraordinary document, horse races occur in the South Slavic Moslem epics. Nevertheless, one song collected by David Bynum and myself in 1964 from Avdo Kevelj in Odžak, Hercegovina, is devoted entirely to an elaborate horse race for the hands of two captive maidens.[25] It has 1,434 lines. A. T. Hatto has published an article about horses in the Kirghiz epic and in the *Iliad*.[26]

Horses play a large role in the South Slavic epic and reflect a horse culture that is not native to the Balkans. This can be seen very clearly from the fact that most of the words for the several kinds of horses are of Turkic, Arabic, or Persian origin. For example, in addition to *šarac* (piebald), from Slavic *šar* (spotted) plus the Slavic ending *-ac,* or possibly combined with Turkish *at* (horse), there are *dorat* (chestnut), from Turkish *doru* (brown) and Turkish *at* (horse), *đogat* (white), from Turkish *gök* (light blue, azure, bright) and Turkish *at* (horse), *kulaš* (mouse gray, ash gray, color of lead), from Turkish *kula* (brown, reddish, dun, sorrel) and Turkish *at* (horse), *alat* (strawberry roan), from Turkish *al* (light red, rose colored) from Persian *al* (light red, rose colored) and Turkish *at* (horse), *bedevija* (Bedouin mare), from Turkish *bedevi* (Bedouin, nomad), from Arabic *badawiyy, badawi* (desert, wilderness, Bedouin), *menzilski konj* (post-horse), (Turkish *menzil-beygiri*), from Turkish *menzil* (halting-place), from Arabic *manzil* (place where one dismounts, unsaddles), or simply *menzil* (post-horse), and so forth.

Karl Reichl quotes Chodzko's comments on Kurroglou's relationship to his horse, Kyrat, and points to the model description of Rawšan's horse, Džijranquš, in the fifth set of verse passages in the epic.[27] The passage is too long to quote in its entirety, but here is a sample, in Reichl's German translation:

> Höre die vielstimmige Musik!
> Schwere Tage stehen dem Jungling jetzt bevor.
> Seht den Helden Rawšan-Chan,
> Kraftvoll geht er in den Pferdestall.

[24] More on the horse, horse culture, and related subjects can be found in Lord, A., 1972, especially 301–307.
[25] "Halil izbavlja na košiji dvije šćeri Osman Alibega" (Halil in a Horse Race Rescues the Two Daughters of Osman Alibey), Lord and Bynum, 1964, 10. This collection is presently with the Milman Parry Collection in Widener Library, Harvard University.
[26] Hatto, 1980, 179–281.
[27] Reichl, 1985a, 56–59.

5   Die Liebe ist Bek Rawšan ins Herz gedrungen,
     Sein Kragen ist nass von den Tränen, die ihm aus den Augen
         fliessen.
     Seht jetzt den Helden Bek Rawšan,
     Kraftvoll geht er zum Pferd.

     Schaut jetzt auf Rawšan, das unerfahrene Kind;
10   Es möge dem jungen Knaben kein Unglück zustossen.
     Betrachtet den Helden Bek Rawšan,
     Er fuhrt Džijranquš ins Freie.

     Er glaubt, dass die vergängliche Welt vergehen wird,
     Ein kleines Kind spricht vielerei.
15   Er führt Džijranquš ins Freie,
     Nimmt ihn und bindet ihn an einem Holzpflock fest.

     Jetzt füllen sich dem Kind beide Augen mit Tränen,
     Der Jüngling entblösst das geflügelte Ross.
     Den Sattelgurt und die Decke des schnellfüssigen Pferds knüpft er
         auf.
20   Über die Ohren zieht er die goldbestickte Pferdedecke.

     Der Gärtner pflückt die reine Rose des Gartens;
     Die Helden bahnen sich an schweren Tagen eine Bahn.
     Den Sattelgurt und die Decke des schnellfüssigen Pferds knüpft er
         auf.
     Er nimmt geschwind von oben die Pferdedecke weg.

25   Die Gläubigen setzen ihr Vertrauen nicht allein in das Leben;
     Rot färbt sich im Tod der Glaubenszeuge in seinem Blut.
     Mit einem Besen aus Rosenholz, einem Striegel aus Gold in der
         Hand
     Scheuert er den Körper von Džijran.

     Wer fern der Heimat reitet, erduldet Leid;
30   Der Jigit, der den Renner bestiegen hat, vollbringt Heldentaten.
     Bek Rawšan legt dem Pferd auf die Kruppe
     Die weiche, dicke Schabracke aus reiner Seide.

     Weit von der Heimat blicken die Beks durchs Fernrohr.
     Die Meister betätigen die Axt, die Klinge.
35   Auf das Pferd legt Bek Rawšan,
     Wirft geschwind die samtene Schabracke.

In seinem Tun zeigt Bek Rawšan Standhaftigkeit,
Als Lieblingskind aufgewachsen, fehlt es ihm nicht an
    Starrköpfigkeit.
Betrachtete jetzt den Helden Bek Rawšan-Chan,
40   Auf die Schabracke legt er den Sattelgurt.

Auf Čambil schlägt Bek Rawšan das Herz in der Brust,
Seht jetzt, wie er von dem Helden Awaz gekränkt wurde.
Schaut den Herrn Bek Rawšan an,
Er legt die Schabracke aus Biberpelz auf.

45   Die Mullas lesen das 'i' und das 'a',
Die Meister betätigen die Axt, das Beil.
Auf den Falken legt Bek Rawšan
Den goldenen Sattelbogen, den silbernen Sattel.[28]

The song has 99 lines. After the saddle, Bek Rawšan places the two golden stirrups at Džijranquš's side and fastens the silken saddle-girth. There follows the horse-blanket with golden fringe; the blanket reaches to Džijranquš's fetlocks. Next comes the crupper of rhinoceros leather, folded twelve times. On the horse's flanks Rawšan places the reins, which reach to his hoofs, and on his breast a golden plastron. He puts a neck ornament on Džijranquš's long neck, and over his head he places a bridle with forty decorative spheres. Finally Rawšan girds on his sword, mounts, and departs. Such a passage is indeed difficult to match!

Some of the most elaborate descriptions of a horse in the South Slavic epic songs show a similar type of expansion of detail. For example, here is a passage from Avdo Međedović's *The Wedding of Smailagić Meho* in the Milman Parry Collection.[29] Meho's uncle is telling him in the opening assembly of the favor with which the sultan had held him since the boy's birth:

When your thirteenth year dawned, my son, the imperial chamberlain came from the halls of Sultan Sulejman, bringing an Egyptian chestnut horse for you, one that had been bought from the Shah of Egypt. Golden-winged, its mane reached to its hoofs. Then a two-year-old, it was like a horse of seven. The trappings were fashioned in Afghanistan especially for the chestnut steed when it grew up. The saddle was decorated with coral; the upper portion was woven of pure gold. Beneath the saddle an

---

[28] Ibid., 56–57. For the remainder of the song see Appendix 2 at the end of this chapter.
[29] Međedović, 1974a and 1974b.

Osmanli cloth, not like any other, my son, but of Syrian damask silk, that it should not chafe the horse's back. The saddle of gold, the trappings of gold. On the Egyptian chestnut horse next to his skin are silken girths, soft silk that they may not chafe his flesh. The upper part of them is ornamented with pearl. If God grants, my son, you shall see them when you become the alajbey of the Border. It is now nineteen years, my dear son, since that day when you were born, and this is the ninth year since the chestnut steed with its trappings came to you as a gift. Whatever the sultan could think of by way of trappings for the steed was prepared for him.[30]

After the assembly has decided to send Meho on a mission to Buda, Meho returns home, and eventually his father has this wonderful steed prepared for his son's journey. The following description of the trappings as they are placed on Meho's horse merits comparison with that of the caparisoning of Rawšan's horse Džijranquš quoted earlier:

First they took a Hungarian saddlecloth and placed it on the chestnut steed. On this they set the coral saddle, which was adorned round about with gold. The coral was decorated with Egyptian agates of various colors, one of which was worth a golden florin. The gold was yellow, white was the pearl. Among the pearls were agates, some blue, some green, some yellow, and some red. On the background of gold and pearl the colors of the agates were enhanced. On the front of the saddle instead of a pommel there was a sphere of gold worth a chest of ducats. The holsters for his pistols were of Syrian silk, embroidered with white pearl. In them they put his two Venetian guns, covered with gold. Their cover was adorned with so many golden sequins that you could scarcely see the Venetian cloth; around them was a border of Venetian ducats. Over the saddle were four girths and a fifth beneath to protect the horse's flesh, whenever the steed jumped or galloped. All four were woven of silk and the one next to the horse's body was of black marten fur, while the outer ones were adorned with pearl. The stewards tightened and buckled the girths and adjusted the crupper on his back; the crupper of silk was ornamented with ducats and a moon-plate made of gold glittered on it. The two shabracques were of gold and down the horse's breast hung shining bosses. On them diamonds flashed. He fastened the martingales

---

[30] Međedović, 1974a, 89–90; 1974b, lines 783–814. This passage has been quoted also in "Avdo Međedović, Guslar," Chapter 4 in this volume; it and the following passages from "The Wedding of Smailagić Meho" are repeated here so that they may the more easily be compared with the quotations from Rawšan.

from the girths to the double-ring snaffles; all the fastenings were of gold. Next came the golden breast-strap. Over his mane from ears to shoulder they cast a piece of embroidered mesh from Egypt, fastening it under the pommel of the saddle. The embroidery was of gold. Through it the dark mane hung, shining through the gold like the moon through the branches of a pine tree. They brought then a golden bridle and attached the Egyptian reins to the four chains on the bit that fitted over the horse's teeth and were fastened under its neck. All four were ornamented with pearl and the bridle beside them was of gold. Down each cheek flashed a band of pure gold, the two fastened by a clasp between the ears. Atop the clasp shone the morning star and in its center a diamond. There is no darkness before the horse, but midnight is as bright as midday.

My God, thanks be to thee for all things. When they had harnessed his mighty steed with golden saddle and golden shabracques, with girths and martingales and shining bosses on its chest, a golden mesh over its mane and the golden breast-straps, the bridle, and bands covering him from the tips of his ears to the bottom of his cheeks, no hair was visible except a bit of tail, no mane at all. The yellow gold confined and covered it.

The passage concludes with the following:

The horse was like a mountain *vila,* and people say that it had wings. It knew not how to speak and yet it knew the way to go. When he flared his nostrils and snorted, he was so strong and fiery that from them burst forth smoke and blue flame.[31]

The smoke and flame are found also in the description of the horse ridden by the captain of the contingent assigned to escort Fatima in a coach as she is being taken away to be wed to General Peter:

He was leader of a hundred men and rode a chestnut stallion, with imperial Osmanli saddle, studded shabraques on either side, shining bosses down his chest, and martingales from the snaffle beneath his neck. His reins were decorated with wild animals, especially a wolf and a fox. What a cloud of smoke surrounded the steed! From his nostrils spouted smoke and blue flame, as though fires were burning within him. They lighted up the coats of the fox and the gray wolf. Great was the noise of the horses' hoofs, still greater the rumbling of the wondrous coach, and greatest of all was that of the imperial captain![32]

[31] Međedović, 1974a, 105–106; 1974b, lines 1885–1974.
[32] Međedović, 1974a, 119; 1974b, lines 2956–2972.

The fire-breathing horse is also found in Mongolian Geser epics, and elsewhere. From Heissig's *Geser-Studien* I quote:

> Aus den vier Hufen des bläulichgrauen Rosses, das sie ritt,
> Quoll der Rauch, und beim Laufen blitzte
> Aus seinem Maul und seinen Nüstern Feuer.[33]

> From the four hoofs of the light gray horse that she was riding
> Welled forth smoke, and as it ran there flashed
> Fire from its mouth and nostrils.

Thus was described the mount of Alu Mergen in the Peking manuscript.

It behooves us to make a few comments on the two descriptions from Uzbek and from Serbo-Croatian which were just quoted. Clearly, some elements in the South Slavic passage belong to the Balkans. At least I believe that references to a "Hungarian saddlecloth," to "two Venetian guns," "Venetian cloth," and "Venetian ducats" seem to belong more properly to the Balkans than to Central Asia. "Egyptian agates," "Syrian silk," "mesh from Egypt," and "Egyptian reins" might also be peculiar to the eastern Mediterranean area.

It is clear as well that some elements in *Rawšan* are peculiar to the style of Uzbek epic, such as the general character of the first two lines of each stanza, which give a very special atmosphere to the poetry. More specifically, references, for example, to Čagataj, the son of Dschingis Chan, in line 73, or to Nu in line 96, and to Čambil in lines 89 and 99, are appropriate only in Central Asia, but would be strange in the Balkans.

Other similarities between the two descriptions, however, call for comment. The shabracque of pure silk (but not that of beaver), the tightening of the saddle girths, the horse-blankets, including the covering that reaches to the horse's fetlocks, the plastron on the horse's breast, with its ornaments, all these and more are familiar in the Balkan epic. The trappings are the same in both traditions, and on the whole the order of putting them on the horse is the same. We are dealing with a basic common tradition, adapted to different cultural backgrounds. Moreover, a device of narrative in which the teller speaks to the audience and invites them to listen, or to see the hero's action is shared by both traditions. In Reichl's German (line 3), for example, we have:

[33] Heissig, 1983a, 456–457.

"Seht den Helden Rawšan-Chan!" (See the heathen Rawšan-Chan!); in line 7, "Seht jetzt den Helden Bek Rawšan!" (Now see the hero Bek Rawšan!); in line 9, "Schaut jetzt auf Rawšan, das unerfahrene Kind!" (Now look upon Rawšan, the inexperienced boy!); in line 11, "Betrachtet den Helden Bek Rawšan!" (Now observe the hero Bek Rawšan!); and in line 39, "Betrachtete jetzt den Helden Bek Rawšan-Chan!" (Now observe the hero Bek Rawšan-Chan!). This construction is found frequently also in South Slavic epic.

The Nurture of Horses

In the South Slavic songs the description of the way in which horses are nurtured is reminiscent of Central Asiatic epic. For example, in the Moslem epics among the South Slavs horses are kept in the dark for long periods of time. This reminds one of the manner in which Kurroglou's horse was treated at the beginning by Kurroglou's father, as described in Meeting I of Chodzko's "Adventures and Improvisations of Kurroglou."[34] The reason for such treatment was to allow the wondrous horse to grow wings, as we know from that tale.

South Slavic examples can be found in Salih Ugljanin's "Ropstvo Đulić Ibrahima" (The Captivity of Đulić Ibrahim) of which there are three versions.[35] The story begins with the capture of a Bosnian named Radovan, who is placed in a dungeon with other prisoners from Bosnia, among whom is Đulić Ibrahim, who asks Radovan for news of home, since he has been in prison for many years. In one of Salih's three texts, no. 6, Radovan asks Đulić how he was captured and he relates how he was called out of the marriage chamber to join the fighting with the governor on the Border. When he left, he said to his wife that she should take care of his mother and sister and his horse (lines 59–61):

"I čuva' mi kanali dorata!	"Take care of my hennaed chestnut horse!
Hran'te konja u mračne podrume,	Feed him in the dark stable,
Hel ja hoću peše na nogama!"	For I am going on foot!"

Later Đulić asks Radovan how things are at home, including a question about his horse (lines 167–168):

[34] Chodzko, 1842, 3–4.
[35] Parry, 1953 and 1954, nos. 4, 5, and 6.

"A sedi l' mi dorat u podrume?	"Is my horse in the stable?
Da ga njesu čete zajagmili?"	Raiders have not taken him?"

To which Radovan replies (lines 207–222):

"A sedi ti dorat u podrume;	"Your horse is in the stable;
Hranu konja, bolje bit' ne more.	They feed your horse, it could not be better.
Te se dora hasi učinijo.	The horse has become wild.
Ne da nikom sebe prilaziti;	He lets no one approach him;
Zubom griže, čivtetima bije.	He bites and kicks.
Na čustek je na noge četiri;	His four feet are hobbled;
Na čusteke veljiki sinđiri.	Great chains are in the hobbles.
Zapučili halke za jaslima.	They have attached the chains to the stalls.
Sam prilazi Huso kahveđija,	Only Huso the steward approaches,
Te timari konja Đulićeva,	And grooms Đulić's horse,
I tura mu zobi i sijena.	And gives him barley and hay.
Donosi mu vodu na nogama.	He brings him water as he stands.
Mlaku vodu sve daju doratu,	They give tepid water to the horse,
Da se ne bi dorat ištetijo,	That he might not become ill,
Ištetijo, pa se požegao;	Become ill, and catch cold;
Od studene požegnut' se more."	One can catch cold from a chill."

In another of Salih's versions, no. 5, Đulić asks the newly arrived prisoner, Radovan (lines 65–70):

"A sedi lj' mi dorat u podrumu;	"Is my horse in the stable?
Sedi lj' dorat u toplom podrumu?	Is my horse in the warm stable?
Hranu lj' dora konja mojega,	Do they feed my horse?
A goru lj' mu četiri svijeće?	Do four candles burn for him?
Sve mu goru danjem i po noći,	Burn day and night,
Ka' što ga je Đulić naučijo?"	As Đulić taught him to expect?"

There is here, of course, a contradiction to the concept of keeping a horse in the darkness! As other passages show, however, it is the light of the sun or moon that must be avoided; perhaps candle light, or, as we shall see shortly, the light of torches, did not count. At any rate, Radovan replies to the newly arrived prisoner (lines 72–78):

"Sedi dorat u topla podruma;	"Your horse is in the warm stable.
Hranu konja, bolje bit' ne more.	They feed the horse, it could not be better.
Tek se dorat hasi učinijo.	The horse has become wild.
Niti daje kome prilaziti;	He lets no one approach him.
Na čusteku na noge četiri,	His four feet are hobbled.
Zubom griže, čiftetima bije.	He bites and kicks.
Ne da nikom, Đulić, prilaziti."	He lets no one approach him, Đulić!"

In Međedović's *The Wedding of Smailagić Meho*, after telling Meho about the horse that the sultan had sent him at the time of his birth, Meho's uncle tells him how they had taken care of the horse while they waited for Meho to grow up:

We hid the horse from you and made a special stall for him in the side of the stable. There is no other horse with him. Two servants are in the stable, and four torches burn the whole night long beside your horse. They exercise him within the stable. They groom him four times every twenty-four hours; not as any other horse is groomed, but with a scarf of silk. You should see how well cared for the horse has been; he has seen neither sun nor moon, my dear son, for nine years.

When the horse is later prepared for Meho to ride with the standard-bearer Osman to Buda, the preparation is described as follows (lines 1870–84):

And when the steward heard, he went down to the manger where the chestnut horse was. He unfastened the twelve buckles forged of silver and took from the horse his twelve blankets. Then he called for the groom Ibrahim, and they brought a cauldron of warm water and a piece of perfumed soap. They washed the horse's coat as they had trained him to expect. With a sponge they dried him and they smoothed his coat with a towel. Then with a key they opened a hamper ornamented with gold and brought forth the horse's trappings.

Up to this point we have been thinking of similarities and differences between Central Asiatic and Balkan epics, primarily with the implication that many elements in the latter derive from the former. This has been intended as an ongoing concern with the history of oral-traditional epic in the Balkan peninsula. The pages of Walther Heissig's work on Mongolian epic, especially his *Geser-Studien* mentioned earlier, as well as the many valuable monographs that he has edited in *Asiatische Forschungen*, including Nekljudov and Tomorceren's *Mongolische Erzählungen über Geser*, provide excellent material for further comparative research.[36]

Practice and Performance of Balkan and Central Asiatic Epic

We have reviewed a number of ways in which the narratives and motifs of Balkan epic tradition are similar to those in several epic traditions in Central Asia. There are also similarities in the practice and performance of the poetries in the two general areas insofar as one can judge from the field reports of Reichl and his predecessors in the Central Asiatic regions. Radloff's descriptions of the methods of composition, transmission, and performance of Kara-Kirghiz epic singing in the last century are justly famous.[37] They bear close resemblance to the methods of composition and performance in the Balkans. Reichl, in his works mentioned earlier, has elaborated on the practice in other areas, which are different in the twentieth century from those recounted by Radloff, and Reichl has indicated the possible usefulness of these latter Central Asiatic epics in studying European medieval epics. His field work suggests that there have been similar developments in the Balkans, which have only recently begun to be described and evaluated.

According to Reichl, it seems that there are in general two ways in which oral-traditional epic and romance in Central Asia are composed and transmitted, the one by "improvisation," the other by "memorization." The first type, the improvisational, is the same as that described

---

[36] Nekljudov and Tomorceren, 1985.
[37] Radloff, 1885, Part V, Introduction, i–xxviii, especially xv–xxvii.

by Radloff, and it is roughly equivalent to the normal practice of oral-traditional epic in the Balkans, as described in Part I of *The Singer of Tales*.

It is important to clarify what is meant by "improvisation," because "composition in performance," the term I prefer, has at least two meanings. The first would be what might be called "pure improvisation," if there is such a thing, a story or a song, or poem, thought up on the spur of the moment. Some of the African praise poems appear to be "pure improvisations." Such texts are usually short and nontraditional, and often of a topical nature. The second kind of "composition in performance" includes those traditional and inherited items composed in the oral-formulaic and thematic technique described by Parry for Homer and for the South Slavic epic songs. Although we already know a fair amount about this technique, it needs further study—and perhaps a more precise definition and certainly greater elaboration—but it is a recognizable and known process. It is exactly this method of composition in performance, rather than the "spur of the moment" type, with which we are concerned, I believe, in most oral-traditional epic studies.

The practice of performing memorized texts also has its counterpart in the Balkans in the twentieth century. There are performers—I do not call them oral-traditional singers—who memorize written fixed texts and perform them.[38] In some cases the written texts that they memorize are oral-traditional texts someone has dictated for a scribe to write down. In other instances the memorized texts are poems or songs written in the style of oral-traditional texts, and still others are straight written literature. It does not matter which of these types of texts the performer memorizes. The performer is like an actor reciting from memory, or reading, lines that a dramatist has written. Such performers should not, I believe, be termed oral-traditional singers, any more than the present-day "folk singer" who memorizes "folk" ballads is a real folk singer. The poetry or songs that they perform should not be considered to be oral poetry or song, except in the most literal sense, unless the texts memorized were oral-traditional texts to begin with.

Moreover, and this is a key point, in such cases the performance is of no lasting significance; it is, indeed, irrelevant. The only question that is worthwhile is to ask whether the text is oral-traditional poetry, produced during performance by an oral-traditional singer, or poet. On the

---

[38] See my discussion of "The Memorizing Oral Poet" in Lord, A., 1985b.

other hand, in considering the performance of the oral-traditional singer, the performance (be it the normal one before an audience or that of
dictation) which produced that text, *is* important, and it is the only one
of importance, so far as oral-traditional literature is concerned. Homer's
dictation of his songs as we know them, and his normal singing of them
to his normal traditional audience, are the only events of significance so
far as the poems themselves are concerned. What happened to them
once recorded, whether they were preserved or not, how they were
sung by other people, and so on are entirely different matters. They
concern the "use" of Homer's text, or the history of his text, not the text
itself.

Reichl has presented brief sections of both Chorezmian and Karakalpak poems, noting the variations in other versions of them by the
same singer. Reichl notes five points (I abbreviate them): (1) "The closeness of the texts to one another suggests a basically memorized transmission of the poem as opposed to an improvised transmission." (2)
"We find an ever-changing correspondence between the various versions, making the construction of a stemma impossible." (3) "We find
that the rhymes are more stable than the beginning of the lines; here the
variants often lie within the same semantic range." (4) "There are a
number of positional variants: interchange of stanzas (but typically stability of the first stanza), lines, words, and phrases." (5) "Variants are
often phonetically/graphemically so close that they look like reading of
aural mistakes." He concludes: "The interweaving of a written and an
oral textual transmission, the predominance of memorization and the
metrical structure of the *dastans* in the Chorezmian tradition furnish a
close parallel to at least a portion of medieval epics, which merits further
study."[39]

I have quoted Reichl at length because the points in his summary and
his conclusion are worthy of our attention, and he has noted important
elements in his parallel texts. I hesitate mostly in regard to memorization. It is true that the variations are not great, and yet, I wonder if they
are really consonant with memorization. Even as Reichl summarizes
them, the variations seem greater than he implies they are. I have seen
the same phenomenon with parallel passages from the Pabuji epic collected by John D. Smith from western India, and with passages from
praise poetry collected by Trevor Cope among the Zulu in South Af-

[39] Reichl, 1985b, 628–632 and 638–640.

rica.[40] Ruth Finnegan has quoted two versions of the Mandinka epic *Sunjata* by the same singer as examples of texts in which "memorisation is to some extent involved."[41] She quotes passages from Gordon Innes's article, "Stability and Change in Griots' Narrations."[42] Smith concluded that his material from Pabuji epic was memorized. If one looks in detail, as I have done with all three of those cases, one finds that something other than conscious memorization has been taking place. An analysis of the syntactic, acoustic, and metric, or rhythmic structures of the individual groups of lines, couplets, triplets, and so forth, shows that they are easily remembered. They are memorable, and they are frequently repeated. Singers have not memorized them; they have remembered them.

Moreover, most of the "minor variations," as noted by Smith, Cope, Innes, and Finnegan, are substitutions within common, repeated structures. Variations are not mere synonyms; they are not always predictable or readily anticipated. Reichl has in essence noted the same characteristics in his five points. In short, these common, repeated structures operate in very much the same way in which formulas operate in the "improvisational" technique. I have analyzed such structures in Latvian *dainas* and in South Slavic lyric and epic songs.[43] The difference between this type of so-called memorial composition and "improvisation" is really one of degree, not of basic technique. In my article on Latvian *dainas* I suggested that behind both methods of composition is the remembering of a basic core of lines, themselves variable, which may then be further varied to suit context. This applies well enough to shorter forms. If one considers the "themes" of longer epics as being made up of short segments constructed as I have just described, then it may be that longer epics too are composed in this way. Yet, one must add, in long epics larger patterns, such as ring-composition, emerge from the shorter segments and hold them together. A long epic is not just a series of short pieces. Perhaps what we are doing is refining the concept of "composition by formula and theme." This phenomenon requires much further detailed study, and the Chorezmian and Karakalpak texts can provide

---

[40] Smith, 1977. My discussion of Smith's article can be found in my article "Characteristics of Orality," Lord, A., 1987, 65–67. Cope, 1968, especially 35–38. My discussion of these pages can be found in Lord, A., 1985b.

[41] Finnegan, 1977, 75–78.

[42] Innes, 1973. I have discussed these passages also in Lord, A., 1985b.

[43] See Lord, A., 1989.

useful material for further analysis by experts in the languages and cultures involved.

The Central Asiatic epic traditions can be invaluable in reaching a full appreciation of the history of some of the stories and story elements in South Slavic epic and lyric song, and of the techniques of their composition and transmission. This would include possible vestiges of shamanic motifs, which would explain some puzzling situations in Balkan epic and ballad. Much remains to be done as we continue to increase our knowledge of this extraordinarily rich cultural continuum.

Appendix 1

Alpamyš

The first part of *Alpamyš* relates to the birth of a son and daughter to Bajburi and a daughter to his brother Bajsary. Bajburi's son's name was Hakim, his daughter was Kaldyrgač and Bajsary's daughter's name was Barčin. When Hakim was seven years old, he strung his grandfather Alpinbic's bow and received the new name Alpamyš. The two brothers quarreled and Bajsary moved to the land of the Kalmyks. The Kalmyk Surhajnil' sought to marry Barčin to his son Karadžan. When Alpamyš heard of this, he set out for the land of the Kalmyks on his wondrous, winged horse, Bajčibar, against the advice of all. He met Karadžan, they became friends, and Karadžan became a Moslem. Barčin declared that she would marry the one whose horse could win a certain race, who could string a given bow, and shoot a coin at a distance of 1,000 "shags," and overcome a host of the enemy. Bajčibar won the race, and Alpamyš won the stringing of the bow, the shooting of the coin, and the battle with the opposing champions. On the way home after the wedding, Alpamyš, Barčin, Karadžan, and their Kungrat friends repulsed the attack by the Kalmyks who had pursued them under the Kalmyk shah Tajča-han and Surhajnil'. Barčin's father, Bajsary, still remained among the Kalmyks.

The second part begins by telling how Tajča-han took away all of Bajsary's possessions. When Alpamyš heard of that, he again went with his forty comrades to the land of the Kalmyks, where he was overpowered and imprisoned. Another son of Bajburi, Ultan-taz, took over the rule of the Kungrats when he heard of Alpamyš's fate, since Bajburi was now aged, and Ultan exiled Karadžan. Alpamyš wrote a letter in blood and sent it by a bird, who delivered it to Alpamyš's sister Kaldyrgač. She sent Karadžan to rescue him, but the attempt failed. The daughter of the Kalmyk shah, Tavka-aim, fell in love with Alpamyš. With her help he escaped and Bajčibar also freed himself. They overcame the Kalmyks and killed the shah, and Alpamyš set out for home.

On the way he met some of Ultan's caravan drivers, and they told him of what had happened at home after the news came that Alpamyš was dead. Alpamyš killed them. His horse, Bajčibar, neighed when he saw his native land and Bajčibar's mother came to join him. The young herder of the caravan told what had passed in Alpamyš's family after his death. He next met his sister, barefooted and in rags, tending a herd of camels. An old camel that had not stirred for seven years suddenly arose to greet its master and to run seven times around him. It seemed to his sister Kaldyrgač that she recognized her brother, but he went past without revealing who he was. Next he met old Kultaj with a herd of Bajburi's rams. Alpamyš told him who he was, but the old man had lost all hope and did not believe him, and Alpamyš did not disclose the mark on his shoulders that the old man had put there when Alpamyš was a boy.

Alpamyš exchanged clothes with Kultaj so that he would not be recognized when he reached home. The hero observed the treatment that Ultan had meeted out to his family, namely to his mother, his father, the boy Jadgar, and Barčin. There followed then a competition with the bow. Alpamyš broke the bow that was given him and called for his grandfather's bow, which none of Ultan's people was able to string, but young Jadgar had the power to do so. Alpamyš strung it without difficulty and hit the target. In the evening Alpamyš participated in the singing and exchanged songs with Barčin, from which he was convinced of her faithfulness. By this time many of the guests had come to realize that this Kultaj was actually the returned Alpamyš, and he acknowledged it to be true. Justice was rendered upon Ultan and his followers. Bajsary returned from the land of the Kalmyks, and Alpamyš reestablished his rule over the Kungrats.

Bamsi Beyrek of the Grey Horse

The tale of Bamsi Beyrek begins with the birth of a son to Bay Bure and of a daughter to Bay Bijan, who eventually have the names of

Bamsi Beyrek and Lady Chichek. Bamsi overcame Lady Chichek's crazy brother, who killed all seeking to marry her, and they were betrothed. She gave him a red caftan as a wedding gift. The night before their marriage, he and his thirty-nine friends were captured by the Infidel while they were feasting.

Sixteen years later Yaltajuk brought a shirt of Beyrek's that Beyrek had once given him, which Yaltajuk had dipped in blood. They all thought Bamsi Beyrek was dead, and preparations were made to wed Lady Chichek to Yaltajuk. Beyrek's father sent merchants to seek his son. They eventually came to the castle where Beyrek was kept and where a feast was in progress, at which Beyrek had been brought to sing to the lute. He saw the merchants, and in his song asked them for news of the Oghuz, including Lady Chichek. When he learned that she was betrothed, he asked the Infidel's daughter to help him escape, promising to marry her.

When Beyrek, disguised as a minstrel, reached his father's encampment he met his little sister weeping at a spring and speaking her brother's name. He next met his older sisters, the eldest of whom thought he looked much like her brother. He put on ragged clothing then and continued to the wedding feast. At it, he shot with Beyrek's bow, and recognized Lady Chichek among other women by the ring that he had given her. When he was brought to his father, who had become blind with weeping, he cured his blindness with blood from his finger. Yaltajuk was forgiven. Beyrek returned to the castle where he had been kept, released his thirty-nine companions, and brought back the Infidel's daughter. The tale ends with multiple weddings.

The South Slavic epics with the generic return pattern fall into two traditions: Christian and Moslem. The two best known of the classic texts in the Christian tradition are "The Captivity of Janković Stojan" (Ropstvo Janković Stojana), and "Marko Kraljević and Mina of Kostur" (Marko Kraljević i Mina od Kostura).[44]

The Captivity of Janković Stojan

The story of Janković Stojan begins with the capture of Janković Stojan and Smiljanić Ilija by the Turks. "Ilija left behind a young wife of

[44] Karadžić, 1958, vol. 3, no. 25 (151 lines), and vol. 2, no. 61 (336 lines).

fifteen days; Stojan left a younger wife of a week of days." In short, our hero had just been married. The Turks gave the two friends to the sultan; they became Moslems and stayed in Stambol for nine years and seven months. After all that time, they decided to go home. They stole two horses and fled. When they were close to their home in Kotar, Ilija parted from Stojan, and Stojan continued to his vineyard, where he found his mother pruning and binding up the vines, weeping and speaking her son's name. Stojan asked if she had nobody to help her in her old age, and she said that she had none but the son whom the Turks had captured. She tells Stojan that his wife had waited for him for nine years, but she was about to be married again that very day! The scene is somewhat reminiscent, of course, of Odysseus and his father Laertes, which occurs, it is to be noted, after recognition with Penelope and everyone else and after the slaughter of the suitors. Stojan joined the wedding guests and asked permission to sing a little. In his song, he told about a swallow which had built its nest for nine years, but was undoing it that very morning. The wedding guests payed no attention to the song, but Stojan's wife called his sister and told her that her brother had returned. She ran downstairs and embraced her brother. The wedding guests asked what they should do, and Stojan gave the bridegroom his sister. These are not evil suitors, as in the *Odyssey*. When Stojan's mother came home from the vineyard, her daughter ran to meet her and told her that Stojan had returned. When she saw her son, she fell down dead. Stojan buried her in a fitting manner.

I do not know whether Žirmunskij knew this song or not, although it is perfectly possible that he did. But, if so, it is not surprising that he did not find it particularly germaine to his study of *Alpamyš!*

Marko Kraljević and Mina of Kostur

In the song about Marko Kraljević, he is already married—nothing said of how long. He receives a letter from the sultan asking him to come to aid him in fighting with the Arabs. When he leaves home he advises his mother to guard well against Mina of Kostur, with whom Marko has quarreled. He departs with his servant Goluban. (Note that the heroes in both these songs have companions.) After defeating the Arabs for the sultan, Marko receives news that his wife has been abducted by Mina of Kostur, and he makes his way to Mina's tower with a number of janisseries disguised as monks. Marko drinks with Mina, and his wife serves them. Mina asks him where he got the piebald horse, and Marko tells him that he had been given the horse for burying Marko Kraljević after he had died in Arabia. Mina asks him to perform the marriage ceremony for him and Marko's wife, and he does so. Mina sends her to fetch some ducats, and she brings them together with Marko's rusty sword, which she gives to the monk! Marko asks permission to dance a little in monkish fashion, and in the course of the dance he cuts off Mina's head. The janisseries raze Mina's tower, and Marko takes his wife and Mina's treasures home to Prilip.

In the foregoing description I have followed the version of "Marko and Mina" in the Karadžić collection. In other versions, such as those in the Milman Parry Collection from Petar Vidić of Stolac, Marko meets his wife as she is drawing water from a spring near Mina's tower, and she asks about the horse Šarac, and is told the same deceptive story.[45]

The Captivity of Đulić Ibrahim

There are many versions of the generic song of return in the Moslem tradition. I have taken as a model "The Captivity of Đulić Ibrahim" by Salih Ugljanin of Novi Pazar.[46] In this case the story opens with the hero in prison for many years. A new prisoner from his town is put into the prison and Đulić asks how things are at home. The prisoner tells him all is well, but his wife is about to marry again. Đulić shouts to get the attention of his jailer. The jailer's wife asks that the prisoner be brought before the jailer and after some negotiation he is released for ransom. He is challenged at the border, but overcomes the opposition. At home he meets an old family retainer, who does not recognize him and asks for news of Đulić. The hero says that Đulić is dead, and he is taken to see Đulić's mother and sister, who also ask about Đulić and are told the same deceptive story. Đulić's request to see his *tambura* and to play it is granted, and he sings that he does not wonder that his mother and sister did not recognize him, but he does wonder that Huso did not. At the news of her son's return his mother dies. Đulić asks his sister not to tell his wife that he has returned, and they bury his mother. He goes to see his wife, who asks about Đulić. When she hears his deceptive story of the death of Đulić, she weeps and says that she would never find a husband like him again. The hero then reveals his identity.

[45] See Lord, A., 1960, Appendix II, 236–241.
[46] Parry, M., 1954, no. 4.

At this point the wedding guests arrive and Đulić tells them his deceptive story. He then goes to his chestnut horse, which recognizes him and weeps! His master saddles him and leads him into the courtyard, after which, with the assistance of his sister, he dresses in his best clothing. He mounts his horse and joins the wedding guests. He eventually agrees to give his sister to the disappointed bridegroom. The rest of the song is taken up with the return of Đulić with Halil, the disappointed bridegroom, and the rescuing of Đulić's imprisoned comrades.

Appendix 2

Continuation of Song 5 in *Rawšan*

Er hatte sich in der Nacht vor dem Grab der Heiligen verbeugt.
50   In seine verliebten Narzissenaugen waren die Tränen gestiegen.
Zwei Steigbügel, beide aus Gold,
Poliert, bringt er an beiden Seiten an.

Die Mähne des Džijranquš, sein Schweif sind fein.
Über die Taten des Helden begeistern sich alle.
55   Ein Verlangen nach Ehre beseelt den jungen Helden Rawšan,
Fest zieht er den Sattelgurt aus feiner Seide.

Perlengleich sind die Zähne einer Schönheit.
Er geht auf die Suche nach der schönen Zulchumar.
Er wirft auf den Pferderücken, breitet aus
60   Die wertvolle, mit goldenen Fransen verzierte Pferdedecke.

Die Nachtigall ist mit dem Paradiesgarten befreundet.
Der Tod möge zugrunde gehen! Wer wäre dann noch betrübt?
Die Decke, die Bek Rawšan aufgelegt hatte,
Reicht Džijran bis zu den Fesseln.

65   Das Tier schmückt er vom Kopf bis zu den Fesseln,
Das vom Pir gesegnete Fohlen, jünger als drei Jahre alt.
An dem Schweif des Pferdes befestigt Bek Rawšan
Einen zwölfmal gefalteten Schwanzriemen aus Nashornleder.

Eine jede Zierkugel ist grösser als ein Tarkaš.
70   Das Tier macht beim Passgang keinen Fehler.
Wenn er 'Hü!' sagt, lässt er den geflügelten Vogel los.

An die Flanke legt Bek Rawšan dem Pferd
Die bis zu den Hufen reichended čaġatajischen Zügel.

Betrachtet das Tun des Rawšan-Bek—
75   Sein Kragen ist nass von den Tränen, die ihm aus den Augen
        quellen—:
Wie er einen goldenen Brustlatz an die Brust heftet,
Einen Halsschmuck Džijran an seinem langen Hals befestigt,
Einen Zaum mit vierzig Zierkugeln ihm über den Kopf wirft.

Das Pferd des Bek beisst in ein stählernes Mundstück,
80   In Rot gekleidet strahlt es wie eine Rose.
Den schlangenzüngigen, blitzgleichen Chandžar
Bindet er sich, um Ehre zu erlangen, an die schmale Hüfte.

Betrachtet den Chan, den Recken Rawšan,
Er strebt nach dem Land Širwan.
85   Rawšan steigt Džijranquš auf die Kruppe,
Furcht verbreitet der Jigit zu seiner Rechten und zu seiner Linken.
Vom Volk seines Vaters, den Taka-Jawmit,
Strebt er, seht, zu Širwans Volk.

Betrachtet den Jagdfalken Čambils,
90   Es besteigt der Jigit das Pferd Džijranquš.
Er macht weinen seinen Vater, den Helden Hasan,
Blut macht er weinen die schöne Chan Dalli,
Rawšan strebt nach dem Land Širwan.

Seht den Sohn Hasans,
95   Den unerfahrenen Liebling Chan Dallis.
Im Nu steigt der Jigit aufs Pferd,
Er spornt sein Ross an und verlässt den Hof:
Das Land Čambil macht er zum Trauerhaus.

Bibliography

Abbreviations

AJP   *American Journal of Philology*
HSCP *Harvard Studies in Classical Philology*
PMLA *Publications of the Modern Language Association*
Prilozi *Prilozi za književnost, jesik, istoriju i folklor*
TAPA *Transactions of the American Philological Association*

Alexiou, 1974. Alexiou, Margaret. *The Ritual Lament in Greek Tradition*. Cambridge: Cambridge University Press, 1974.
Alpamyš, 1949. *Alpamyš*, uzbekskij narodnyi epos, po variantu Fazila Juldasa, perevod L'va Pen'kovskogo. Moscow: Gosudarstvennoe izdatel'stvo khudozhestvennoj literatury (State Publishing House for Literature), 1949.
Alter, 1989. Alter, Robert. *The Pleasures of Reading in an Ideological Age*. New York: Simon and Schuster, 1989.
Arend, 1933. Arend, Walter. *Die typischen Scenen bei Homer, Problemata: Forschungen zur Klassischen Philologie*, Heft 7. Berlin: Weidmannsche Buchhandlung, 1933.
Armstrong, 1958. Armstrong, J. I. "The Arming Motif in the *Iliad*." *AJP* 79 (1958), 337–354.
Arrian, 1967. Flavius Arrianus. Vol. 1, *Alexandri anabasis*. Ed. A. G. Roos, Leipzig: Teubner, 1967.
ASPR (The Anglo-Saxon Poetic Records) 2, 1932. Krapp, George Philip, ed. *The Vercelli Book*. New York: Columbia University Press, 1932.
Atlas, 1963. K. Vertkov, G. Blagodatov, and E. Jazovitskaja. *Atlas muzykal'nyh instrumentov narodov SSSR*. Moscow: n.p., 1963.
Austin, 1975. Austin, Norman. *Archery at the Dark of the Moon: Poetic Problems in Homer's Odyssey*. Berkeley: University of California Press, 1975.
Bailey, 1947. Bailey, Cyril, ed. and trans. Titi Lucreti Cari, *De Rerum Natura*, Libri sex. 3 vols. Oxford: Clarendon Press, 1947.

Bartók and Lord, 1951. Bartók, Béla, and Albert B. Lord. *Serbo-Croatian Folk Songs: Texts and Transcriptions of Seventy-Five Folk Songs from the Milman Parry Collection and a Morphology of Serbo-Croatian Folk Melodies*. Foreword by George Herzog. New York: Columbia University Press, 1951.

Bäuml, 1980. Bäuml, Franz H. "Varieties and Consequences of Medieval Literacy and Illiteracy." *Speculum* 55 (1980), 237–265.

Benoist. *Histoire des Albigeois et des Vaudois ou Barbets* (1691). 1:283 ff.

Benson, 1966. Benson, Larry D. "The Literary Character of Anglo-Saxon Formulaic Poetry." *PMLA* 81 (1966), 334–441.

Beowulf, 1950. *Beowulf and the Fight at Finnsburg*. Ed. with introduction, bibliography, notes, glossary, and appendixes by Frederick Klaeber, 3d ed., with first and second supplements. Boston: D. C. Heath, 1950.

Beowulf, 1968. *Beowulf*. Trans. Kevin Crossley-Holland. New York: Farrar, Straus and Giroux, 1968.

Beowulf and Its Analogues. Trans. G. N. Garmonsway and Jaqueline Şimpson, including *Archaeology and Beowulf*, by Hilda Ellis Davidson. New York: E. P. Dutton, 1971.

Biebuyck, 1978. Biebuyck, Daniel. *Hero and Chief: Epic Literature from the Banyanga Zaire Republic*. Berkeley: University of California Press, 1978.

Biebuyck and Mateene, 1969. Biebuyck, Daniel, and Kahombo C. Mateene. *The Mwindo Epic, from the Banyanga (Congo Republic)*. Berkeley and Los Angeles: University of California Press, 1969.

B'lgarski junaški epos, 1971. *B'lgarski junaški epos, Sbornik za narodni umotvorenija i narodopis*, vol. 53. Sofia: B'lgarska akademija na naukite, Etnografski institut i muzej, 1971.

BNT. Vols. 1–13, 1961–1965. *B'lgarsko narodno tvorčestvo*, vol. 1, *Junaški pesni*, ed. Ivan Burin, vol. 11, *Narodni predanija i legendi*. Ed. Tsvetana Romanska and Elena Ognjanova. Sofia: B'lgarski pisatel, 1961–1965.

Bogišić, 1878. Bogišić, Valtazar. *Narodne pjesme iz starijih, najviše primorskih napisa*. Belgrade: Državna štamparija, 1878.

Boratav and Bazin, 1965. Boratav, Pertev, and Louis Bazin. *Aventures merveilleuses sous terre et ailleurs de Er-Töshtük, le géant des steppes. Épopée du cycle de Manas*. Kirghiz trans. Pertev Boratav, introduction and notes by Pertev Boratav and Louis Bazin. Paris: Gallimard, 1965.

Bosanac, 1897. Bosanac, Stjepan, ed. *Hrvatske narodne pjesme*, vol. 2. Zagreb: Matica hrvatska, 1897.

Bowra, 1952. Bowra, Cecil Maurice. *Heroic Poetry*. London: Macmillan, 1952.

Broz and Bosanac, 1896. Broz, Ivan, and Stjepan Bosanac, eds. *Hrvatske narodne pjesme, Odio prvi, Junačke pjesme*, vol. 1. Zagreb: Matica hrvatska, 1896.

Bynum, 1964. Bynum, David E. "Kult dvaju junaka u kulturnoj istoriji Balkana" (The Cult of Two Heroes in the Cultural History of the Balkans). *Anali filološkog fakulteta* (Annals of the Philological Faculty, Belgrade) 4 (1964) 65–73.

Bynum, 1968. "Themes of the Young Hero in Serbocroatian Oral Epic Tradition." *PMLA* 83 (1968), 1296–1303.

Bynum, 1969. "The Generic Nature of Oral Epic Poetry." *Genre* 2 (1969), 236–258.

Bynum, 1978. *The Daemon in the Wood: A Study of Oral Narrative Patterns*. Foreword by Albert B. Lord. Cambridge, Mass.: Center for the Study of Oral Literature, Harvard University, 1978.

Bynum, 1979. See Parry, M., 1979.

Carpenter, 1946. Carpenter, Rhys. *Folk Tale, Fiction and Saga in the Homeric Epics.* Berkeley: University of California Press, 1946.

Cavalcanti, 1967. Cavalcanti, Guido. *Rime.* Ed. with introduction and notes by Giulio Cattaneo. Turin: Giulio Einaudi, 1967.

Child, 1965. Child, Francis James, ed. *The English and Scottish Popular Ballads,* vols. 1–5. New York: Dover, 1965.

Chodzko, 1842. Chodzko, Alexander. *Specimens of Popular Poetry of Persia.* London: Oriental Translation Fund of Great Britain and Ireland, 1842.

Clover, 1980. Clover, Carol J. "The Germanic Context of the Unferth Episode." *Speculum* 55 (1980), 444–468.

Combellack, 1950. Combellack, Frederick M. "Contemporary Unitarians and Homeric Originality." *AJP* 71 (1950), 337–64.

Comparetti, 1898. Comparetti, Domenico. *The Traditional Poetry of the Finns.* Trans. Isabella M. Anderton, with introduction by Andrew Lang. New York: Longmans, Green, 1898). Originally published as *Il Kalevala; o, la poesia tradizionale dei Finni; studio storico-critico sulle origini delle grandi epopee nazional.* Rome: Reale Academia dei Lincei, 1891.

Cope, 1968. Cope, Trevor. *Izibongo: Zulu Praise Poems.* Collected by James Stuart, trans. Daniel Malcolm, and ed. with introduction and annotations by Trevor Cope. Oxford: Clarendon Press, 1968.

Cope, 1978. Cope, Trevor. "Towards an Appreciation of Zulu Folktales as Literary Art." In *Social System and Tradition in Southern Africa,* ed. John Argyle and Eleanor Preston-Whyte. New York: Oxford University Press, 1978, 183–205.

Creed, 1962. Creed, Robert Payson. "The Singer Looks at His Sources." *Comparative Literature* 14 (1962), 44–52.

David-Neel and Lama Yongden, 1933. David-Neel, Alexandra, and the Lama Yongden. *The Superhuman Life of Gesar of Ling.* 1933; New York: Arno Press, 1978.

Dede Korkut, 1974. *The Book of Dede Korkut.* Trans. with introduction and notes by Geoffrey Lewis. Harmondsworth: Penguin Books, 1974.

Dillon, 1971. Dillon, Myles, trans. *There Was a King in Ireland.* Austin: University of Texas Press, 1971.

Döllinger, 1890. Döllinger, Johann Joseph Ignatius von. *Beiträge zur Sektengeschichte des Mittelalters,* vols. 1–2. Munich: C. H. Beck, 1890.

Dunbar, 1880. Dunbar, Henry. *A Complete Concordance to the Odyssey and Hymns of Homer, to which is added a Concordance to the Parallel Passages in the Iliad, Odyssey, and Hymns.* Oxford: Clarendon Press, 1880.

Edwards and Vasse, 1957. Edwards, John Hamilton, and William W. Vasse. *Annotated Index to the Cantos of Ezra Pound, Cantos I–LXXXIV.* Berkeley: University of California Press, 1957.

Elevterov, 1978. Elevterov, Stevan. *Antologija na b'lgarskata literatura: Izbrani tekstove i harakteristiki.* Sofia: Izdatelstvo nauka i izkustvo, n.d. [ca. 1978].

Elezović, 1923. Elezović, G. "Jedna arnautska varianta o boju na Kosovu." *Arhiv za arbansku starinu, jezik i etnologiju* 1 (Seminar za arbanašku filologiju, University of Belgrade, 1923), 54–67.

Eliade, 1964. Eliade, Mircea. *Shamanism: Archaic Techniques of Ecstacy.* Trans. Willard R. Trask, Bollingen Series 76. New York: Pantheon, 1964.

Elliott, 1959. Elliott, Ralph W. V. *Runes: An Introduction.* Manchester: Manchester University Press, 1959.

Ellis, 1983. Ellis, John M. *One Fairy Story Too Many: The Brothers Grimm and Their Tales.* Chicago: University of Chicago Press, 1983.

Erdelyi, 1972. Erdelyi, Istvan. *Ostjakische Heldenlieder aus Jozsej Papay Nachlass.* Budapest: Kiadó, 1972.

Ethé, 1871. Ethé, Hermann. *Die Fahrten des Sajjid Batthal: Ein alttürkischer Volks- und Sittenroman.* Trans. for the first time by Dr. Hermann Ethé. Leipzig: F. A. Brockhaus, 1871.

Fenik, 1968. Fenik, Bernard. *Typical Battle Scenes in the Iliad: Studies in the Narrative Techniques of Homeric Battle Description. Hermes* Einzelschriften, Heft 21. Wiesbaden: Franz Steiner Verlag, 1968.

Finnegan, 1970. Finnegan, Ruth. *Oral Literature in Africa.* Oxford: Clarendon Press, 1970.

Finnegan, 1977. *Oral Poetry: Its Nature, Significance and Social Context.* Cambridge: Cambridge University Press, 1977.

Finnish Folk Poetry, Epic, 1977. *Finnish Folk Poetry, Epic, an Anthology in Finnish and English.* Ed. and trans. Matti Kuusi, Keith Bosley, and Michael Branch. Helsinki: Finnish Literature Society, 1977.

Fleischer, 1888. Fleischer, H. L. "Über den türkischen Volksroman Sireti Sejjid Battal." In *Kleinere Schriften,* collected, edited and augmented by H. L. Fleischer. Leipzig: Verlag von S. Hirzel, 1888, 3:226–254.

Foley, 1980. Foley, John Miles. "*Beowulf* and Traditional Narrative Song: The Potential and Limits of Comparison." In *Old English Literature in Context: Ten Essays,* ed. John D. Niles. London and Totowa, N.J.: Rowman & Littlefield, 1980, 117–136.

Foley, 1981. *Oral Traditional Literature: A Festschrift for Albert Bates Lord.* Ed. John Miles Foley. Columbus, Ohio: Slavica, 1981.

Foley, 1985. *Oral-Formulaic Theory and Research: An Introduction and Annotated Bibliography.* New York: Garland, 1985.

Foley, 1986. *Oral Tradition in Literature: Interpretation in Context.* Ed. John Miles Foley. Columbia: University of Missouri Press, 1986.

Foley, 1987. *Comparative Research on Oral Traditions: A Memorial for Milman Parry.* Ed. John Miles Foley. Columbus, Ohio: Slavica, 1987.

Foley, 1988. *The Theory of Oral Composition: History and Methodology.* Bloomington: Indiana University Press, 1988.

Ford, 1977. Ford, Patrick K., trans. and ed. *The Mabinogi, and Other Medieval Welsh Tales.* Berkeley and Los Angeles: University of California Press, 1977.

Fortgesetzte Sammlung von alten und neuen theologischen Sachen (1734), 703 ff.

Franciplegius, 1965. *Franciplegius: Medieval and Linguistic Studies in Honor of Francis Peabody Magoun, Jr.,* ed. Jess B. Bessinger, Jr., and Robert P. Creed. New York: New York University Press, 1965.

Fry, 1967. Fry, Donald K., Jr. "Old English Formulas and Systems." *English Studies* 48 (1967), 193–204.

Golden Legend, The, 1969. *The Golden Legend of Jacobus de Voragine.* Trans. from

Latin by Granger Ryan and Helmust Ripperger. New York: Arno Press, 1969.

Göller, 1981. Göller, Karl H., ed. *The Alliterative Morte Arthure: A Reassessment of the Poem*. Arthurian Studies 3. Totowa, N.J.: Rowan & Littlefield, 1981.

Goold, 1977. Goold, G. P. "The Nature of Homeric Composition." *Illinois Classical Studies* 2 (1977), 1–34.

Green, 1990. Green, D. H. "Orality and Reading: The State of Research in Medieval Studies," *Speculum* 65 (1990), 267–280.

Grégoire, 1949. Grégoire, Henri. "Le Digénis russe." In *Russian Epic Studies*, ed. Roman Jakobson and Ernest J. Simmons. Memoirs of the American Folklore Society, no. 42. Philadelphia: American Folklore Society (1949), 131–169.

Haavio, 1952. Haavio, Martti. *Väinämöinen, Eternal Sage, Folklore Fellows Communications* 144. Helsinki: Academia scientiarum fennica, 1952.

Hainsworth, 1968. Hainsworth, John Brian. *The Flexibility of the Homeric Formula*. Oxford: Clarendon Press, 1968.

Hall, 1901. Hall, Joseph, ed. *King Horn: A Middle-English Romance*. Oxford: Clarendon Press, 1901.

Hatto, 1977. Hatto, Arthur T. *The Memorial Feast for Kökötöy-Khan (Kökötöydun Asi) A Kirghiz Epic Poem*. Ed. for the first time from a photocopy of the unique manuscript with translation and commentary by A. T. Hatto. New York: Oxford University Press, 1977.

Hatto, 1979. "Plot and Character in Mid-Nineteenth-Century Kirghiz Epic." In *Die mongolischen Epen, Bezüge, Sinndeutung, und Überlieferung*, ed. Walther Heissig. Wiesbaden: Otto Harrassowitz, 1979, 95–112.

Hatto, 1980. "Das Pferd in der älteren kirghisischen Heldenepik und in der Ilias." *Fragen der mongolischen Heldendichtung*, Teil 2, *Asiatische Forschungen*, Band 73. Wiesbaden: Otto Harrassowitz, 1980, 179–201.

Havelock, 1963. Havelock, Eric A. *Preface to Plato*. Cambridge, Mass.: Belknap Press of Harvard University Press, 1963.

Havelock, 1978. Havelock, Eric A., and Jackson P. Hershbell, eds. *Communication Arts in the Ancient World*. New York: Hasting House, 1978, 3–29.

Heissig, 1983a. Heissig, Walther. *Geser-Studien*. Untersuchungen zu den Erzählstoffen in den "neuen" Kapiteln des mongolischen Geser-Zyklus, *Abhandlungen der Rheinisch-Westfälischen Akademie der Wissenschaften*, Band 69. Opladen: Westdeutscher Verlag, 1983.

Heissig, 1983b. *Westliche Motivparallelen in zentralischen Epen*. Bayerische Akademie der Wissenschaften, Philosophisch-historische Klasse, Sitzungsberichte, Jahrgang, 1983, Heft 2. Munich: Bayerische Akademie der Wissenschaften, 1983.

Hennecke, 1959. Hennecke, Edgar. *New Testament Apocrypha*. Ed. Wilhelm Schneemelcher, English trans. ed. R. McL. Wilson, vol. 1, Gospels and Related Writings. Philadelphia: Westminster Press, 1959.

Hilferding, 1950. Hilferding, A. F. *Onežskie byliny*, zapisannye A. F. Gilferdingom, 1871, 2 vols., 4th ed. Moscow: Akademija nauk SSSR, 1949–1950.

Hoekstra, 1964. Hoekstra, A. *Homeric Modifications of Formulaic Prototypes: Studies in the Development of Greek Epic Diction*. Verhandelingen der Koninklijke Nederlandse Akademie van Wetenschappen, afd. Letterkunde, n. r., Deel 71, no. 1. Amsterdam: N. V. Noord-Hollandsche Uitgevers Maatschappij 1964, repr. 1969.

Homeri opera, 1976. 2d ed., ed. Thomas W. Allen, *Iliad,* vols. 1–2; *Odyssea,* vols. 3–4. Oxford: Clarendon Press, 1976.

Hörmann, 1933. Hörmann, Kosta. *Narodne pjesme muslimana u Bosni i Hercegovini,* vols. 1–2. Sarajevo: J. Kusan, 1933. Originally published as *Narodne pjesme muhamedovaca u Bosni i Hercegovini.* Sarejevo: Zemaljska štamparija, 1888–89.

Hrvatske narodne pjesme, vols. 1–10. Zagreb: Matica hrvatska, 1896–1942.

Huppé, 1970. Huppé, Bernard Felix, trans. *The Web of Words; Structural Analyses of the Old English Poems: Vainglory, The Wonder of Creation, The Dream of the Rood, and Judith.* Albany: State University of New York, 1970.

Huxley, 1969. Huxley, George Leonard. *Greek Epic Poetry from Eumelos to Panyassis.* London: Faber and Faber, 1969.

Innes, 1973. Innes, Gordon. "Stability and Change in Griots' Narrations." *African Language Studies* 14 (1973), 105–118.

Innes, 1974. *Sunjata: Three Mandinka Versions.* London: School of Oriental and African Studies, University of London, 1974.

Ivanov, 1925. Ivanov, Jordan. *Bogomilski knigi i legendi.* Sofia: B'lgarska akademija na naukite, 1925, photocopy published in 1970.

Ivanov, 1935. *Starob'lgarski razkazi: Tekstove, novob'lgarski prevod i belezki.* Sofia: Prisdvorna pečatnica, 1935.

Janko, 1981. Janko, Richard. "Equivalent Formulae in the Greek Epos," *Mnemosyne,* vol. 24, fasc. 3–4 (1981), 251–264.

Janko, 1982. *Homer, Hesiod, and the Hymns.* Cambridge: Cambridge University Press, 1982.

Johnson, 1986. Johnson, John William, trans. *The Epic of Son-Jara: A West African Tradition.* Bloomington: Indiana University Press, 1986.

Jousse, 1925. Jousse, Marcel. *Le Style oral rhythmique et mnémnotechique chez les Verbo-Moteurs.* Paris: Gabriel Beauchesne, 1925.

Jousse, 1990. *The Oral Style.* Trans. from French by Edgard Sienaert and Richard Whitaker. The Albert Bates Lord Studies in Oral Tradition, John Miles Foley, gen. ed. New York: Garland, 1990.

Kačić-Miošić, 1967. Kačić-Miošić, Andrija. *Razgovor ugodni naroda slovinskoga, Djela Andrije Kačić-Miošić, Stari pisci hrvatski,* vol. 1. Zagreb: Hrvatska akademija znanosti i umjestnosti, 1967, first published Venice, 1756.

Kalonaros, 1941. Kalonaros, P. *Digenes Akritas,* vols. 1–2. Athens: Archaios ekdotikos oikos Dem. Demetrakou A. E., 1941.

Karadžić, 1932–36. Karadžić, Vuk Stefanović. *Srpske narodne pjesme,* vols. 1–9. Belgrade: Državna štamparija, 1932–36.

Karadžić, 1958. *Srpske narodne pjesme,* vols. 1–4. Belgrade: Prosveta, 1958.

Khalanskii, 1893. Khalanskii, M. *Južnoslavjanskija skazanija o Kraleviče Markě v' svjazi s' proizvedenijami russkago bylevogo eposa.* Warsaw: Tipografija varšavskago učenago okruga, 1893.

Konstantinov, 1946. Konstantinov, Georgi. *Stara b'lgarska literatura.* Sofia: Xemus, 1946.

Kunene, 1971. Kunene, Daniel P. *Heroic Poetry of the Basotho.* Oxford: Oxford Library of African Literature, Clarendon Press, 1971.

Latacz, 1979. Latacz, Joachim. *Homer: Tradition und Neuerung*. Darmstadt: Wisenchaftliche Buchgesellschaft, 1979.

Lattimore, 1951. Lattimore, Richmond, trans. *The Iliad of Homer*. Chicago: University of Chicago Press, 1951.

Lattimore, 1965. *The Odyssey of Homer*. Trans. with introduction by Richmond Lattimore. New York: Harper and Row, 1965.

Latvian Folk Songs, 1989. *Linguistics and Poetics of Latvian Folk Songs: Essays in Honour of the Sesquicentennial of the Birth of Kr. Barons*. Ed. Vaira Vīkiş-Freibergs. Kingston: McGill-Queens University Press, 1989.

Laude-Circautas, 1979. Laude-Circautas, Ilse. "Einige Gemeinsamkeiten und Unterschiede in den Epen der Mongolen und der Türken Mittelasiens." In *Die Mongolischen Epen, Bezüge. Sinndeutung und Überlieferung: (Ein Symposium)*, ed. Walther Heissig. Wiesbaden: Otto Harrassowitz, 1979, 113–126.

Lesky, 1954. Lesky, Albin. "Mündlichkeit und Schriftlichkeit im homerischen Epos." In *Festschrift für Dietrich Kralik*. Horn, N.-Ö.: Verlag Ferdinand Berger, 1954, 1–9.

Levy, 1953. Levy, Gertrude R. *The Sword from the Rock: An Investigation into the Origin of Epic Literature and the Development of the Hero*. London: Faber and Faber, 1953.

Lönnrot, 1963. Lönnrot, Elias. *The Kalevala, or Poems of the Kaleva District*. Comp. Elias Lönnrot, prose trans. with foreword and appendixes by Francis Peabody Magoun, Jr. Cambridge, Mass.: Harvard University Press, 1963.

Lönnrot, 1969. *The Old Kalevala and Certain Antecedents*. Comp. Elias Lönnrot, prose trans. with foreword and appendixes by Francis Peabody Magoun, Jr. Cambridge, Mass.: Harvard University Press, 1969.

Lord, A., 1936. Lord, Albert B. "Homer and Huso I: The Singer's Rests in Homer and Southslavic Heroic Song." *TAPA* 67 (1936), 106–113.

Lord, A., 1938. "Homer and Huso II: Narrative Inconsistencies in Homer and Oral Poetry." *TAPA* 69 (1938), 439–445.

Lord, A., 1948. "Homer and Huso III: Enjambement in Greek and Southslavic Heroic Song." *TAPA* 79 (1948), 113–124.

Lord, A., 1951. "Composition by Theme in Homer and Southslavic Epos." *TAPA* 82 (1951), 71–80.

Lord, A., 1953. "Homer's Originality: Oral Dictated Texts." *TAPA* 84 (1953), 124–133.

Lord, A., 1960. *The Singer of Tales*. Cambridge, Mass.: Harvard University Press, 1960.

Lord, A., 1962. "Homeric Echoes in Bihać." *Zbornik za narodni život i običaje*, vol. 40. Zagreb: Jugoslavenska akademija znanosti i umjetnosti, 1962, 313–320.

Lord, A., 1965. "Beowulf and Odysseus." In *Franciplegius: Medieval and Linguistic Studies in Honor of Francis Peabody Magoun, Jr.*, ed. Jess B. Bessinger, Jr., and Robert P. Creed. New York: New York University Press, 1965, 86–91.

Lord, A., 1969. "The Theme of the Withdrawn Hero in Serbo-Croatian Oral Epic." *Prilozi* 35 (1969), 18–30.

Lord, A., 1972. "The Effect of the Turkish Conquest on Balkan Epic Tradition." In

Aspects of the Balkans: Continuity and Change, ed. Henrik Birnbaum and Speros Vryonis, Jr. The Hague: Mouton, 1972, 298–318.

Lord, A., 1975. "Perspectives on Recent Work on Oral Literature." In *Oral Literature: Seven Essays,* ed. Joseph J. Duggan. New York: Barnes and Noble, 1975, 1–24.

Lord, A., 1976a. "Formula and Non-Narrative Theme in South Slavic Oral Epic and the OT." *Semeia* 5, "Oral Tradition and Old Testament Studies," ed. Robert C. Culley. Missoula, Mont.: Society of Biblical Literature, 1976, 93–105.

Lord, A., 1976b. "Studies in the Bulgarian Epic Tradition: Thematic Parallels." In *Bulgaria, Past and Present: Studies in History, Literature, Economics, Music, Sociology, Folklore, and Linguistics.* Columbus, Ohio: American Association for the Advancement of Slavic Studies, 1976, 349–358.

Lord, A., 1978a. "The Ancient Greek Heritage in Modern Balkan Epic." *Slavjanskie kul'tury i Balkany* 2 (Sofia, 1978), 337–355.

Lord, A., 1978b. "The Gospels as Oral Traditional Literature." In *The Relationships among the Gospels: An Interdisciplinary Dialogue,* ed. William O. Walker, Jr. San Antonio: Trinity University Press, 1978, 33–91.

Lord, A., 1980. "Interlocking Mythic Patterns in *Beowulf.*" In *Old English Literature in Context: Ten Essays,* ed. John D. Niles. Totowa, N.J.: Rowan & Littlefield, 1980, 137–142.

Lord, A., 1982. "Béla Bartók as a Collector of Folk Music." In *Cross Currents: A Yearbook of Central European Culture,* ed. by Ladislav Matejka and Benjamin Stolz. Ann Arbor: University of Michigan, 1982, 295–304.

Lord, A., 1984. "The Battle of Kosovo in Albanian and Serbocroatian Oral Epic Songs." In *Studies on Kosova.* Boulder, Colo.: East European Monographs, 1984, 65–83.

Lord, A., 1985a. "Béla Bartók and Text Stanzas in Yugoslav Folk Music." In *Music in Context: Essays for John M. Ward,* ed. Anne Dhu Shapiro. Cambridge, Mass.: Department of Music, Harvard University, 1985, 385–403.

Lord, A., 1985b. "The Nature of Oral Poetry." In *Comparative Research on Oral Traditions: A Memorial for Milman Parry,* ed. John Miles Foley. Columbus, Ohio: Slavica, 1985, 313–349.

Lord, A., 1986. "The Merging of Two Worlds: Oral and Written Poetics and Poetry as Carriers of Ancient Values." In *Oral Tradition in Literature: Interpretation in Context,* ed. John Miles Foley. Columbia: University of Missouri Press, 1986, 19–64.

Lord, A., 1987. "Characteristics of Orality." In festschrift for Walter J. Ong, *Oral Tradition,* vol. 2, no. 1 (January 1987), 54–72.

Lord, A., 1989. "Theories of Oral Literature and the Latvian Dainas." In *Linguistics and Poetics of Latvian Folk Songs: Essays in Honour of the Sesquicentennial of Kr. Barons,* ed. Vaira Vīķis-Freibergs. Kingston: McGill-Queen's University Press, 1989, 35–48.

Lord, A., 1990. "Patterns of Lives of Patriarchs from Abraham to Samson and Samuel." In *Text and Tradition: The Hebrew Bible and Folklore,* edited with introductions by Susan Niditch. Scholars Press, Atlanta, Georgia, 1990.

Lord, M., 1967. Lord, Mary Louise. "Withdrawal and Return: An Epic Story

Pattern in the Homeric Hymn to Demeter and in the Homeric Poems." *Classical Journal* 62 (1967), 241–48.

Lucretius, 1943. Lucretius. *De rerum natura.* Trans. W. H. D. Rouse. Cambridge, Mass.: Loeb Classical Library, 1943.

McLuhan, 1962. McLuhan, Marshall. *The Gutenberg Galaxy: The Making of Typographic Man.* Toronto: University of Toronto Press, 1962.

Manas, 1946. *Manas, Kirgizskij epos velikij pohod.* Trans. Semen Lipkin, Lev Pen'kovskij, and Mark Tarlovski. Moscow: Gosudarstvennoe izdatel'stvo khudozhestvenoj literatury (State Publishing House for Literature), 1946.

Mandelbaum, 1971. Mandelbaum, Allen, trans. Vergil, *Aeneid.* New York: Bantam, 1971.

Marjanović, 1898–99. Marjanović, Luka. *Hrvatske narodne pjesme,* Odio prvi, Junačke (muhamedovske), vols. 3 and 4. Zagreb: Matica hrvatska, 1898–99.

Mavrogordato, 1956. Mavrogordato, John, ed. and trans. *Digenes Akrites.* Oxford: Clarendon Press, 1956.

Međedović, 1974a. Međedović, Avdo. *The Wedding of Smailagić Meho.* Trans. with introduction, notes, and commentary by Albert B. Lord, with trans. of conversations concerning the singer's life and times by David E. Bynum. *Serbo-Croatian Heroic Songs,* collected by Milman Parry, vol. 3. Cambridge, Mass.: Publications of the Milman Parry Collection, 1974.

Međedović, 1974b. *Ženidba Smailagina Sina.* Ed. David E. Bynum, *Serbo-Croatian Heroic Songs,* collected by Milman Parry, vol. 4. Cambridge, Mass.: Publications of the Milman Parry Collection, 1974.

Međedović, 1980. *Ženidba Vlahinjić Alije, Osmanbeg Delibegović i Pavičević Luka.* Ed. with prolegomena and notes by David E. Bynum, *Serbo-Croatian Heroic Songs,* collected by Milman Parry, vol. 6. Cambridge, Mass.: Publications of the Milman Parry Collection, 1980.

Melia, 1977. Melia, Daniel F. "'Empty figures' in Irish syllabic poetry." *Philological Quarterly* 56, no. 3 (Summer 1977), 285–300.

Menendez Pidal, 1967. Menendez Pidal, Ramon. "Los cantores épicos yugoslavos y los occidentales. El *Mio Cid* y dos refundidores primitivos." *Boletin de la Real Academia de Buenas Letras de Barcelona* 31 (1965–66), 195–225.

Mertens-Fonck, 1978. Mertens-Fonck, Paule. "Structure des passages introduisants le discours direct dans *Beowulf.* In *Mélanges de philologie et de littératures romanes offerts à Jeanne Wathelet-Willem.* Liège: Marché Romane 1978, 433–445.

Miletich, 1990. Miletich, John S. *The Bugarštica: A Bilingual Anthology of the Earliest Extant South Slavic Folk Narrative Song.* Ed., verse trans., introduction, and bibliography by John S. Miletich, foreword by Albert B. Lord, afterword by Samuel G. Armistead. Illinois Medieval Monographs, no. 3. Urbana: University of Illinois Press, 1990.

Milojević, 1870. Milojević, M. S. *Pesme i običaji ukupnog naroda srpskog,* vol. 2. Belgrade: Državna pečatnica, 1870.

Mladenović and Nedić, 1974. Mladenović, Živomir, and Vladan Nedić, eds. *Srpske narodne pjesme iz neobljavljenih rukopisa Vuka Stef. Karadžića,* Knjiga druga, Pjesme junačke najstarije. Belgrade: Srpka akademija nauka i umetnosti, Odeljenje jezika i književnosti, 1974.

Mwindo, 1969. *The Mwindo Epic from the Banyanga (Congo Republic)*. Ed. and trans. Daniel Biebyck and Kahombo C. Mateene. Berkeley: University of California Press, 1969.

Mzolo, 1978. Mzolo, Douglas. "Zulu Clan Praises." In *Social System and Tradition in Southern Africa*, ed. John Argyle and Eleanor Preston-Whyte. New York: Oxford University Press, 1978, 206–221.

Nagler, 1974. Nagler, Michael N. *Spontaneity and Tradition: A Study in the Oral Art of Homer*. Berkeley: University of California Press, 1974.

Nagy, G., 1979. Nagy, Gregory. *The Best of the Achaeans: Concepts of the Hero in Archaic Greek Poetry*. Baltimore: Johns Hopkins University Press, 1979.

Nagy, G., 1990a. *Greek Mythology and Poetics*. Ithaca: Cornell University Press, 1990.

Nagy, G., 1990b. *Pindar's Homer: The Lyric Possession of an Epic Past*. Baltimore: Johns Hopkins University Press, 1990.

Nagy, J., 1985. Nagy, Joseph Falaky. *The Wisdom of the Outlaw*. Berkeley: University of California Press, 1985.

Nekljudov and Tomorceren, 1985. Nekljudov, S. Ju., and Tomorceren, Z. *Mongolische Erzählungen über Geser, Asiatische Forschungen* Band 92. Wiesbaden: Otto Harrassowitz, 1985.

Nicoloff, 1979. Nicoloff, Assen, ed. and trans. *Bulgarian Folktales*. Cleveland: published by the editor, 1979.

Notopoulos, 1959. Notopoulos, James A. *Modern Greek Heroic Oral Poetry*. Ethnic Folkways Library, Album FE 4468, 1959.

Obolensky, 1948. Obolensky, Dmitri. *The Bogomils: A Study in Balkan Neo-Manichaeism*. Cambridge: Cambridge University Press, 1948.

Okpewho, 1979. Okpewho, Isidore. *The Epic in Africa*. New York: Columbia University Press, 1979.

Ong, 1982. Ong, Walter J. *Orality and Literacy: The Technologizing of the Word*. New York: Methuen, 1982.

O'Nolan, 1982. O'Nolan, Kevin. *Eochair, A King's Son in Ireland*, told by Eamon Bourke, recorded by Liam Costello, ed. and trans. Kevin O'Nolan. Dublin: Comhairle Bhéaloideas Éireann, University College, 1982.

Opland, 1975. Opland, Jeff. "Imbongi Nezibongo: The Xhosa Tribal Poet and the Contemporary Poetic Tradition." *PMLA* 90 (1975), 185–208.

Opland, 1983. *Xhosa Oral Poetry: Aspects of a Black South African Tradition*. Cambridge: Cambridge University Press, 1983.

Oral Tradition. Ed. John Miles Foley. Columbus, Ohio: *Slavica*, vol. 1, no. 1, January 1986, and subsequent numbers.

Oral Tradition and Literacy, 1986. *Oral Tradition and Literacy: Changing Visions of the World*. Ed. Richard A. Whitaker and Edgard R. Sienaert. Durban: Natal University Oral Documentation and Research Centre, 1986.

Palmer, 1912. Palmer, George Herbert, trans. *The Odyssey of Homer*. Boston: Houghton Mifflin, 1912, first edition 1884.

Panzer, 1910. Panzer, Friedrich. *Studien zur germanischen Sagengeschichte I. Beowulf*. Munich: Oskar Beck, 1910.

Pàroli, 1975. Pàroli, Teresa. *Sull' elemento formulare nella poesia germanica antica*. Rome: Instituto di glottologia, Università di Roma, 1975.

Parry, A., 1971. Parry, Adam. *The Making of Homeric Verse.* Oxford: Clarendon Press, 1971.

Parry, M., 1928. Parry, Milman. *L'Épithète traditionelle dans Homère.* Paris: Société Éditrice "Les Belles Lettres," 1928.

Parry, M., 1930. "Studies in the Epic Technique of Oral Verse-Making. I. Homer and Homeric Style." *HSCP* 41 (1930), 73–147.

Parry, M., 1932. "Studies in the Epic Technique of Oral Verse-Making. II. The Homeric Language as the Language of an Oral Poetry," *HSCP* 43 (1932), 1–50.

Parry, M., 1936. "On Typical Scenes in Homer." *Classical Philology* 61 (1936), 357–360. Review of Walter Arend, *Die typischen Scenen bei Homer,* q.v.

Parry, M., 1953. *Serbocroatian Heroic Songs,* vol. 2, *Novi Pazar: Serbocroatian Texts.* Collected by Milman Parry. Ed. Albert B. Lord. Cambridge, Mass., and Belgrade: Harvard University Press and Serbian Academy of Sciences, 1953.

Parry, M., 1954. *Serbocroatian Heroic Songs,* vol. 1, *Novi Pazar: English Translations.* Collected by Milman Parry. Trans. Albert B. Lord. Cambridge, Mass., and Belgrade: Harvard University Press and Serbian Academy of Sciences, 1954.

Parry, M., 1979. *Serbocroatian Heroic Songs,* vol. 14, *Bihačka Krajina, Serbo-Croatian Texts.* Collected by Milman Parry, Albert B. Lord, and David E. Bynum. Ed. David E. Bynum. Cambridge, Mass.: Publications of the Milman Parry Collection, 1979.

Pešić, 1967. Pešić, Radmila. *Vuk Vrčević,* Monografije 14. Belgrade: Filološki fakultet, Belgrade University, 1967.

Pope, M. W. M., 1963. Pope, M. W. M. "The Parry-Lord Theory of Homeric Composition." *Acta classica* 6 (1963), 1–21.

"Porče ot Avale," 1891. *Živaja Starina* 1, 3. St. Petersburg: S. H. Khudekova, 1891, 159–160.

Post, 1951. Post, L. A. *From Homer to Menander.* Berkeley: University of California Press, 1951.

Pound, 1970. Pound, Ezra. *The Cantos of Ezra Pound.* New York: New Directions, 1970.

Prendergast, 1962. Prendergast, Guy Lushington. *A Complete Concordance to the Iliad of Homer.* New ed. rev. and enlarged by Benedetto Marzullo. Hildesheim: G. Olms, 1962.

Radloff, 1885. Radloff, W. von. *Proben der Volksliteratur der nordlichen türkischen Stämme,* gesammelt und übersetzt von W. Radloff, Part V. St. Petersburg: Kaiserliche Akademie der Wissenschaften 1885.

Reichl, 1985a. Reichl, Karl, trans. *Rawšan, Ein usbekische mündliches Epos, Asiatische Forschungen,* Band 93. Wiesbaden: Otto Harrassowitz, 1985.

Reichl, 1985b. "Oral Tradition and Performance of the Uzbek and Karakalpak Epic Singers." In *Fragen der mongolischen Heldendichtung,* Teil III, ed. Walther Heissig. Wiesbaden: Otto Harrassowitz, 1985, 613–643.

Rieu, 1946. Rieu, E. V., trans. *The Odyssey.* Harmondsworth: Penguin Books, 1946.

Ritzke-Rutherford, 1981a. Ritzke-Rutherford, Jean. "Formulaic Microstructure: The Cluster." In *The Alliterative Morte Arthure,* ed. Karl H. Göller. London: D. S. Brewer, 1981, 70–82, 167–169.

Ritzke-Rutherford, 1981b. "Formulaic Microstructure: The Theme of Battle." In *The Alliterative Morte Arthure*, ed. Karl H. Göller. London: D. S. Brewer, 1981, 83–95, 169–171.

Roland, 1937. *La Chanson de Roland*, published according to the Oxford manuscript and trans. Joseph Bédier de l'Académie française, Paris: L'Édition d'Art H. Piazza, 1937.

Rouse, 1943. Rouse, W. H. D. Lucretius. *De rerum natura*. Trans. W. H. D. Rouse. Cambridge, Mass.: Loeb Classical Library, 1943.

Rybnikov, 1909. Rybnikov, P. N. *Pjesni sobrannyja P. N. Rybnikovym'*, 3 vols., 2d ed. Ed. A. E. Gruzinski. Moscow: Izdanie firmy "Sotrudnik' Škol'," 1909.

Rychner, 1955. Rychner, Jean. *La Chanson de geste: Essai sur l'art épique des jongleurs*. Geneva: Droz, 1955.

Schadewaldt, 1966. Schadewaldt, Wolfgang. *Iliasstudien*. Darmstadt: Wissenschaftliche Buchgesellschaft, 1966.

Schadewaldt, 1975. *Der Aufbau der Ilias: Strukturen und Konzeptionen*. Frankfurt am Main: Insel, 1975.

Schadewaldt, 1979. "Die Epische Tradition." *Homer: Tradition und Neuerung*. Ed. Joachim Latacz. Darmstadt: Wissenschaftliche Buchgesellschaft, 1979, 529–539.

Shalian, 1964. Shalian, Artin K., trans. *David of Sassoun: The Armenian Folk Epic in Four Cycles, The Original Text*. Athens: Ohio University Press, 1964.

Smith, 1977. Smith, John D. "The Singer or the Song? A Reassessment of Lord's Oral Theory." *Man* n.s. 12 (1977), 141–153.

Sokolov', 1910. Sokolov', M. I. *Slavjanskata kniga Enoha Pravednoga* (The Slavic Book of Enoch the Just). Moscow: n.p., 1910, 165 ff.

Stojković, 1927. Stojković, Sr. J. *Lazarica, ili boj na Kosovu, narodna epopeja u 25 pesama iz narodnih pesama i njihovih odlomaka sastavio Sr. J. Stojković* ("Lazarica, or the battle of Kosovo, national epic in 25 songs, from traditional songs and their fragments, put together by Sr. J. Stojković"). 3d ed., Srpska književna zadruga, no. 101, Belgrade, 1908; 6th ed., Belgrade: Izdavačka knjižarnica Geče Kona, 1927.

Surmelian, 1964. Surmelian, Leon. *Daredevils of Sassoun: The Armenian National Epic*. Denver: Alan Swallow, 1964.

Tatar, 1987. Tatar, Maria. *The Hard Facts of Grimms' Fairy Tales*. Princeton: Princeton University Press, 1987.

Thilo, 1832. Thilo, J. C. *Codex apocryphus Novi Testamenti*. Leipzig: n.p., 1832, 1:884 ff.

Thompson, 1955. Thompson, Stith. *Motif Index of Folk Literature*, vols. 1–6. Bloomington: Indiana University Press, 1955.

To Honor Roman Jakobson: Essays on the Occasion of His Seventieth Birthday (11 October 1966). Janua Linguarum, Series Maior, 32, vol. 2. The Hague: Mouton, 1967, 1199–1206.

Trautmann, 1935. Trautmann, Reinhold. *Die Volksdichtung der Grossrussen*, 1. Band, Das Heldenlied (Die Byline). Heidelberg: Carl Winter, 1935.

Vansina, 1965. Vansina, Jan. *Oral Tradition: A Study in Historical Methodology*. Trans. H. M. Wright. Chicago: Aldine, 1965.

Veit, 1981. Veit, Veronika. "Einige Überlegungen zu natürlichen und übernatürlichen Aspekten bezüglich des Pferdes im mongolischen Epos." *Fragen der mongolischen Heldendichtung* 1 (1981), 109–117.

Veit, 1985. "Das Pferd—Alter ego des Mongolen." *Fragen der mongolischen Heldendichtung* 3 (1985), 58–88.

Vergil, 1969. P. *Vergili Maronis opera.* Ed. R. A. B. Mynors. Oxford: Clarendon Press, 1969.

Vergil, 1977. P. *Vergili Maronis Aeneidos, Liber sextus.* Commentary by R. G. Austin. Oxford: Clarendon Press, 1977.

Vivante, 1982. Vivante, Paolo. *The Epithets of Homer: A Study in Poetic Values.* New Haven: Yale University Press, 1982.

Wade-Gery, 1952. Wade-Gery, H. T. *The Poet of the Iliad.* Cambridge: Cambridge University Press, 1952.

Walker, 1978. Walker, William O., Jr., ed. *The Relationships among the Gospels: An Interdisciplinary Dialogue.* San Antonio: Trinity University Press, 1978.

Watts, 1969. Watts, Ann Chalmers. *The Lyre and the Harp: A Comparative Reconsideration of Oral Tradition in Homer and Old English Epic Poetry.* New Haven: Yale University Press, 1969, repr. University Microfilms, Ann Arbor, Mich., 1980.

Whitman, 1958. Whitman, Cedric H. *Homer and the Homeric Tradition.* Cambridge, Mass.: Harvard University Press, 1958.

Work, 1930. Work, J. A. "Odyssean Influence on the *Beowulf.*" *Philological Quarterly* 9 (1930), 399–402.

Yeats, 1983. Yeats, William Butler. *The Poems.* Ed. Richard J. Finneran. New York: Macmillan, 1983.

Žirmunskij, 1960. Žirmunskij, V. M. *Skazanie ob Alpamyše i bogatyrskaja skazka.* Moscow: Izdatel'stvo vostochnoi literatury, 1960.

Index

Library of Congress Cataloging-in-Publication Data

Lord, Albert Bates.
    Epic singers and oral tradition / Albert Bates Lord.
        p.   cm. — (Myth and poetics)
    Includes bibliographical references and index.
    ISBN 0-8014-2472-0 (alk. paper). — ISBN 0-8014-9717-5 (pbk. : alk. paper)
    1. Oral tradition—History and criticism.   2. Oral-formulaic analysis.   3. Epic poetry—
History and criticism.   I. Title.   II. Series.
GR72.L66   1991
809.1'32—dc20   90-55888